PRO/CON VOLUME 1

INDIVIDUAL
and SOCIETY

Fluvanna County High School
3717 Central Plains Road
Palmyra, VA 22963

Published 2002 by Grolier Educational
Sherman Turnpike
Danbury, Connecticut 06816

© 2002 Brown Partworks Limited

Library of Congress Cataloging-in-Publication Data

Pro/con
   p. cm
Includes bibliographical references and index.
Contents: v. 1. The individual and society – v. 2. Government – v. 3. Economics – v.
4. Environment – v. 5. Science – v. 6. Media.
   ISBN 0-7172-5638-3 (set : alk. paper) – ISBN 0-7172-5639-1 (vol. 1 : alk. paper) –
ISBN 0-7172-5640-5 (vol. 2 : alk. paper) – ISBN 0-7172-5641-3 (vol. 3 : alk. paper) –
ISBN 0-7172-5642-1 (vol. 4 : alk. paper) – ISBN 0-7172-5643-X (vol. 5 : alk. paper) –
ISBN 0-7172-5644-8 (vol. 6 : alk. paper)
   1. Social problems. I. Grolier Educational (Firm)

HN17.5 P756 2002
361.1–dc21

                                                                    2001053234

Printed and bound in Singapore

SET ISBN 0-7172-5638-3
VOLUME ISBN 0-7172-5639-1

For Brown Partworks Limited
Project Editor: Fiona Plowman
Editors: Sally McFall, Dawn Titmus, Matt Turner,
Chris Marshall, Ben Hoare, Dennis Cove
Consultant Editors: Aruna Vasudevan and Timothy Buzzell,
Associate Professor of Sociology, Baker University, Kansas
Designer: Sarah Williams
Picture Researcher: Clare Newman
Set Index: Kay Ollerenshaw

Managing Editor: Tim Cooke
Design Manager: Lynne Ross
Production Manager: Matt Weyland

GENERAL PREFACE

> *"All that is necessary for evil to triumph is for good men to do nothing."*
> —Edmund Burke, 18th-century British political philosopher

Decisions

Life is full of choices and decisions. Some are more important than others. Some affect only your daily life—the route you take to school, for example, or what you prefer to eat for supper—while others are more abstract and concern questions of right and wrong rather than practicality. That does not mean that your choice of presidential candidate or your views on abortion are necessarily more important than your answers to purely personal questions. But it is likely that those wider questions are more complex and subtle and that you therefore will need to know more information about the subject before you can try to answer them. They are also likely to be questions about which you might have to justify your views to other people. In order to do that, you need to be able to make informed decisions, to be able to analyze every fact at your disposal, and evaluate them in an unbiased manner.

What is *Pro/Con*?

Pro/Con is a collection of debates that presents conflicting views on some of the more complex and general issues facing Americans today. By bringing together extracts from a wide range of sources—mainstream newspapers and magazines, books, famous speeches, legal judgments, religious tracts, government surveys—the set reflects current informed attitudes toward dilemmas that range from the best way to feed the world's growing population to gay rights, and from the connection between political freedom and capitalism to the fate of Napster.

The people whose arguments make up the set are all acknowledged experts in their fields, and that makes the vast differences in their points of view even more remarkable. The arguments are presented in the form of debates for and against various propositions, such as "Does Global Warming Threaten Humankind"? or "Should the Media Be Subject to Censorship"? This question format reflects the way in which ideas often occur in daily life: in the classroom, on TV shows, in business meetings, or even in state or federal politics.

The contents

The subjects of the six volumes of the *Pro/Con* set—*Individual and Society, Government, Economics, Environment, Science,* and *Media*—are issues on which it is preferable that people's opinions are based on information rather than simply on personal bias.

Special boxes throughout *Pro/Con* comment on the debates as you are reading them, pointing out facts or analyzing arguments to help you think about what is being said.

Introductions and summaries within each topic also provide background information that might help you reach your own conclusions. There are also comments and tips about how to structure an argument that you can apply on an everyday basis to any debate or conversation, learning how to present your point of view as effectively and as persuasively as possible.

3

VOLUME PREFACE
Individual and society

In liberal democracies like the United States citizens have certain natural rights, such as equality and free speech, that are protected by laws. In the United States the Bill of Rights and the Constitution help preserve those rights. But sometimes the laws that help preserve one person's freedom restrict someone else's. The right to free speech, for example, enables people to say things that others might find offensive; it also protects those who argue against the idea of free speech itself.

The relationship between individuals and society is highly complex. There are many issues of potential conflict or possible compromise. How do you know what is right? Most people are influenced in their attitudes by outside factors, such as education, upbringing, family values, religion, the media. It is important to learn how to make unbiased decisions about controversies. In order to do so, it is vital to get as much information as possible from reliable sources, to clarify and evaluate the facts, and finally, to make a proper judgment based on them.

The consequences of decisions
Every decision people make has a subsequent effect. On a day-to-day basis other people might suffer from unethical or uninformed decisions that you make about your relationship to society. Ultimately, everyone has to recognize that they are accountable or "responsible" for their choices. To do this, it is important to appreciate that in deciding to do or not do something, your choice could affect other people and, indeed, society as a whole. Say, for example, that you object to a specific law outlawing people of a certain race from traveling on a bus or train. You may decide to protest against that law on the grounds that it is unfair.

Your actions may help other people realize the unfairness of that law and may eventually lead to the government changing it. But while on the one hand you have shown that you are socially responsible—that you think that all people should be treated equally—on the other you have challenged laws accepted by your society. Does that mean you were wrong to do so? How do you decide what is right?

How this book will help
That issue and others are discussed in the *Individual and Society*. "Should People Have to Obey Unjust Laws?" is only one of around 15 debates on topical issues. By showing you both sides of the argument in each case, the book will help you make your own mind up about what you feel about these everyday, but vital, issues.

HOW TO USE THIS BOOK

Each volume of *Pro/Con* is divided into sections, each of which has an introduction that examines its theme. Within each section are a series of debates that present arguments for and against a proposition, such as whether or not the death penalty should be abolished. An introduction to each debate puts it into its wider context, and a summary and key map (see below) highlight the main points of the debate clearly and concisely. Each debate has marginal boxes that focus on particular points, give tips on

how to present an argument, or help question the writer's case. The summaries to the debates have supplementary material to help you do further research.

Boxes and other materials provide additional background information. There are also special materials on how to improve your debating and writing skills. At the end of each book is a glossary that provides brief explanations of key words in the volume. The index covers all six books, so it will help you trace topics throughout the set.

background information
Frequent text boxes provide background information on important concepts and key individuals or events.

summary boxes
Summary boxes are useful reminders of both sides of the argument.

further information
Further Reading lists for each debate direct you to related books, articles, and websites so you can do your own research.

other articles in the *Pro/Con* series
See Also boxes list related debates throughout the Pro/Con series.

marginal boxes
Margin boxes highlight key points in the argument, give extra information, or help you question the author's meaning.

key map
Key maps provide a graphic representation of the central points of the debate.

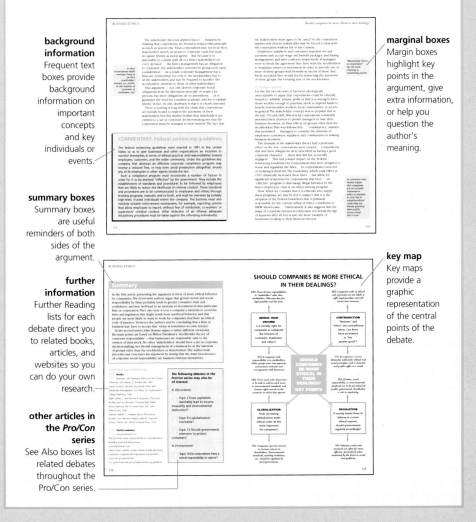

CONTENTS

PART 1
ISSUES OF EQUALITY AND INEQUALITY

INTRODUCTION

The "individual," according to the *Merriam-Webster Collegiate Dictionary*, is a "particular being or thing as distinguished from a class, species, or collection." "Society," on the other hand, is "a part of a community bound together by common interests and standards." The apparently contradictory relationship between an individual and the society in which he or she lives has fascinated people since the beginning of humankind. It is still hotly debated.

Writer Emma Goldman wrote in 1940 that life "begins and ends with man, the individual. Without him there is no race, no humanity, no State. No, not even 'society' is possible without man." In 19th-century Germany the philosopher Nietzsche shared this view, arguing that it is a fundamental error to place an emphasis on the society when the individual is more important. Many people still hold this view; yet, others argue that society actually shapes the actions and behavior of the individuals living in it.

Individual v. society

One of the chief contradictions in the individual's relationship with society is that society brings inequality. Not every individual is the same or has similar abilities or opportunities. Yet every individual has a consciousness of his or her own uniqueness and worth. By and large, individuals see themselves as worthwhile and as deserving as anyone else, even if their position in society does not reflect this.

The tension this creates between individuals and society has gone on throughout history. In most cases achieving equality—that is, having the same status, measure, quantity, or value as another—has been based on the attainment of power. Power has been the motivating factor in most political, social, or cultural change.

In theory most modern societies try to achieve some kind of equality in which all citizens have the same civil rights and political status. Yet this is often difficult to achieve, as are economic and social equality. The "American Dream" promotes the idea that anyone can achieve anything. In doing so, it also endorses inequality. Such a dream will inevitably create individuals with money, status, and power—and those without. Nietzsche argued that inequality is natural: "Every living thing reaches out as far from itself with its forces as it can and overwhelms what is weaker."

Critics of imbalance in society argue that most inequalities are the result of discrimination by powerful social groups over weaker. This discrimination is often based on minority status, such as race, gender, sexual orientation, or poverty. This section of the volume looks at various aspects of the question of equality.

Is inequality a problem?

If most societies suffer from economic, social, or cultural imbalance, then is equality a realistic aim? Is it even a real problem? In Topic 1 Bonnie Lefkowitz explores these questions through the relationship between inequality and health, while Richard Freeman argues that inequality is a solvable problem.

been perceived historically as the inferior sex, suffering inequalities in the workplace, home, and society at large, the feminist movement has done much to redress the balance. But recently the media have focused on another group—gays and lesbians—who have been discriminated against on the grounds of sexuality. In Topic 3 extracts from Simone de Beauvoir and Christina Hoff Sommers question whether women remain what de Beauvoir calls "the second sex." Topics 4 and 5 look at gay issues, particularly in regard to the

"It is correct to say that society is objective fact, coercing and even creating us. But it is also correct to say that our meaningful acts help to support the edifice of society and may on occasion help to change it ... society defines us, but is in turn defined by us."

—PETER BERGER, *AN INVITATION TO SOCIOLOGY*

Race

Many scholars of inequality argue that race is a key determinant of a group's or individual's position in society. Ethnic minorities tend to inhabit the bottom rungs of society. Topic 2 asks if it is possible to live in a nonracist society. Feminist bell hooks argues that a society in which color is irrelevant is attainable, while Richard Rayner argues that most people are inherently racist, even if they are not aware of it.

Gender and sexuality

Studies have shown that gender and sexuality are also factors in determining status in society. While women have

legal status of gay relationships as compared to that of heterosexual ones.

Redressing the balance

Affirmative action policies were introduced in the 1960s to help groups that had previously been discriminated against achieve equal status. Topic 6 looks at whether these policies are still needed and if they are discriminatory in themselves.

Linguistic minorities can also find themselves discriminated against. Topic 7 presents the debate about whether English should be America's official language, or whether such a policy is racist and unfair.

Topic 1
IS INEQUALITY A PROBLEM?

YES
"DOLLARS COUNT MORE THAN DOCTORS"
WWW.INEQUALITY.COM/HEALTHDC.HTML
BONNIE LEFKOWITZ

NO
"SOLVING THE NEW INEQUALITY"
BOSTON REVIEW, DECEMBER 1996/JANUARY 1997
RICHARD B. FREEMAN

INTRODUCTION

The concept of inequality means different things to different people, but for the most part the term is used to refer to the disparity in distribution of a specific resource or item, be it income, employment, education, health care, energy, or food. Even in comparatively rich countries societies are divided into rich and poor citizens: Some people always have more than others.

The same seems to be true on a larger scale. The global economy is divided between the developed, industrialized rich countries, such as the United States and the nations of Europe, and the poor, developing countries, such as India or Nigeria. In the world order the latter have less political and economic power than the former, and there is a constant battle to redress the balance.

But is inequality a natural occurrence that will always exist in any political or social order, or is it something that can be solved? Is it worth society and governments trying to do away with inequality? It may be unfair, but is inequality really even a problem at all?

One of the best indicators of inequality is poverty. The poorer a person is, the more likely it is that not only does he or she have fewer material possessions, but that he or she also will have fewer rights or status within a society. The same is true of countries and their influence in the global order. For countries poverty means that they can provide no financial or social backup for their worse-off citizens. For those individuals it means that they might find it hard to feed their children adequately or to afford vital medical care. The diets and therefore the health of the poor tend to be worse than those of the better off. It is not only a question of money. Some groups who have suffered from inequality are not financially poor but are discriminated against because of their race or their sexual orientation.

How much poverty is there? According to PovertyNet, which provides international information on poverty and inequality, extreme poverty fell slowly in the 1990s in developing countries. In 1987 around 28 percent of people living in these areas survived on less than $1 per day; by 1998 the figure had fallen to around 23 percent, although the actual numbers of poor remained fairly constant. China—in 1990 home to one-quarter of the world's poor—was by the end of 1998 home to only one-fifth after the Gross Domestic Product (GDP) rose by 9 percent a year.

"You are lost if you forget that the fruits of the earth belong to everyone and that the earth itself belongs to no one."

—JEAN-JACQUES ROUSSEAU,
A DISCOURSE ON INEQUALITY

A reduction in extreme poverty, however, does not necessarily mean a decrease in inequality. Inequality, for example, can only be understood by also looking at high and middle incomes to establish the width of the gap between various incomes. And the decline in poverty in increased-income countries was matched by an increase in inequality in other countries with a large, poverty-stricken population, such as in India, Nigeria, and Bangladesh.

How do Americans feel about the issue? The Pew Research Center conducted a survey on inequality in the United States in June 2001. It found that 44 percent of people interviewed believed that U.S. society was split between haves and have-nots; in 1988 only 26 percent believed this was the case. Similarly, 55 percent stated that they were in fair or poor financial shape; 26 percent said that they could not make ends meet; and 15 percent said that they were struggling. In 1976, 15 percent of those interviewed said that they could not afford health care; in 2001 that figure had risen to 27 percent. A significant percentage said that their credit card and loan repayments exceeded their monthly salary. Issues of gender and race often come into the equation since the people most badly affected by inequality, not only in terms of financial status but politically and socially too, tend to come from minority groups.

Nevertheless, can the inequalities suffered by people in an advanced, wealthy society be compared to those of people living in a poor society? At the end of the 20th century many nations called for a total eradication of world debt so that poor countries saddled with huge debt repayments could start the millennium afresh. Advocates argued that the world community had a responsibility to help those countries in need, and that huge debt repayments were crippling already weak economies, making it difficult for them to become financially and socially independent. That issue has caused much controversy, and antidebt and anticapitalist protests are taking place all over the world.

The following two articles take a more detailed look at inequality. The first article, by Bonnie Lefkowitz, analyzes the link between inequality and health. In the second article Richard B. Freeman believes that inequality is solvable and gives several broad pointers on how the United States could solve the divide between rich and poor.

DOLLARS COUNT MORE THAN DOCTORS
Bonnie Lefkowitz

YES

The scene was a familiar one in the nation's capital. Two hundred or so movers and shakers in the health policy world had gathered in a darkened meeting room to await the presentation of new research.

But the message flashed on the screen was not the kind they were accustomed to hearing. The first speaker, Leonard Syme of the University of California at Berkeley, declared that the dramatic decline in mortality since 1900 was the result more of basic long-term improvements in the social and physical environment than of advances in medical care. Moreover, he observed, increasingly expensive technology like the human genome project wasn't likely to improve population health in the future. A focus on individual health habits probably wouldn't help a great deal, either.

That's partly because behavior hasn't changed much, even in the face of massive public education efforts. The exception is smoking, which has declined in adults but increased among the young over the last 15 years. But mostly, when you're dealing with whole populations, new generations are constantly exposed to such powerful social problems as poverty, inequality, substandard housing, and inadequate education.

The influence of socioeconomic status

What affects health most, Syme and others at the conference argued, is socioeconomic status. And though most public health researchers have not been very interested in studying issues outside their sphere of influence, there has been an explosion of work on this topic in recent years. That's why it was chosen as the focal point of a conference (on Income Inequality, Socioeconomic Status and Health) held at the Washington Court Hotel on April 27, 2000.

The basics … were covered by leading experts in the field, including Syme, Richard Wilkinson of the University of Sussex in England, and George Kaplan of the University of Michigan. At every ascending rung of income, education or job status, they explained, there is a corresponding improvement in health status. In poorer nations, the general health level tracks closely with per capita income. But in the developed

Syme's declaration introduces the author's central point: that a society's health is rooted firmly in its social environment.

Why do you think smoking has declined in adults but increased among the young?

world, the degree of income inequality is critically important. In the United States, it was argued, the effects of poverty and income inequality have a devastating effect on the health of a significant portion of the population. According to Kaplan, the "burden of mortality" related to these factors equals "the combined total from lung cancer, HIV/AIDS, unintentional injuries, diabetes, suicide, and homicide."

What's the causal link between inequality and poor health? The speakers pointed to several pathways. At the lower end of the scale, there's true material deprivation as well as lack of knowledge and opportunity, and the psychosocial impact of stress, frustration, and a culture devoid of trust and caring. Wilkinson pointed to two- and threefold differences in mortality associated with social connections and status—or, in his words, "orderings based on power and coercion which determine access to scarce resources, regardless of the needs of others." The health-sustaining opposite side of the coin, he added, is "friendship and mutual assistance."

More recent contributors to the field presented findings on such topics as the linkage of income and race, the role of early childhood development, the biologic role of stress, and the applicability of "social capital," as espoused by Robert Putnam and others. In the United States, income and race were inextricably linked, according to David Williams of the University of Michigan. Race exerted an independent effect on health in every income group, he said. The black/white gap in health status has not decreased and in some cases is growing. Among other culprits, he pointed to persistent racism, employment impacts, and increasing residential segregation.

The author points to a correlation between inequality and health. In what ways are poor health and poverty part of a downward spiral?

See also Topic 6 Should affirmative action continue? on pages 72–83.

"Hard wired" at an early age

Clyde Hertzman of the University of British Columbia reported on his studies showing that certain aspects of development affected by socioeconomic status were "hard wired" at a very young age, while other forces exert a cumulative effect from childhood to maturity. The United States would do well, he said, to focus on disparities in health and development among young children, as Canada has done.

Bruce Kennedy discussed his work with Ichiro Kawachi on mechanisms linking income distribution and health, including a breakdown in social cohesion and social capital—catch-all terms for trust, political participation, and power. Social capital, according to the two Harvard School of Public Health researchers, is related in turn to investment in such public goods as education and health care. As the gap between rich and poor increases, according to their theory, the well-off have less of a stake in what happens to the rest of the population and are less likely to support social spending.

Finally, the audience heard and participated in a vigorous debate about the policy implications of the new work. Luncheon speaker Jim Lardner of *U.S. News and World Report* (and Inequality.org director) compared the "paltry investments" in today's safety-net programs with sweeping remedies of the past like the G.I. Bill. Yet in a society that tends to see the market as "natural" and government as "unnatural," he suggested, large-scale efforts to redistribute income and wealth are almost bound to be resisted; an effective remedy might have to tackle the way they're distributed before the government gets into the act.

> *The Serviceman's Readjustment Act (G.I. Bill) was passed in 1944 to help U.S. veterans of World War II reintegrate into society.*

Big gains for modest spending

Even as the researchers espoused different theories about how inequality affects health, they supported similar solutions. These focused primarily on tax, transfer, and employment policies to soften the impact of the market, plus increased investments in housing, education, transportation, and health care for those at the lower end of the income scale. "We don't need a revolution to achieve this," Wilkinson argued. "Small differences in socioeconomic status matter to health." In other words, there are significant gains to be made with relatively moderate spending.

Several issues emerged as flashpoints for panelists and audience members. Some … were reluctant to surrender their preoccupation with universal insurance coverage, despite evidence that health care is not the most important determinant of health. Others took a middle position, urging that the United States address inequalities in the health care system itself, along with other social investments. "We can't just play in the health care sandbox," said Nicole Lurie of the U.S. Department of Health and Human Services. But disparities in access to and quality of care [demand] action.

> *The economic wisdom of federal health subsidies is often questioned. See the* Science *volume, Topic 6* Should government limit the price of drugs?

Some [participants] called for additional research on the costs and benefits of socioeconomic remedies. As a point of departure, Katherine Newman of Harvard's Kennedy School of Government took the United Kingdom's ambitious Independent Inquiry into Inequalities in Health chaired by Sir Donald Acheson. The United States should consider a similar undertaking, she said, but with better data and more explicit cost/benefit analysis, since critics of the Acheson report have derided it as "nothing more than a liberal agenda dressed in the clothing of a concern for health care costs."

A "zero-sum game"?

[One] question was whether improving health is a "zero-sum game." Several of the scientists claimed that improvements in health through socioeconomic status offered opportunities to garner universal support, since improvements for those at the lower end of the scale would not come at the expense of the better off. International evidence from countries like Japan and Sweden was cited in support of this view. But economist Len Nichols of the Urban Institute noted that the funds to support social investments, however small, had to come from somewhere. He urged attention to the net costs of such actions for each income group.

In the zero-sum game, a game-theory model used by mathematicians and strategists, one contestant wins at the other's expense. How does it apply to the situation described here?

"The man of great wealth owes a peculiar obligation to the state because he derives special advantages from the mere existence of government."

—THEODORE F. ROOSEVELT, 26TH U.S. PRESIDENT

William Rogers of the U.S. Department of Labor questioned the firmness of the evidence for a causal link between socioeconomic status and health. "We know more than we think we do," Kaplan replied. There is work in progress on the degree to which long-established social programs such as Medicare and Social Security have improved health, and on the impact of inequality and socioeconomic status on health care costs. But we need not wait for more studies before we act, Kaplan said. He pointed to official action taken on the smoking front, where a similarly strong relationship was demonstrated without the kind of random trials that would usually be required to prove cause and effect.

Questions of political feasibility and strategy provoked discussion as well. Some thought the goal was one of social justice; others suggested that a healthy and competitive workforce had greater practical appeal. Whatever the questions of timing and rationale, there was general agreement on the urgency of the health/wealth issue. Noting that the United States will soon be a "majority minority" nation, Newman asked rhetorically: "Can we afford to let the present patterns of premature mortality and early morbidity run unchecked as the country's population shifts?"

What would be a uniformly just motive for social equality?

15

SOLVING THE NEW INEQUALITY
Richard B. Freeman

NO

Over the past two decades, income inequality in the United States has massively increased. This jump owes to the unprecedentedly abysmal earnings experience of low-paid Americans, income stagnation covering about 80 percent of all families, and an increase in upper-end incomes. The rise in inequality—greater than in most other developed countries—has reversed the equalization in income and wealth we experienced between 1945 and 1970. The United States has now cemented its traditional position as the leader in inequality among advanced countries.

I would recommend five broad strategies of reform that would take us "out of the box" of conventional remedies and constitute radical reform, in the best sense:

Breaking your argument into numbered points is an effective debating tool.

Asset-based redistribution

Consider a two-step approach in this direction. First, give workers themselves control of the most important assets they already own but do not control—the $5 trillion in deferred wages now residing in pension and other retirement funds. Amounting to nearly a third of all U.S. financial assets, this money could be used in ways that ... reduce inequality.

Can you see benefits to government from releasing such deferred funds ahead of schedule?

Assume that worker-owners, no less than capitalists, use their assets to advance their interests. This would have positive effects on economic growth and allow management to focus on long-run business problems, including business strategies to improve the position of the worse-off.

But there is no need to stop here. As a second and longer-term step toward an asset-based egalitarian strategy, we should move toward more fundamental asset redistribution. Imagine if instead of being promised at birth that you will get a Social Security pension decades in the future ... you were given a trust fund based on bonds or stocks whose returns would constitute your social transfer. Such a fund would give citizens a share of the nation's capital endowment similar to the privatization vouchers in the transitional economies. The incompetent poor would then be more like the incompetent rich: they would have income from assets that would let them live at some basic level, without depending on income transfers.

How might we fund such a redistribution and set up a citizen asset trust fund? Through progressive taxes, in part on inheritance and other forms of wealth, but also through the income tax, or some consumption or value-added tax. There are important design issues on which we would have to strike compromises in any such scheme. To prevent new cross-generational equity problems or perverse savings incentives, we might stipulate that only the income from the individual capital account could be consumed by its holder. Individuals might allot their trust fund investments in different ways (subject to some fiduciary responsibility limits). But the capital itself would, upon the holder's death, revert to the national pool for disbursement to the next round of babies.

All manner of critical details need to be worked out, of course—from the precise dimensions of such accounts and their funding, to the speed at which this sort of social funding base could supplement or supplant traditional entitlement programs. But as a general proposition, asset redistribution, coupled with the accountability-inducing possibilities of the market, makes more compelling sense in a society based on private capital than after-tax income transfer and insurance. Instead of demonizing welfare mothers, we'd all be tending our social stock portfolios—and so would they.

Starting-gate equality

Most Americans would, I believe, prefer generating equality naturally, from more equal labor-market endowments, to generating it unnaturally by correcting market outcomes through taxes and transfers. If that could be done, egalitarian policies would have a more stable base. To do it, however, we of course need to invest in people before they reach those labor markets. How much might all this cost? Another $200 billion a year? It would be a Marshall Plan for the poorest among us—our nation's children—and an investment in our future. Properly developed, no economic strategy is more likely to excite popular imagination, bring us together as a nation, or reverse the new inequality than a massive investment in starting-gate equality for children.

Like asset redistribution, shifting social expenditures forward in the life cycle fits with the broad goal of remaking America as the land of equal opportunity within a market economy. Indeed, just as asset redistribution is an effort to level the playing field by providing capital resources to those without such, starting-gate equality is an effort to level the field by providing educational or human capital resources to

What is a common factor among the sources of capital suggested here?

A "social stock" program would, the author claims, promote social harmony as well as financial equality.

Equality, suggests Freeman, could start in the cradle. But might such social engineering meddle with civil liberties?

them as well. These strategies are the same approach applied to different aspects of the inequality problem. The effect of both would be to raise living standards of the least well-off.

A higher social wage, progressively taxed

One way is to expand the safety net of supports for the very poor. Get some social agreement on the minimum acceptable income level, and when individuals fall below that, fill in the gaps. At one time both conservatives and liberals supported a negative income tax. But this seemingly economically rational solution no longer commands much support anywhere. Workers … tend to be skeptical of programs that fund those who do not work. If the very poor have a serious physical or mental defect, we are willing to provide them with some funds, but if they are able-bodied, we are suspicious. Given this skepticism, means-tested programs for poor people risk becoming poor programs.…

Can you think of ways in which the dominance of the work ethic already stigmatizes the unemployed?

"The contrast of affluence and wretchedness, continually meeting and offending the eye, is like the dead and living bodies, chained together."
—THOMAS PAINE, PHILOSOPHER, 1796

We could treat social benefits the same as private incomes in the tax system, or perhaps even tax them more progressively. Imagine a scheme in which social benefits were universal but in which the better-off who didn't really need them had the vast bulk taxed away. This is what President Reagan tried, in part, to do with his proposed taxation of the Social Security/medical benefits going to the wealthy elderly—but on which he was creamed by the AARP and Democrats and Republicans in the Congress. This is what President Clinton did by reducing the amount of Social Security that receives a tax break—leading Republicans to denounce him for raising taxes when they could just as easily have praised him for reducing entitlements.

The American Association for Retired People (AARP) looks after the interests of middle-aged and senior citizens. With the rising proportion of elderly in the U.S. population, the AARP has gained a powerful voice in politics.

Whatever the … details, there is a strong case for taxing income that comes in the form of social benefits at least as high as income that comes in the form of earnings. This is not a left/right issue. Taxing social-wage income even higher than private incomes may make sense to some, but not to others. However … recentering the welfare state in this way is a way to institutionalize commitments to greater equality.

Build unions

U.S. labor law stifles other forms of employee workplace activity or organization for fear that they will become old-fashioned company unions…. This must change. Although the proportion of the U.S. workforce covered by unions has been falling for years, unions are still the single largest group of Americans concerned with, and committed to fighting, the new inequality. Indeed, without an enhanced union movement I cannot imagine how the United States can ever get itself organized to reduce the new inequality. The only measure adopted by the last Congress to combat inequality— the increase in the minimum wage—was passed through union pressure. Survey after survey shows that low-paid workers—particularly low-paid African-American workers— want to join unions. Concentrated in the service sector, and thus largely safe from foreign competition, the lives of these workers could be substantially improved through the benefits of organization. If private sector unionization rose to 20 or 30 percent—and the polling data indicate that it would rise to that if workers had free choice—we would see a huge increase in pay and benefits at the bottom of the distribution.

Research U.S. labor history, especially the decline of the unions since the late 1940s, and list reasons why government might not welcome a return of strong labor unions.

Rebuild cities

Resuscitating cities will require some reduction of regulatory red tape and elimination of municipal corruption…. It will be enhanced by local adoption of metropolitan forms of governance and taxation. We've made it too easy to avoid the burdens of city life without sacrificing the benefits by moving a few miles out. Rebuilding our metro regions could be accompanied by institutionalizing regional government.

How to think about this

The unifying theme of the five strategies is to achieve equal opportunity by leveling the playing field. We ensure people the resources they need to compete … on fair terms: through asset redistribution, starting-gate intervention, and a social safety net of universal but taxed benefits. We ensure that those who are better off don't exploit their advantages by easing the conditions of organization for workers. And we concentrate resources on cities, where concentrations of poverty are greatest and social investments most likely to pay off.

The author sums up his essay in the phrase "equal opportunity"— giving everyone an equal start.

Summary

The issue of inequality has been examined for centuries by leading philosophers, such as Plato and Jean-Jacques Rousseau. In the two preceding articles Bonnie Lefkowitz reports on a conference held in Washington, D.C., that links socioeconomic status with health. Delegates found that at every "ascending rung of income, education, or job status ... there is a corresponding improvement in health status. In poorer nations, the general health level tracks closely with per capita income," but in rich countries income inequality levels are critical and thus important in determining whether people receive adequate health care or not. Richard B. Freeman argues that inequality is a problem, but one that can be solved. He proposes several different options for doing so, including asset-based redistribution, building up unions, and rebuilding inner cities.

FURTHER INFORMATION:

Books:

Arrow, Kenneth, Samuel Bowles, and Steven Durlauf (editors), *Meritocracy and Economic Inequality.* Princeton, NJ: Princeton University Press, 1999.

Barker, Paul (editor), *Living as Equals.* New York: Oxford University Press, 1996.

Daniels, Norman, Bruce Kennedy, Ichiro Kawachi, and Amartya Sen, *Is Inequality Bad for Our Health?* Boston, MA: Beacon Press, 2000.

Rousseau, Jean-Jacques, *A Discourse on Inequality.* London: Penguin, 1984.

Wilkinson, Richard, *Unhealthy Societies: The Afflictions of Inequality.* New York: Routledge, 1997.

Useful websites:

www.inequality. org
Inequality.org provides useful links to other sites on poverty and inequality, as well as links to current articles on the subjects.
www.people-press.org/june01rpt.htm
Gives the results of a study on inequality by the Pew Research Center.
www.inequality.org/conbudstudyfr.html
Findings of a Congressional Budget Office study that shows an increase in the wealth gap in the United States.
www.urban.org/oppor/opp_02.htm
Isabel V. Sawhill and Daniel P. McMurrer, "Are Justice and Inequality Compatible"?

The following debates in the Pro/Con series may also be of interest:

In this volume:
 Topic 6 Should affirmative action continue?

 Topic 14 Should society make reparations to the descendants of slaves?

In *Government*:
 Topic 2 Are all human beings created equal?

In *Economics*:
 Topic 2 Does capitalism lead to income inequality and environmental destruction?

 Topic 6 Should welfare be abolished?

 Topic 8 Should wealth redistribution be part of government policy?

IS INEQUALITY A PROBLEM?

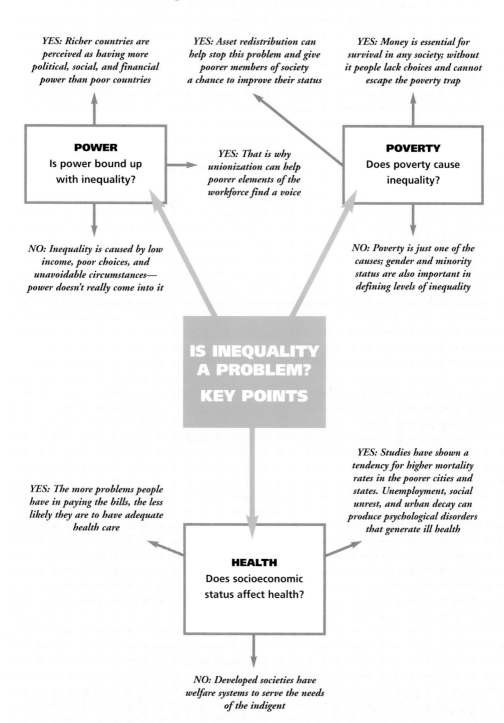

YES: Richer countries are perceived as having more political, social, and financial power than poor countries

YES: Asset redistribution can help stop this problem and give poorer members of society a chance to improve their status

YES: Money is essential for survival in any society; without it people lack choices and cannot escape the poverty trap

POWER
Is power bound up with inequality?

YES: That is why unionization can help poorer elements of the workforce find a voice

POVERTY
Does poverty cause inequality?

NO: Inequality is caused by low income, poor choices, and unavoidable circumstances—power doesn't really come into it

NO: Poverty is just one of the causes; gender and minority status are also important in defining levels of inequality

IS INEQUALITY A PROBLEM? KEY POINTS

YES: Studies have shown a tendency for higher mortality rates in the poorer cities and states. Unemployment, social unrest, and urban decay can produce psychological disorders that generate ill health

YES: The more problems people have in paying the bills, the less likely they are to have adequate health care

HEALTH
Does socioeconomic status affect health?

NO: Developed societies have welfare systems to serve the needs of the indigent

Topic 2
IS IT POSSIBLE TO LIVE IN A NONRACIST SOCIETY?

YES
"BELOVED COMMUNITY: A WORLD WITHOUT RACISM"
FROM *KILLING RAGE, ENDING RACISM*
BELL HOOKS

NO
"LOS ANGELES"
FROM *THE GRANTA BOOK OF REPORTAGE*
RICHARD RAYNER

INTRODUCTION

According to the *Merriam-Webster Dictionary*, racism is defined as "a belief that by nature some races are superior to others" and also as "discrimination based on that belief."

Since the beginning of humankind different social groups—from the Aztecs of Central America to the Nazis in 1930s and '40s Germany—have persecuted races that they considered inferior—sometimes through ignorance, sometimes through fear, sometimes just through innate hatred and savagery.

Although civil rights groups have for many centuries campaigned against such practices, racism in some form or another still exists in most countries of the world today and in some regions, such as the former Yugoslavia and Rwanda, has resulted in "ethnic cleansing" and genocide. With continuing ethnic conflict on every continent in the world, is a nonracist society really possible, or is it just an impossible ideal?

From the 16th century, when the first European settlers came to the New World, indigenous peoples have been persecuted and discriminated against. The Native American population declined after the introduction of previously unknown diseases, alcohol, and guns by European settlers. While some enlightened men and women mixed with the native populations, learning from them and sometimes marrying into them, the majority arrived with the idea firmly entrenched that the natives were little more than savages and were far inferior to the white race. This idea permeated European colonization in Africa, Asia, and Australasia too.

The introduction of large numbers of slaves, predominantly from Africa and sometimes China and India, further complicated matters, and the foundations of a racially divided society were quickly laid in which the white population became the "masters," and everyone else was seen to be inferior. This idea has been endorsed by right-wing groups such as the Ku Klux Klan and the Aryan Brotherhood.

Although slavery was made illegal in 1865 (see Topic 14), the majority of blacks continued to live in poor conditions and were still discriminated against. While Mahatma Gandhi campaigned against racism in South Africa and later India in the early 20th century, the United States began to see the emergence of its own civil rights movement fighting for equal rights for all U.S. citizens. It drew on Gandhi's techniques of nonviolent resistance and noncooperation.

> *"I have a dream that one day this nation will use up and live out its creed: 'We hold these truths to be self evident: that all men are created equal.'"*
> —MARTIN LUTHER KING JR., AUGUST 28, 1963

The 1950s and '60s were turbulent times when race riots erupted in several U.S. states and segregation came to an end. Despite desegregation, the United States is still accused of being a racist country. Every day in the media we read about "racist" incidents, the criminal justice system, and "discriminatory" affirmative action policies. Against this background advances in transportation and technology have now made the world a comparatively small place. Immigration has risen, and increasingly society is made up of a mixture of races, who increasingly intermarry and have children.

The 2000 Census reflected the racial diversity. It found that the U.S. population was 281,421,906, and that almost 98 percent of that figure classed themselves as deriving from one race—that is White, Black/African American, American Indian and Alaska Native, Asian, Native Hawaiian and Other Pacific Islanders, and Some Other Race. The Census defined "White" as "people having origins of the original peoples of Europe, the Middle East, or North Africa." Around 75 percent of the population stated their race as "White"; that figure included almost half of the 12.5 percent Hispanic population. The Black/African American population totaled around 12 percent, and around 2.4 percent of the figure claimed to originate from two or more races. Critics of U.S. racism argue that every group has to be represented fairly, otherwise society will suffer problems like those witnessed during the race riots in Los Angeles in the 1990s.

Some people see the solution to racial problems as "integration," but there is arguably a very fine line between integration, under which different races live side by side, and "assimilation," in which the traditions and cultural traits of an ethnic group are absorbed by the main, dominant culture.

The following articles examine the debate. Feminist bell hooks argues that a "beloved community" in which skin color is invisible is still attainable. But Richard Rayner uses the Rodney King affair and the consequent riots in Los Angeles as showing that most people are innately racist in certain situations.

BELOVED COMMUNITY: A WORLD WITHOUT RACISM
bell hooks

YES

Rev. Martin Luther King, Jr. (1929–1968) was a Baptist minister who became a leading advocate for the Civil Rights Movement in the 1950s and '60s. He was assassinated in Memphis in 1968. See box, page 104.

✓ Early on in his work for civil rights, long before his consciousness had been deeply radicalized by resistance to militarism and global Western Imperialism, Martin Luther King imagined a beloved community where race would be transcended, forgotten, where no one would see skin color. This dream has not been realized. From its inception it was a flawed vision. That flaw, however, was not the imagining of the beloved community; it was the insistence that such a community could exist only if we erased and forgot racial difference.

hooks repeats the phrase "beloved community" throughout the article to reinforce her argument. bell hooks is a pseudonym of Gloria Watson, and by using it the author is making an antipatriarchal statement.

Is a "beloved community" possible?

Many citizens of these United States still long to live in a society where beloved community can be formed—where loving ties of care and knowing bind us together in our differences. We cannot surrender that longing—if we do we will never see an end to racism. These days it is an untalked about longing. Most folks in this society have become so cynical about ending racism, so convinced that solidarity across racial differences can never be a reality, that they make no effort to build a community. Those of us who are not cynical, who still cherish the vision of beloved community, sustain our conviction that we need such bonding not because we cling to utopian fantasies but because we have struggled all our lives to create this community. In my blackness I have struggled together with white comrades in the segregated South. Sharing that struggle we came to know deeply, intimately, with all our minds and hearts that we can all divest of racism and white supremacy if we so desire. We divest through our commitment to and engagement with anti-racist struggle. Even though that commitment was first made in the mind and heart, it is realized by concrete action, by anti-racist living and being.

The term "segregation" means the official or unofficial practice of limiting physical contact or personal interaction between the races.

Over the years my love and admiration for those black and white southerners in my hometown who worked together to realize racial justice deepens, as does theirs of me. We have gone on from that time of legalized segregation to create intimate lives for ourselves that include loving engagement with all races and ethnicities. The small circle of love we have managed to form in our individual lives represents a concrete realistic reminder that beloved community is not a dream, that it already exists for those of us who have done the work of educating ourselves for critical consciousness in ways that enabled a letting go of white supremacist assumptions and values. The process of decolonization (unlearning white supremacy by divesting of white privilege if we were white, or vestiges of internalized racism if we were black) transformed our minds and our habits of being.

Do you agree with the author that it is possible to unlearn racial prejudices? Do you think that human beings are born with racist views, or that such attitudes are acquired through experience of the world?

In the segregated South those black and white folks who struggled together for racial justice (many of whom grounded their actions not in radical politics but in religious conviction) were bound by a shared belief in the transformative power of love. Understanding that love was the antithesis of the will to dominate and subjugate, we allowed that longing to know love, to love one another, to radicalize us politically. That love was not sentimental. It did not blind us to the reality that racism was deeply systemic, and that only by realizing that love in concrete political actions that might involve sacrifice, even the surrender of one's life, would white supremacy be fundamentally challenged. We knew the sweetness of beloved community.

Identity and culture

What those of us who have not died now know, that generations before us did not grasp, was that beloved community is formed not by the eradication of difference but by its affirmation, by each of us claiming the identities and cultural legacies that shape who we are and how we live in the world. To form beloved community we do not surrender ties to precious origins. We deepen those bondings by connecting them with an anti-racist struggle which is at the heart always a movement to disrupt that clinging to cultural legacies that demands investment in notions of racial purity, authenticity, national fundamentalism. The notion that differences of skin color, class background, and cultural heritage must be erased for justice and equality to prevail is a brand of popular false consciousness that helps [keep] racist thinking and action intact. Most folks are threatened by the notion that they must give up allegiances to specific cultural legacies in order to have harmony. Such suspicion is healthy. Unfortunately, as long as our society holds up a vision of democracy that requires the surrender of bonds and ties to legacies folks hold dear, challenging

Do you agree that the "beloved community" of which the author writes would need to be based on respect? Are there other ways to achieve it?

Members of the white supremacy group, the Ku Klux Klan, stand in a square formation at a rally in West Virginia in 1924.

racism and white supremacy will seem like an action that diminishes and destabilizes....

More than ever before in our history, black Americans are succumbing to and internalizing the racist assumptions that there can be no meaningful bonds of intimacy between blacks and whites. It is fascinating to explore why it is that black people trapped in the worst situation of racial oppression—enslavement—had the foresight to see that it would be disempowering for them to lose sight of the capacity of white people to transform themselves and divest of white supremacy, even as many black folks today who in no way suffer such extreme racist oppression and exploitation are convinced that white people will not repudiate racism. Contemporary black folks, like their white counterparts, have passively accepted the internalization of white supremacist assumptions. Organized white supremacists have always taught that there can never be trust and intimacy between the superior white race and the inferior black race. When black people internalize these sentiments, no resistance to white supremacy is taking place; rather we become complicit in spreading racist notions.... We must not allow the actions of white folks who blindly endorse racism to determine the direction of our resistance. Like our white allies in struggle we must consistently keep the faith, by always sharing the truth that white people can be anti-racist, that racism is not some immutable flaw....

Renewing the faith

To live in an anti-racist society we must collectively renew our commitment to a democratic vision of racial justice and equality. Pursuing that vision we create a culture where beloved community flourishes and is sustained. Those of us who know the joy of being with folks from all walks of life, all races, who are fundamentally anti-racist in their habits of being, need to give public testimony. We need to share not only what we have experienced but the conditions of change that make such an experience possible. The interracial circle of love that I know can happen because each individual present in it has made his or her own commitment to living an anti-racist life and to furthering the struggle to end white supremacy will become a reality for everyone only if those of us who have created these communities share how they emerge in our lives and the strategies we use to sustain them.... Those of us who are anti-racist long for a world in which everyone can form a beloved community where borders can be crossed and cultural hybridity celebrated.

The slave trade to the Americas began in the 16th century with the transportation of men, women, and children from Africa to work on plantations. The system remained in place until it was finally abolished by the Thirteenth Amendment in 1865.

Is the expression of racist beliefs and attitudes confined to people of any one particular color or ethnic background, or can racism manifest itself in any individual or societal group?

LOS ANGELES
Richard Rayner

The Taser stun gun and the LAPD

The Taser stun gun was introduced by the LAPD in 1980, and it was used against Rodney King, the black motorist whom LAPD officers Lawrence Powell, Ted Briseno, Timothy Wind, and Sergeant Stacey Koon were accused of unlawfully beating shortly after midnight on March 3, 1991. Despite all that had been written about the incident, I had read very little about the operation of the Taser. It was, I discovered, a weird-looking device: a crude, chunky grey pistol which fired darts into people. The darts were attached to wires, which on pushing a button administered a shock of 50,000 volts. "Seems to cool off most people pretty good," said a representative of Rays Guns of Hollywood. It had been used more and more to restrain suspects following the banning of the carotid chokehold in 1984.

The background to Rodney King

Rodney King was stopped after a high speed pursuit, first on the Foothill freeway, and then on the streets of Pacoima, during which he drove at speeds in excess of 100 miles per hour and ignored a number of red lights. The initial pursuit was made by Melanie and Timothy Singer, a husband and wife team of the California Highway Patrol, but when LAPD cars arrived on the scene it was Sergeant Stacey Koon who took charge. As Koon notes in an as yet unpublished autobiography, he looked at the petite Melanie Singer and then at the 6 foot 3 inch, 225 pound Rodney King (who, according to Koon, had dropped his trousers and was waving his buttocks in the air) and decided that this was about to develop into a "Mandingo type sex encounter," a reference to a Hollywood movie which involves black slaves raping white women.

Koon used his Taser stun gun, firing two darts into Rodney King and giving him two shocks. One was enough to subdue most suspects and even the Mandingo Rodney King himself was on the ground by now, showing little sign of resistance. Koon and the three other officers then kicked him and hit him 56 times with their batons, breaking his ankle, his cheekbone, and causing 11 fractures at the base of his skull, as well as concussion and nerve damage to the face. The force of the blows knocked fillings from his teeth.

The last of the not-guilty verdicts was announced in Simi Valley at 3.45 p.m. on Wednesday April 29, 1992. As Stacey Koon left the courthouse, it was declared that he had hired an entertainment attorney to sell the movie and book rights to his story, which would be titled The Ides of March, since he had been indicted on March 15 of the previous year.

For more on the Rodney King case and a transcript of the trial proceedings visit www.law.umkc. edu/faculty/ projects/ftrials/ lapd/lapd.html.

The riots

After the verdict, I went to the Mayfair Market, to a bookstore, to a bar on Franklin. People were nervous, excited. Something was going to happen in South-Central; the question was how bad it would be. When I got home the phone was ringing. Crowds had gathered at Park Center, the LAPD Police Headquarters. A car had been turned over. Looting was said to have started in other places, though the moment the riots began in earnest was easy to spot: it was broadcast live on TV.

At 6.30 p.m, Reginald Denny stopped at a traffic-light at the intersection of Florence and Normandie.... While waiting for the light to change he was pulled from his rig by five or six black youths. Two news helicopters were overhead, watching the crowd that had been gathering since the verdict was announced, and the incident turned into an uncanny mirror-image of the Rodney King beating, though where the King video had been dim and murky ... what I now saw was shot by professionals....

Later I watched a video shot by an eyewitness—again the uncanny mirror image. In this one there was sound; you could hear the voices: "No mercy for the white man, no mercy for the white man ...." Watching the Rodney King video I had thought it reasonable for American blacks to hate the police and be suspicious of all whites. This didn't make me suspicious of these particular blacks; it made me want to kill them.... I actually saw myself with a gun in my hand. Pow. Pow. Pow.

Here Rayner expresses strong feelings about the black men involved in the violence he sees on his TV screen. Are his thoughts racist?

Simi Valley

I had never seen Simi Valley, the town where the four officers had been found not guilty of beating Rodney King, and from where, every morning, more than 2,000 LAPD officers, county sheriffs, and other law enforcement personnel commuted to their jobs in distant Los Angeles. I wanted to make the journey myself. My girlfriend and I drove there from South-Central.

The journey took us about an hour; in traffic, it could take two hours: the Harbor freeway to the Hollywood freeway, short stretches of the Ventura and San Diego freeways and the bland sprawl of the San Fernando Valley. It was on our last freeway, the Simi Valley, that the landscape changed. This had all been part of Southern California's ranch country; its 19th-century history concerned trails and horses and men who did what men had to do. But now housing estates could be seen on most hillsides, and freeway exit ramps were marked "CONSTRUCTION VEHICLES ONLY," where new dormitory suburbs were being built. It was like a passage between continents.

What are the "continents" that Rayner refers to here?

At the far end of Los Angeles Avenue, there was a sale of "recreational vehicles," where a short man called Ted said that, while he had been shocked by the verdicts, and horrified by the riots, this was all good news for him. He was a real estate agent. He predicted a boom in Simi Valley, and indeed throughout the whole of Ventura Country, as more and more fled black street crime and the Dickensian hell of Los Angeles. "You know the worst thing about the looting all those niggers did down there?" he asked. "They couldn't afford it." Ted paused, "Just kidding," he said.

Ted reveals himself to be a racist through his sense of humor. In what other ways might people display their racist beliefs?

The American Dream

We drove through the city. Los Angeles Avenue itself consisted of shopping malls: Simi Valley Plaza, Mountain Gate Plaza, Madre Plaza, the Westgate Center. In these plazas huge parking lots were surrounded by stores of all kinds.... Everything else issued the smell of air conditioning. You could buy things here: a new Ford, a taco, a garden hose, an ice cream, an airline ticket to Lake Tahoe, a pair of jeans, a carton of frozen yoghurt, a CD player, a haircut, a chilli burger, a spade, a doughnut, a bag of enriched soil fertilizer, a vegetarian health sandwich, the Simi Valley Advertiser, a novel by Stephen King, a new tie, a bathing suit that dries in minutes, spark plugs, a suit for $250.... You could collect interest on your savings, wash your car, or go bowling. You could buy beer, Gatorade, and many different kinds of California Chardonnay. You could buy a Coca-Cola. I bought a Coca-Cola.

Rayner deliberately lists all the items on sale in the Simi Valley plazas to make the point that this is a prosperous white area, unlike the black neighborhoods of LA where poverty is rife.

You could tell who lived in Simi Valley (they were white), and who worked there but lived elsewhere (they were hispanic). We didn't see any blacks but we may not have stayed long enough. I'm sure there were blacks in Simi Valley.

At the East County courthouse, where the King verdicts had been reached, I was confronted by a local resident, a middle-aged woman in a beige suit made of an indeterminate fabric. She smiled at me coldly.

"You're not from here, are you?"

"No," I replied, a little surprised. Was I really so obvious? Perhaps I looked a little thin. Simi Valley seemed to be a place where fat people got fatter.

"I thought so," she said. "And you've come because of that Rodney King thing."
I said yes.

"I don't feel guilty," she said, answering a question I hadn't asked. "I refuse to feel guilty. I did everything I could back in the sixties for those people. They just refused to make the most of their opportunities."

"Why was that?"

"Oh, they're lazy," she said, "Go back to Los Angeles and take your issue with you. It has nothing to do with Simi Valley. Those people on the jury did the best job they could, and for you to assume that 12 white people can't hand down a fair verdict in a case like that, well, that's racist in itself, isn't it?"

What does this conversation reveal about the woman who is talking to Rayner?

Innate racism or reality?

She was right: if thinking that 12 people like her couldn't be relied upon to hand down a fair verdict was racist, then I was racist. I hated her. I wanted to hurt her. I didn't want to argue or protest. I wanted her injured. I saw myself doing it. Pow. Pow. Pow. We returned to Los Angeles.

What differences are there between the way in which Rayner judges a white woman and the way racists judge black or Hispanic people?

The riots began on Wednesday April 29, 1992. Monday May 4 was the first day—the first of many—that gun sales topped 2,000 in Southern California, twice the normal figure, a gun sale every 40 seconds. By that Monday, this was the riot toll: 228 people had suffered critical injuries (second and third degree skin burns; blindness; gunshot wounds to the lung, stomach, neck, shoulder, and limbs; knife wounds; life-threatening injuries from broken glass), and 2,383 people had suffered non-critical injuries (requiring hospital treatment); there were more than 7,000 fire emergency calls; 3,100 businesses were affected by burning or looting; 12,111 arrests. As this goes to press there are reports of 18,000 arrests. Fifty-eight people are dead.

Richard Rayner is a white reporter living in a black neighborhood of Los Angeles. For a full version of this article see The Granta Book of Reportage. London: Granta Publications, 1998.

Summary

"Racism" is a pervasive and destructive force in any society, but is it possible to eradicate it completely? Is it an innate, inherent feeling that even the most liberal of us have, or does it exist primarily through ignorance and lack of education? Feminist bell hooks draws on Martin Luther King Jr.'s idea of the "beloved community" in which people can live together regardless of skin color or ethnicity. She argues that it is still an attainable dream if society works together, and that to achieve this end it is not necessary to surrender cultural diversity; rather, it should be celebrated.

Journalist Richard Rayner, however, draws on the Rodney King affair in Los Angeles and on the riots that followed the acquittal of the police officers concerned. Rayner shows through sharp observations and subtle comments about our media-based culture that most people are inherently racist—including himself—in certain situations.

FURTHER INFORMATION:

Books:

Brittan, Arthur, and Mary Maynard, *Sexism, Racism, and Oppression.* New York: Basil Blackwell, 1984.

hooks, bell, *Yearning: Race, Gender, and Cultural Politics.* Boston: South End Press, 1991.

Terkel, Studs, *Race: How Blacks and Whites Think and Feel about the American Obsession.* New York: The New York Press, 1992.

Useful websites:

www.udayton.edu/~race
A study of institutional racism in America.

www.worldracism.com
Race issues in the news.

www.aclu.org/profiling
Racial profiling in America.

www.american-pictures.com
Illustrated lectures on race issues.

www.magenta.nl/crosspoint
Lists 2000 organizations dealing with race issues.

www.igc.org/gateway
AntiRacismNet information and articles.

www.pocho.com./racism
Racism issues concerning immigrants to the U.S.

www.arc.org
The Applied Research Center is a public policy, educational and research institute for race issues.

The following debates in the Pro/Con series may also be of interest:

In this volume:

Topic 1 Is inequality a problem?

Topic 6 Should affirmative action continue?

Topic 8 Should people have to obey unjust laws?

Topic 10 Is violent protest ever justified?

Topic 11 Is hate speech a right?

In *Government*:

Topic 2 Are all human beings created equal?

IS IT POSSIBLE TO LIVE IN A NONRACIST SOCIETY?

YES: The United States has a long record of discriminatory practices against ethnic minorities, and more blacks and hispanics live in poverty and are unemployed

YES: This is why affirmative action policies are in place

YES: Rodney King and O.J. Simpson showed that the criminal justice system is racist and flawed

YES: More ethnic minorities are sentenced to death and to prison than other groups

CRIMINAL JUSTICE
Is the criminal justice system racist?

DISCRIMINATION
Does racial discrimination cause disproportionate unemployment and poverty among ethnic groups?

NO: It's not racist. The United States has one of the fairest legal systems in the world.

NO: The number of ethnic minorities in prison reflects the high incidence of people in these groups who commit crimes

NO: They are not caused by discrimination but by poor education, language problems, and work status

IS IT POSSIBLE TO LIVE IN A NONRACIST SOCIETY?

KEY POINTS

YES: The current system is harsh and penalizes immigrants

YES: Immigration officials often behave unfairly, and immigrants have no redress under the current system

IMMIGRATION
Do tough U.S. immigration policies reflect an innately racist way of thinking?

NO: The United States is a wealthy country and must protect itself from exploitation

NO: The United States immigration policies are no tougher than those of other industrialized countries, such as the United Kingdom

CIVIL RIGHTS TIMELINE
1942–1992

People in the United States today often take their civil rights for granted. It is easy to forget that until as recently as the 1960s, many laws and customs discriminated against African Americans, for instance. Today some groups in society continue to struggle for their rights in areas such as employment.

1942 The Congress of Racial Equality (CORE) is founded in Chicago, Illinois, and becomes a national organization in 1943.

1945 President Roosevelt dies, and Democratic president Harry S. Truman continues the use of executive action as the principal means of furthering black civil rights.

1946 Congress abolishes the Fair Employment Practices Committee, wiping out some of the employment advances made by blacks.

1947 First freedom rides on previously segregated bus routes. CORE sends "integrated" teams of black and white members on freedom rides and to sit-ins.

1950 The House of Representatives votes to create a Fair Employment Practices Commission, but the Senate rejects the bill.

1951 Harry T. Moore, the Florida secretary of the National Association for the Advancement of Colored People, and his wife are killed by a bomb. Moore had been organizing Florida blacks to register to vote. The House of Representatives votes to create a Fair Employment Practices Commission, but the Senate rejects the bill.

1952 Republican Dwight D. Eisenhower is elected president of the U.S. He follows Roosevelt's and Truman's example of using the powers of the presidency to further the cause of black civil rights. The Supreme Court hears a number of school segregation cases.

1954 In *Brown v. Board of Education of Topeka, Kansas*, the Supreme Court unanimously bans segregation in public schools.

1955 A bus boycott is launched by 50 leaders of the black community, including Dr. Martin Luther King Jr., in Montgomery, Alabama, after an African American woman, Rosa Parks, is arrested for refusing to give up her seat to a white person. Eight months later the Supreme Court decides that bus segregation violates the Constitution.

December 21, 1956 After more than a year of the boycott and a legal fight the Montgomery buses desegregate.

1957 One thousand paratroopers are called in by President Eisenhower to restore order at the previously all-white Central High in Little Rock, Arkansas and escort nine black students to classes.

1960 February 1: The sit-in protest movement begins at a Woolworth's lunch counter in Greensboro, North Carolina, when Joseph McNeill, a black college student, is refused service. He returns daily with three classmates to sit at the counter until they are served. An article in the *New York Times* highlights the students' protest, and they are joined by other students, black and white. On November 8, John F. Kennedy is elected president. He has strong support from the black community.

1961 An interracial group of CORE activists attempt to ride buses from Washington, D.C. to the South to challenge segregation. Other freedom rides follow.

1962 James Meredith is the first black student to enroll at the University of Mississippi. President Kennedy orders 20,000 U.S. soldiers into the campus to restore order. Two people are killed and many more are injured in the ensuing riots.

1963 May 3–5: police arrest Dr. King and other preachers during demonstrations in Birmingham, Alabama. June 11: University of Alabama is desegregated. June 12: Medgar Evers, NAACP leader, is murdered in Jackson, Mississippi. August 28: 250,000 people attend a march on Washington, D.C., urging support for pending civil rights legislation. The event prompts King's "I have a dream" speech. September 15: four girls are killed in the bombing of the Sixteenth Street Baptist Church in Birmingham, Alabama. November 22: President Kennedy is assassinated in Dallas, Texas.

1964 Three civil rights workers are murdered in Mississippi. On July 2 President Johnson signs the Civil Rights Act.

1965 February 21: Malcolm X is murdered. March 7: on "Bloody Sunday" state troopers use tear gas and batons on the people of Selma, Alabama, who intend to march from the city to Montgomery. March 25: King leads another march along the same route. August 6: Johnson signs the Voting Rights Act, which authorizes federal examiners to register qualified voters and suspends devices such as literacy tests that aimed to prevent African Americans from voting. In Selma, Alabama, 15,000 Blacks were eligible to vote but only 355 were registered. August 11–16: Watts riots result in 34 deaths in Los Angeles.

1966 June: the Black Power movement formally begins. October 15: Huey Newton and Bobby Seale create the Black Panther Party. It supports the use of violence in the achievement of equal rights where necessary.

1967 Robert Clark becomes the first black to be elected to the Mississippi House of Representatives since Reconstruction. Thurgood Marshall becomes the first black Supreme Court Justice.

1968 April 4: Martin Luther King is assassinated in Memphis, Tennessee. In *Green v. County School Board,* the Supreme Court Rules that freedom of choice is no longer an acceptable reason for segregation.

1969 The Supreme Court rules that cities must begin to desegregate the schools immediately.

1971 Busing is approved as the primary method of integrating schools.

1978 The U.S. Supreme Court outlaws racial quotas in university enrollment.

1989 Douglas Wilder of Virginia becomes the nation's first African American to be elected state governor.

1990 A new Civil Rights Act is passed.

1992 The first racially based riots in years erupt in Los Angeles and other cities after a jury acquits L.A. police officers in the videotaped beating of Rodney King, an African American.

Topic 3
ARE WOMEN STILL THE SECOND SEX?

YES
"INTRODUCTION"
FROM *THE SECOND SEX*
SIMONE DE BEAUVOIR

NO
"WAR AGAINST BOYS, PART 1"
ATLANTIC MONTHLY, MAY 2000
CHRISTINA HOFF SOMMERS

INTRODUCTION

Argument over the relative status of the sexes has existed for centuries. The title of this topic accepts that women have been, or have been regarded as, the second sex, an issue that U.S. feminist Betty Friedan labeled the "problem that ha[d] no name." But are women still the second sex? And if so, are men largely responsible? Or have women caught up and redressed the balance? And how can parity or otherwise be assessed?

According to the World Bank Group, "gender" refers to the economic, social, cultural, and political "attributes and opportunities associated with being male and female," and they vary from place to place, as do the roles that men and women are required to play in society. In most societies the amount of resources that custom and tradition allow a man or a woman to attain and control illustrates how those societies perceive men and women. The resources may include employment, education, housing, transport, and land ownership. Whereas in some matriarchal or female-dominated

societies—for example, in Kerala in southern India—women have significant political and social status, the majority of women historically have gotten an unequal amount of those resources. Why?

In 1949 the French feminist writer Simone de Beauvoir wrote her famous treatise on women and called it *The Second Sex*. Its central premise argues that women have occupied a secondary status in society since the rise of the patriarchal or male-dominated society. She argues that such status is imposed not by natural "feminine" traits but by strong forces of education and social tradition enforced by men. De Beauvoir's book caused a great stir when it was first published, and it has influenced feminist thinking ever since.

Women's role in both the society and the economy of the United States underwent great change in the last 30 or so years of the 20th century. That was arguably the result of the success of the feminist movement of the 1970s and 1980s, but it was also largely a response to the changing needs of the

global economy. In the 1980s the United States and Europe experienced a shift away from industrially based economies to those based on finance and the public service sectors. As a result many jobs in traditional male-dominated areas such as heavy industry disappeared, opening the market up to women. Thus the sexual makeup of the workplace has changed in what some theorists have called a "feminization of the economy." There was a significant shift in the ratio of men to women working: The proportion of men in full-time work declined from 62 percent in 1970 to 50 percent in 1996.

"I do not wish women to have power over men; but over themselves."

—MARY WOLLSTONECRAFT,

A VINDICATION OF THE RIGHTS OF WOMAN

Some feminists, such as Germaine Greer in her book *The Whole Woman*, argue that the new jobs for women are often in the lower, more poorly paid sectors, while most management posts go to men. A recent study has shown that the average hourly earnings of U.S. women are still only 68 percent of what a man would earn, and that when a woman has children, she will typically lose half the income she would have earned during her lifetime—pregnancy does not affect a man's income.

However, some feminists believe women are in a better position than that outlined above. Rosalind Coward asserted in *Sacred Cows* that in 1997 52 percent of new attorneys, 32 percent of managers and administrators, 34 percent of health professionals, and 27 percent of buyers, brokers, and sales reps were women. She also estimated that by the end of 2001 women would have 44 percent of the professional jobs in the U.S.

Toward the end of the 20th century the U.S. press discussed at length whether feminism—the organized activity to attain equal rights for women—was dead. In 1998 *Time* magazine published a story about the movement's demise and featured three historic women figures on the cover—Susan B. Anthony, Betty Friedan, and Gloria Steinam—along with the fictional television character Ally McBeal. This led to comment about how relevant it was to compare a fictional, idealized media character to three important real women and what it said about the status of women in 20th-century society.

In the two articles that follow, the issue of the second sex is debated. The first extract is from the introduction to Simone de Beauvoir's classic text *The Second Sex* in which she argues, among other things, that woman is defined by man not in relation to herself but in terms of her relationship to him, and that "the most mediocre of males feels himself a demigod as compared with women."

Christina Hoff Sommers's article, "War against Boys, Part I," on the other hand, takes a more modernist approach, looking at the case of girls and boys in the education system. Sommers asserts that girls are currently outshining boys at school and university, and that males are now the second sex.

INTRODUCTION FROM *THE SECOND SEX*
Simone de Beauvoir

Citing various authors, de Beauvoir sets out her central premise: that the world's historically male point of view made woman a kind of second-class being.

"The female is a female by virtue of a certain lack of qualities," said Aristotle; "we should regard the female nature as afflicted with a natural defectiveness." And St. Thomas for his part pronounced woman to be an "imperfect man", an "incidental" being. This is symbolised in Genesis where Eve is depicted as made from what Bossuet called "a supernumerary bone" of Adam.

Thus humanity is male and man defines woman not in herself but as relative to him; she is not regarded as an autonomous being. Michelet writes: "Woman, the relative being…" And Benda is most positive in his *Rapport d'Uriel*: "The body of man makes sense in itself quite apart from that of woman, whereas the latter seems wanting in significance by itself…. Man can think of himself without woman. She cannot think of herself without man." And she is simply what man decrees; thus she is called "the sex", by which is meant that she appears essentially to the male as a sexual being. For him she is sex—absolute sex, no less. She is defined and differentiated with reference to man and not he with reference to her; she is the incidental, the inessential as opposed to the essential. He is the Subject, he is the Absolute—she is the Other."

Unequal throughout history

Now, woman has always been man's dependent, if not his slave; the two sexes have never shared the world in equality. And even today woman is heavily handicapped, though her situation is beginning to change. Almost nowhere is her legal status the same as man's, and frequently it is much to her disadvantage. Even when her rights are legally recognised in the abstract, long-standing custom prevents their full expression in the mores. In the economic sphere men and women can almost be said to make up two castes; other things being equal, the former hold the better jobs, get higher wages, and have more opportunity for success than their new competitors. In industry and politics men have a great many more positions and they monopolise the most important posts. In addition to all this, they enjoy a traditional prestige that the education of children tends in every way to support,

The author argues that even where women's rights were legally recognized, custom and tradition conspired to prevent them being honored in practice.

for the present enshrines the past—and in the past all history has been made by men. At the present time, when women are beginning to take part in the affairs of the world, it is still a world that belongs to men—they have no doubt of it at all and women have scarcely any. To decline to be the Other, to refuse to be a party to the deal—this would be for women to renounce all the advantages conferred upon them by their alliance with the superior caste. Man-the-sovereign will provide woman-the-liege with material protection and will undertake the moral justification of her existence; thus she can evade at once both economic risk and the metaphysical risk of a liberty in which ends and aims must be contrived without assistance. Indeed, along with the ethical urge of each individual to affirm his subjective existence, there is also the temptation to forgo liberty and become a thing. This is an inauspicious road, for he who takes it—passive, lost, ruined— becomes henceforth the creature of another's will, frustrated in his transcendence and deprived of every value. But it is an easy road; on it one avoids the strain involved in undertaking an authentic existence. When man makes of woman the Other, he may, then, expect to manifest deep-seated tendencies towards complicity. Thus, woman may fail to lay claim to the status of subject because she lacks definite resources, because she feels the necessary bond that ties her to man regardless of reciprocity, and because she is often very well pleased with her role as the Other.

In the feudal political system of the Middle Ages lords granted land to subordinates in return for loyalty and services. Do you see any connection between this concept and the author's view of relationships between men and women?

In what ways might the women de Beauvoir describes be said to lack "an authentic existence?"

A advantageous subordination—for men

Legislators, priests, philosophers, writers, and scientists have striven to show that the subordinate position of woman is willed in heaven and advantageous on earth. The religions invented by men reflect this wish for domination. In the legends of Eve and Pandora men have taken up arms against women. They have made use of philosophy and theology, as the quotations from Aristotle and St Thomas have shown. Since ancient times satirists and moralists have delighted in showing up the weaknesses of women. ... For instance, the Roman law limiting the rights of woman cited "the imbecility, the instability of the sex" just when the weakening of family ties seemed to threaten the interests of male heirs. And in the effort to keep the married woman under guardianship, appeal was made in the sixteenth century to the authority of St Augustine, who declared that "woman is a creature neither decisive nor constant", at a time when the single woman was thought capable of managing her property.

De Beauvoir explains how for centuries men managed to keep women in a subordinate position by invoking learned or sacred writings.

COMMENTARY: Simone de Beauvoir (1908–1986)

The French feminist thinker Simone de Beauvoir.

The French philosopher and writer Simone de Beauvoir was born in Paris in 1908, the elder daughter of a lawyer. After attending schools in and around the French capital, she took a philosophy course at the University of Paris, the Sorbonne, where her fellow students included the future philosopher Maurice Merleau-Ponty and anthropologist Claude Lévi-Strauss. In 1929 de Beauvoir took the philosophy *agrégation*, a competitive examination for teachers in France. She was placed a very close second behind Jean-Paul Sartre, the existentialist philosopher and writer, with whom she began a personal and professional relationship that lasted until Sartre's death in 1980.

Philosophy and politics

From 1931 de Beauvoir taught in schools in Marseille, Rouen, and Paris; but with the publication in 1943 of her first novel, *She Came to Stay*, she turned her attention to writing as a career. Her works of both fiction and nonfiction were expressions of her existentialist thought. To begin with, she shared Sartre's view that human beings are entirely free to choose how they live their lives and wholly responsible for their choices. In time, though, she modified her stance, putting forward an individual's circumstances and lack of experience as possible limiting factors on his or her freedom of action. Like Sartre's, de Beauvoir's political beliefs were socialist in nature, and the two collaborated on the left-wing magazine *Les Temps Modernes* (*Modern Times*) from 1945.

Feminism

Besides *She Came to Stay*, de Beauvoir's novels include *The Mandarins*, published in 1954 and for which she won the Prix Goncourt, while among her nonfiction works are *The Ethics of Ambiguity* (1947), travel books, and extensive memoirs.

She probably remains best known for *The Second Sex*, which appeared in 1949 and sold more than 20,000 copies in its first week of publication. The book, which became a feminist classic, argues that a male-dominated world enshrined man as the standard human being and regarded woman as an inferior model. De Beauvoir herself was later closely associated with the feminist movement.

It was only later, in the eighteenth century, that genuinely democratic men began to view the matter objectively. Diderot, among others, strove to show that woman is, like man, a human being. Later John Stuart Mill came fervently to her defence. But these philosophers displayed unusual impartiality. In the nineteenth century the feminist quarrel became again a quarrel of partisans. One of the consequences of the industrial revolution was the entrance of women into productive labour, and it was just here that the claims of the feminists emerged from the realm of theory and acquired an economic basis, while their opponents became the more aggressive. Although landed property lost power to some extent, the bourgeoisie clung to the old morality that found the guarantee of private property in the solidity of the family. Woman was ordered back into the home the more harshly as her emancipation became a real menace. Even within the working class the men endeavoured to restrain woman's liberation, because they began to see the women as dangerous competitors—the more so because they were accustomed to work for lower wages.

Woman the reflector of ideas?

[T]he most mediocre of males feels himself a demigod as compared with women. It was much easier for M. de Montherlant to think himself a hero when he faced women (and women chosen for his purpose) than when he was obliged to act the man among men—something many women have done better than he, for that matter. And in September 1948, in one of his articles in the *Figaro Littéraire*, Claude Mauriac—whose great originality is admired by all—could write regarding woman: "We listen on a tone [sic!] of polite indifference … to the most brilliant among them, well knowing that her wit reflects more or less luminously ideas that come from us." Evidently the speaker referred to is not reflecting the ideas of Mauriac himself, for no one knows of his having any. It may be that she reflects ideas originating with men, but then, even among men there are those who have been known to appropriate ideas not their own; and one can well ask whether Claude Mauriac might not find more interesting a conversation reflecting Descartes, Marx, or Gide rather than himself. What is really remarkable is that by using the questionable "we" he identifies himself with St Paul, Hegel, Lenin, and Nietzsche, and from the lofty eminence of their grandeur looks down disdainfully upon the bevy of women who make bold to converse with him on a footing of equality.

Henri de Montherlant (1896–1972) was a French writer who was also a bullfighter and served in World War I. His work tends to be masculine in outlook and condescending toward women.

Son of the Nobel Prize-winning French writer François Mauriac (1885–1970), Claude Mauriac (1914–1996) was a novelist, journalist, and critic. His best-known work is the ten-volume Time Immobilized, *published between 1974 and 1988.*

WAR AGAINST BOYS
Christina Hoff Sommers

NO

On April 20, 1999, Eric Harris and Dylan Klebold walked into Columbine High School, near Littleton, Colorado, and opened fire, killing 13 fellow students and wounding 21 more. They then killed themselves.

It's a bad time to be a boy in America. The triumphant victory of the U.S. women's soccer team at the World Cup last summer has come to symbolize the spirit of American girls. The shooting at Columbine High last spring might be said to symbolize the spirit of American boys…

That boys are in disrepute is not accidental. For many years women's groups have complained that boys benefit from a school system that favors them and is biased against girls. "Schools shortchange girls," declares the American Association of University Women. Girls are "undergoing a kind of psychological foot-binding," two prominent educational psychologists say. A stream of books and pamphlets cite research showing not only that boys are classroom favorites but also that they are given to schoolyard violence and sexual harassment.

In the view that has prevailed in American education over the past decade, boys are resented, both as the unfairly privileged sex and as obstacles on the path to gender justice for girls. This perspective is promoted in schools of education, and many a teacher now feels that girls need and deserve special indemnifying consideration. "It is really clear that boys are Number One in this society and in most of the world," says Patricia O'Reilly, a professor of education and the director of the Gender Equity Center, at the University of Cincinnati.

The author rejects the idea that girls are suffering and boys are benefiting as a result of favoritism between the sexes in schools. Do you agree?

The idea that schools and society grind girls down has given rise to an array of laws and policies intended to curtail the advantage boys have and to redress the harm done to girls. That girls are treated as the second sex in school and consequently suffer, that boys are accorded privileges and consequently benefit—these are things everyone is presumed to know. But they are not true.

Error-ridden research

The research commonly cited to support claims of male privilege and male sinfulness is riddled with errors. Almost none of it has been published in peer-reviewed professional journals. Some of the data turn out to be mysteriously missing. A review of the facts shows boys, not girls, on the

weak side of an education gender gap. The typical boy is a year and a half behind the typical girl in reading and writing; he is less committed to school and less likely to go to college. In 1997 college full-time enrollments were 45 percent male and 55 percent female. The Department of Education predicts that the proportion of boys in college classes will continue to shrink.

Girls forging ahead

Data from the U.S. Department of Education and from several recent university studies show that far from being shy and demoralized, today's girls outshine boys. They get better grades. They have higher educational aspirations. They follow more-rigorous academic programs and participate in advanced-placement classes at higher rates.... Girls, allegedly timorous and lacking in confidence, now outnumber boys in student government, in honor societies, on school newspapers, and in debating clubs. Only in sports are boys ahead, and women's groups are targeting the sports gap with a vengeance. Girls read more books. They outperform boys on tests for artistic and musical ability. More girls than boys study abroad. More join the Peace Corps. At the same time, more boys than girls are suspended from school. More are held back and more drop out. Boys are three times as likely to receive a diagnosis of attention-deficit hyperactivity disorder. More boys than girls are involved in crime, alcohol, and drugs. Girls attempt suicide more often than boys, but it is boys who more often succeed....

In the technical language of education experts, girls are academically more "engaged." Last year an article in *The CQ Researcher* about male and female academic achievement described a common parental observation: "Daughters want to please their teachers by spending extra time on projects, doing extra credit, making homework as neat as possible. Sons rush through homework assignments and run outside to play, unconcerned about how the teacher will regard the sloppy work."

School engagement is a critical measure of student success. The U.S. Department of Education gauges student commitment by the following criteria: "How much time do students devote to homework each night?" and "Do students come to class prepared and ready to learn? (Do they bring books and pencils? Have they completed their homework?)" According to surveys of fourth, eighth, and twelfth graders, girls consistently do more homework than boys. By the twelfth grade boys are four times as likely as girls not to do

In September 2001, 61 percent of the Peace Corps' 7,300 volunteers and trainees were female.

In 1997, a typical year, 4,483 young Americans aged five to 24 committed suicide: 701 females and 3,782 males.

Do you think these criteria for assessing academic engagement are reasonable?

Girls are now said to be outshining boys in their educational achievements.

homework. Similarly, more boys than girls report that they "usually" or "often" come to school without supplies or without having done their homework.

The performance gap between boys and girls in high school leads directly to the growing gap between male and female admissions to college. The Department of Education reports that in 1996 there were 8.4 million women but only 6.7 million men enrolled in college. It predicts that women will hold on to and increase their lead well into the next decade.

Deconstructing the test-score gap

In the July, 1995, issue of *Science*, Larry V. Hedges and Amy Nowell, researchers at the University of Chicago, observed that girls' deficits in math were small but not insignificant. These deficits, they noted, could adversely affect the number of women who "excel in scientific and technical occupations." Of the deficits in boys' writing skills they wrote, "The large sex differences in writing ... are alarming.... The data imply that males are, on average, at a rather profound disadvantage in the performance of this basic skill." They went on to warn,

The generally larger numbers of males who perform near the bottom of the distribution in reading comprehension and writing also have policy implications. It seems likely that individuals with such poor literacy skills will have difficulty finding employment in an increasingly information-driven economy. Thus, some intervention may be required to enable them to participate constructively....

Three years ago Scarsdale High School, in New York, held a gender-equity workshop for faculty members. It was the standard girls-are-being-shortchanged fare, with one notable difference. A male student gave a presentation in which he pointed to evidence suggesting that girls at Scarsdale High were well ahead of boys. David Greene, a social-studies teacher, thought the student must be mistaken, but when he and some colleagues analyzed department grading patterns, they discovered that the student was right. They found little or no difference in the grades of boys and girls in advanced-placement social-studies classes. But in standard classes the girls were doing a lot better.

And Greene discovered one other thing: few wanted to hear about his startling findings.... After so many years of hearing about silenced, diminished girls, teachers do not take seriously the suggestion that boys are not doing as well as girls even if they see it with their own eyes in their own classrooms.

According to the Digest of Education Statistics, 2000, produced by the National Center for Education Statistics, between 1988 and 1998 the number of male full-tme graduate students increased by 17 percent, whereas numbers of full-time women rose by 60 percent.

Can you think of any reasons why girls might be less good at math while boys are less good at reading?

What reasons might people have to ignore such seemingly solid evidence as that produced at Scarsdale High?

Summary

The equality of the sexes has always been a matter of great debate, and the notion of whether feminism is dead or obsolete received a lot of press coverage in the United States in the late 1990s. In her classic text *The Second Sex* French feminist writer Simone de Beauvoir outlines why women are treated differently from men. She calls on several well-known and respected male figures to show how women have been characterized as the inferior and secondary sex in history. She shows how philosophers as famous and influential as Aristotle have put women down.

Christina Hoff Sommers in "War against Boys," on the other hand, asserts that the tables have now turned—women are far from being the second sex; she suggests that men now are. Looking at the case of education, Sommers concludes that girls are doing much better than boys and have higher aspirations and study patterns. She argues that girls are more than equal to their male peers.

FURTHER INFORMATION:

Books:

de Beauvoir, Simone, *The Second Sex*. London: Penguin, 1949.

Faludi, Susan, *Backlash: The Undeclared War against American Women*. New York: Anchor, 1992.

Hoff Sommers, Christina, *The War against Boys: How Misguided Feminism Is Harming Our Young Men*. New York: Simon & Schuster, 2000.

Young, Cathy, *Ceasefire!: Why Women and Men Must Join Forces to Achieve True Equality*. New York: Free Press, 1999.

Useful websites:

www.unfpa.org/swp/2000/english/ch01.html
United Nations Population Fund site on gender issues.

www.time.com/time/magazine/1998/dom/980629/cover1.html
Gina Bellafante, "Feminism: It's All about Me!"

www.mg.co.za/mg/news/99dec2/29dec-women.html
Khadija Magardie, "Women: Still the Second Sex" looks at the situation in South Africa.

www.ericajong.com/nyobserver980713.htm
Erica Jong's monthly column in the *New York Observer*.

www.theatlantic.com/issues/97nov/pollitt.htm
Katha Pollitt, "Feminism's Unfinished Business."

www.worldbank.org/gender/assessment/wig.htm
Gender site of World Bank Group.

www.edc.org/WomensEquity/women/beauvoir.htm
Women's Equity Resource Center tribute to de Beauvoir.

The following debates in the Pro/Con series may also be of interest:

In this volume:

Topic 1 Is inequality a problem?

Topic 6 Should affirmative action continue?

Topic 15 Is abortion a right?

Abortion in the United States, pages 200–201

Topic 16 Is surrogate motherhood wrong?

ARE WOMEN STILL THE SECOND SEX?

YES: Women are still treated as second-class citizens. They earn less than men and are discriminated against in the workplace and at home

YES: Society expects women to be successful in the workplace, to look beautiful, and to have a well-run home

YES: Women are expected to work twice as hard as men to prove themselves, often for less pay

INEQUALITY
Are women discriminated against?

"SUPER WOMEN"
Does society have unfair expectations of women today?

NO: Women are in some of the most important political, economic, and social positions in the United States

NO: Women have proved time and time again that they can do things better than men. The latter, if anything, are at a disadvantage.

ARE WOMEN STILL THE SECOND SEX?
KEY POINTS

YES: Men continually put women down, criticizing them if they are poor mothers and demonizing them if they do well in a job

YES: The Old Boy Network still exists, and women are outsiders

MEN V. WOMEN
Do men perpetuate the myth that women are inferior?

NO: The abilities of women are praised on a daily basis in the press

NO: Women can be each other's worst enemies and sometimes help keep the myth going

Topic 4
SHOULD THE CONSTITUTIONAL "RIGHT TO PRIVACY" PROTECT HOMOSEXUAL CONDUCT?

YES

BOWERS V. HARDWICK
JUSTICE HARRY BLACKMUN

NO

BOWERS V. HARDWICK
JUSTICE BYRON WHITE

INTRODUCTION

The U.S. Constitution makes no explicit provision for a "right to privacy." However, the Supreme Court has from time to time concluded that the Constitution protects certain implied fundamental rights, including a right to privacy. The court sometimes applies general principles of ordered liberty and enforces individual rights even when there is no provision in the Constitution that expressly protects those rights. Cases on abortion rights are perhaps the most famous of this kind.

As Justice White remarks in the second article in this debate, the Supreme Court has been wary of exercising this power too freely because it does not want to usurp power that properly belongs to the people and their elected representatives. In "implied rights" cases, Justice White argues, the Supreme Court must strive to "assure itself and the public that announcing rights not readily identifiable in the Constitution's text involves much more than the imposition of the Justices' own choice of values" on a reluctant people. When does the Supreme Court have the rightful power to overrule the democratic community's own "choice of values"? When is it antidemocratic for the Supreme Court to impose its will or judgment in this way?

In recent years the Supreme Court has grappled with the question of whether the emerging constitutional right to privacy protects homosexual conduct. When the democratic community, acting through its elected representatives, passes laws against homosexual conduct—such as the law against sodomy at issue in the case of *Bowers v. Hardwick*, 1986, from which the following articles are excerpted— does it exceed its rightful authority by infringing on a constitutional right of individual citizens to order their private sexual lives as they see fit without interference from the government?

48

Or is this a case in which the democratic majority must be permitted to make its own "choice of values," including by expressing its disapproval of homosexual conduct?

> "[Disapproval of homosexuality cannot justify] invading the houses, hearts, and minds of citizens who choose to live their lives differently."
> —JUSTICE HARRY BLACKMUN

In order to answer this question, we must think about the meaning of the "right to privacy." The origin of the modern right to privacy can be found in the famous case of *Griswold v. Connecticut*, 1965, in which the court held that "specific guarantees in the Bill of Rights have penumbras, formed by emanations from those guarantees that give them life and substance." Various provisions in the Bill of Rights explicitly protect specific zones of privacy—for example, the Fourth Amendment protects the privacy of persons, homes, and papers from unreasonable searches. However, the court reasoned that it was necessary to recognize a more general "right to privacy" that would protect areas of privacy beyond those protected by the specific provisions of the Bill of Rights. That was necessary in order to be faithful to the spirit of those explicit constitutional provisions.

In *Griswold* the court held that this more general right to privacy includes the right of married persons to use contraceptives. In a number of other cases the court has also proved willing to extend the general right of privacy to protect certain other rights associated with the family—the freedom to make private choices in matters of procreation, child rearing, marriage, and education free from government interference. Indeed, the court has sometimes gone so far as to suggest, without quite saying, that the definition of what constitutes the "family" is a matter of private choice, protected by the Constitution from government interference or regulation.

In *Bowers v. Hardwick* the court was presented with the question of whether a state statute that criminalizes sodomy between homosexuals is an infringement of the constitutional right to privacy. (The statute actually criminalizes sodomy between consenting adults in general, not only between homosexuals, but the court does not address the broader question.) The answer to this question turns out to depend in large measure on how one specifies the particular right in question. Is this case about a right to engage in acts of sodomy, as Justice White sees it, in the second article? (The majority decision of the court was expressed by Justice White when he ruled that the constitutional right to privacy does not protect homosexual conduct.) Or is it, as Justice Blackmun argues, about a right to order one's private sexual conduct and to choose modes of sexual intimacy as one sees fit without interference from the state? Or is it even, as Justice Blackmun puts it (quoting a famous earlier opinion by Justice Brandeis), a case about "the most comprehensive of rights and the right most valued by civilized men," namely, "the right to be let alone"?

BOWERS V. HARDWICK
Justice Harry Blackmun

☑ **JUSTICE BLACKMUN, with whom JUSTICE BRENNAN, JUSTICE MARSHALL, and JUSTICE STEVENS join, dissenting.**

This case is no more about "a fundamental right to engage in homosexual sodomy," as the court purports to declare, than *Stanley v. Georgia* was about a fundamental right to watch obscene movies, or *Katz v. United States* was about a fundamental right to place interstate bets from a telephone booth. Rather, this case is about "the most comprehensive of rights and the right most valued by civilized men," namely, "the right to be let alone" [*Olmstead v. United States*].

Longevity is no justification for law

The statute at issue denies individuals the right to decide for themselves whether to engage in particular forms of private, consensual sexual activity. The court concludes that [it] is valid essentially because "the laws of … many states … still make such conduct illegal and have done so for a very long time." But the fact that the moral judgments expressed by statutes like [this] may be "natural and familiar … ought not to conclude our judgment upon the question whether statutes embodying them conflict with the Constitution of the United States" [*Roe v. Wade*]. Like Justice Holmes, I believe that "[i]t is revolting to have no better reason for a rule of law than that so it was laid down in the time of Henry IV. It is still more revolting if the grounds upon which it was laid down have vanished long since, and the rule simply persists from blind imitation of the past." I believe we must analyze respondent Hardwick's claim in the light of the values that underlie the constitutional right to privacy. If that right means anything, it means that, before Georgia can prosecute its citizens for making choices about the most intimate aspects of their lives, it must do more than assert that the choice they have made is an "abominable crime not fit to be named among Christians."

"Our cases long have recognized that the Constitution embodies a promise that a certain private sphere of individual liberty will be kept largely beyond the reach of government" [*Thornburgh v. American College of*

In Roe v. Wade, 1973, the U.S. Supreme Court ruled that abortion was a constitutional right. For a discussion on abortion see Topic 15 Is abortion a right?, pages 188–199.

Obstetricians & Gynecologists]. In construing the right to privacy, the court has proceeded along two somewhat distinct, albeit complementary, lines. First, it has recognized a privacy interest with reference to certain decisions that are properly for the individual to make. Second, it has recognized a privacy interest with reference to certain places without regard for the particular activities in which the individuals who occupy them are engaged. The case before us implicates both the decisional and the spatial aspects of the right to privacy.

Only the most willful blindness could obscure the fact that sexual intimacy is "a sensitive, key relationship of human existence, central to family life, community welfare, and the development of human personality" [*Paris Adult Theatre I v. Slaton*]. The fact that individuals define themselves in a significant way through their intimate sexual relationships with others suggests, in a nation as diverse as ours, that there may be many "right" ways of conducting those relationships, and that much of the richness of a relationship will come from the freedom an individual has to choose the form and nature of these intensely personal bonds.

Different people make different choices

In a variety of circumstances we have recognized that a necessary corollary of giving individuals freedom to choose how to conduct their lives is acceptance of the fact that different individuals will make different choices. For example, in holding that the clearly important state interest in public education should give way to a competing claim by the Amish to the effect that extended formal schooling threatened their way of life, the court declared: "There can be no assumption that today's majority is 'right' and the Amish and others like them are 'wrong.' A way of life that is odd or even erratic but interferes with no rights or interests of others is not to be condemned because it is different." The court claims that its decision today merely refuses to recognize a fundamental right to engage in homosexual sodomy; what the court really has refused to recognize is the fundamental interest all individuals have in controlling the nature of their intimate associations with others.

For a discussion about this case regarding the Amish and compulsory education see Topic 9 Should there be a right to violate laws for religious reasons?, pages 114–125.

The behavior for which Hardwick faces prosecution occurred in his own home, a place to which the Fourth Amendment attaches special significance. The court's treatment of this aspect of the case is symptomatic of its overall refusal to consider the broad principles that have informed our treatment of privacy in specific cases. Just as the right to privacy is more than the mere aggregation of a

COMMENTARY: U.S. sodomy laws

In general, sodomy laws prohibit oral and anal sex between consenting adults. In theory most of these laws apply to both heterosexual and homosexual people, but in practice they are mainly used against lesbians and gay men. For example, in some cases the courts have used the sodomy law to remove children from their parents (or parent) if the parents are homosexual. That is, under the law homosexual parents are deemed to be engaging in criminal behavior.

In 1961 Illinois became the first state to repeal its sodomy law, at a time when every other state in the U.S. had a sodomy law. In the 1970s and early 1980s 21 states got rid of their sodomy laws. During the 1980s, however, antigay groups mobilized to object to the repeal of sodomy laws. The U.S. Supreme Court's ruling in *Bowers v. Hardwick* greatly hampered legal efforts to overturn sodomy laws.

In recent years gay and lesbian rights and legal groups have mobilized and have been successful in having the law against sodomy overturned in several states. These states include Kentucky (1992), Tennessee (1996), Montana (1997), Georgia (1998), Maryland (1999), and Minnesota (2001). Today 15 states still have such laws.

Sodomy laws that target only same-sex acts

State	Penalty
Kansas	6 months/$1,000
Oklahoma	10 years
Texas	$500

Sodomy laws that target all consenting adults

State	Penalty
Alabama	1 year/$2,000
Florida	60 days/$500
Idaho	5 years to life
Louisiana	5 years/$2,000
Mississippi	10 years
North Carolina	10 years/discretionary fine
South Carolina	5 years/$500
Utah	6 months/$1,000
Virginia	1–5 years

Sodomy laws the status of which is unclear

State	Penalty
Massachusetts	20 years
Michigan	15 years
Missouri	1 year/$1,000

number of entitlements to engage in specific behavior, so too, protecting the physical integrity of the home is more than merely a means of protecting specific activities that often take place there. Even when our understanding of the contours of the right to privacy depends on "reference to a 'place,'" [*Katz v. United States*] "the essence of a Fourth Amendment violation is 'not the breaking of [a person's] doors, and the rummaging of his drawers,' but rather is 'the invasion of his indefensible right of personal security, personal liberty, and private property'" [*California v. Ciraolo*].

The assertion that "traditional Judeo-Christian values proscribe" the conduct involved [Brief for Petitioner 20], cannot provide an adequate justification for [this law]. That certain, but by no means all, religious groups condemn the behavior at issue gives the state no license to impose their judgments on the entire citizenry. The legitimacy of secular legislation depends instead on whether the state can advance some justification for its law beyond its conformity to religious doctrine. Thus, far from buttressing his case, petitioner's invocation of *Leviticus, Romans*, St. Thomas Aquinas, and sodomy's heretical status during the Middle Ages undermines his suggestion that [this law] 16-6-2 represents a legitimate use of secular coercive power. A state can no more punish private behavior because of religious intolerance than it can punish such behavior because of racial animus. "The Constitution cannot control such prejudices, but neither can it tolerate them. Private biases may be outside the reach of the law, but the law cannot, directly or indirectly, give them effect" [*Palmore v. Sidoti*]. No matter how uncomfortable a certain group may make the majority of this court, we have held that "[m]ere public intolerance or animosity cannot constitutionally justify the deprivation of a person's physical liberty" [*O'Connor v. Donaldson*].

> St. Thomas Aquinas (around 1225–1274) was an Italian theologian and philosopher.

It took but three years for the court to see the error in its analysis in *Minersville School District v. Gobitis*, and to recognize that the threat to national cohesion posed by a refusal to salute the flag was vastly outweighed by the threat to those same values posed by compelling such a salute. I can only hope that here, too, the court soon will reconsider its analysis and conclude that depriving individuals of the right to choose for themselves how to conduct their intimate relationships poses a far greater threat to the values most deeply rooted in our nation's history than tolerance of nonconformity could ever do. Because I think the court today betrays those values, I dissent.

BOWERS V. HARDWICK
Justice Byron White

NO

 JUSTICE WHITE delivered the opinion of the court.

This case does not require a judgment on whether laws against sodomy between consenting adults in general, or between homosexuals in particular, are wise or desirable. It raises no question about the right or propriety of state legislative decisions to repeal their laws that criminalize homosexual sodomy, or of state-court decisions invalidating those laws on state constitutional grounds. The issue presented is whether the Federal Constitution confers a fundamental right upon homosexuals to engage in sodomy and hence invalidates the laws of the many states that still make such conduct illegal and have done so for a very long time. The case also calls for some judgment about the limits of the court's role in carrying out its constitutional mandate.

We first register our disagreement with the Court of Appeals and with respondent that the court's prior cases have construed the Constitution to confer a right of privacy that extends to homosexual sodomy and for all intents and purposes have decided this case.

The due process clauses hold that a person has certain procedural rights (the right to a fair trial, for instance) when the government is punishing that person or taking away his or her freedom or property. The Supreme Court has interpreted these clauses also to protect substantive rights, so that there must be appropriate justification for taking away a person's life, freedom, or property.

Substantive interpretation of due process clauses

Precedent aside, however, respondent would have us announce, as the Court of Appeals did, a fundamental right to engage in homosexual sodomy. This we are quite unwilling to do. It is true that despite the language of the Due Process Clauses of the Fifth and Fourteenth Amendments, which appears to focus only on the processes by which life, liberty, or property is taken, the cases are legion in which those clauses have been interpreted to have substantive content, subsuming rights that to a great extent are immune from federal or state regulation or proscription. Among such cases are those recognizing rights that have little or no textual support in the constitutional language.

Defining fundamental liberties

Striving to assure itself and the public that announcing rights not readily identifiable in the Constitution's text involves much more than the imposition of the Justices' own choice of values on the states and the federal government, the court has sought to identify the nature of the rights qualifying for heightened judicial protection. In *Palko v. Connecticut* it was said that this category includes those fundamental liberties that are "implicit in the concept of ordered liberty," such that "neither liberty nor justice would exist if [they] were sacrificed." A different description of fundamental liberties appeared in *Moore v. East Cleveland*, where they are characterized as those liberties that are "deeply rooted in this nation's history and tradition."

Sodomy has long been a criminal offense

It is obvious to us that neither of these formulations would extend a fundamental right to homosexuals to engage in acts of consensual sodomy. Proscriptions against that conduct have ancient roots. Sodomy was a criminal offense at common law and was forbidden by the laws of the original 13 states when they ratified the Bill of Rights. In 1868, when the Fourteenth Amendment was ratified, all but five of the 37 states in the Union had criminal sodomy laws. In fact, until 1961 all 50 states outlawed sodomy, and today 24 states and the District of Columbia continue to provide criminal penalties for sodomy performed in private and between consenting adults. Against this background, to claim that a right to engage in such conduct is "deeply rooted in this nation's history and tradition" or "implicit in the concept of ordered liberty" is, at best, facetious.

In 2001, 15 states still had sodomy laws. See the box on page 52 for more information on current sodomy laws in the United States.

Judge-made constitutional law

Nor are we inclined to take a more expansive view of our authority to discover new fundamental rights imbedded in the Due Process Clause. The court is most vulnerable and comes nearest to illegitimacy when it deals with judge-made constitutional law having little or no cognizable roots in the language or design of the Constitution. That this is so was painfully demonstrated by the face-off between the executive and the court in the 1930s, which resulted in the repudiation of much of the substantive gloss that the court had placed on the Due Process Clauses of the Fifth and Fourteenth Amendments. There should be, therefore, great resistance to expand the substantive reach of those clauses, particularly if it requires redefining the category of rights deemed to be fundamental. Otherwise, the judiciary necessarily takes to itself further authority to govern the country without express constitutional authority. The claimed right pressed on us today falls far short of overcoming this resistance.

The American actress Ellen DeGeneres, pictured above with her former partner Anne Heche, chose to out herself in one of the episodes of her comedy series Ellen.

Respondent, however, asserts that the result should be different where the homosexual conduct occurs in the privacy of the home. He relies on *Stanley v. Georgia*, where the court held that the First Amendment prevents conviction for possessing and reading obscene material in the privacy of one's home: "If the First Amendment means anything, it means that a state has no business telling a man, sitting alone in his house, what books he may read or what films he may watch."

No textual support in the Constitution

Stanley did protect conduct that would not have been protected outside the home, and it partially prevented the enforcement of state obscenity laws; but the decision was firmly grounded in the First Amendment. The right pressed upon us here has no similar support in the text of the Constitution, and it does not qualify for recognition under the prevailing principles for construing the Fourteenth Amendment. Its limits are also difficult to discern. Plainly enough, otherwise illegal conduct is not always immunized whenever it occurs in the home. Victimless crimes, such as the possession and use of illegal drugs, do not escape the law where they are committed at home. *Stanley* itself recognized that its holding offered no protection for the possession in the home of drugs, firearms, or stolen goods. And if respondent's submission is limited to the voluntary sexual conduct between consenting adults, it would be difficult, except by fiat, to limit the claimed right to homosexual conduct while leaving exposed to prosecution adultery, incest, and other sexual crimes even though they are committed in the home. We are unwilling to start down that road.

Should standards of behavior be different in public and in private?

Law is based on notions of morality

Even if the conduct at issue here is not a fundamental right, respondent asserts that there must be a rational basis for the law and that there is none in this case other than the presumed belief of a majority of the electorate in Georgia that homosexual sodomy is immoral and unacceptable. This is said to be an inadequate rationale to support the law. The law, however, is constantly based on notions of morality, and if all laws representing essentially moral choices are to be invalidated under the Due Process Clause, the courts will be very busy indeed. Even respondent makes no such claim, but insists that majority sentiments about the morality of homosexuality should be declared inadequate. We do not agree, and are unpersuaded that the sodomy laws of some 25 states should be invalidated on this basis.

Do you agree that majority sentiments about morality are an adequate basis for law?

Summary

In the first extract Justice Blackmun, in dissent from the majority decision of the court in *Bowers v. Hardwick*, argues that it is not a case about the right to engage in sodomy. Instead, he argues, it is a case about "the fundamental interest all individuals have in controlling the nature of their intimate associations with others." Individuals define themselves in large part "through their intimate sexual relationships," and there may be many "'right' ways of conducting those relationships." A right to privacy in one's intimate associations is fairly comprised within the right to privacy as it has developed since *Griswold*, Justice Blackmun argues. Moreover, courts need not respect the moral judgment of the democratic community in such matters, even if that judgment has a long historical pedigree.

In the second extract Justice White argues on behalf of the majority of the court that the constitutional right to privacy does not protect homosexual conduct. He defines the question narrowly—is there a right to engage in acts of homosexual sodomy?—and he argues that earlier cases establishing and defining the right to privacy are best understood as protecting the family from intrusions by the state.

Since "no connection between family, marriage, or procreation, on the one hand, and homosexual activity, on the other, has been demonstrated," the right to privacy established by those cases does not protect homosexual conduct. Moreover, there is no good reason, Justice White argues, to extend the right to privacy to include homosexual conduct because the law is often properly based on moral questions, and courts should not overrule such democratic judgments without clear authority from the "language or design" of the Constitution to do so, especially in the face of strong evidence of the willingness of the people to act on their moral opinions, as in this case.

FURTHER INFORMATION:

Books:

Cain, Patricia A., *Rainbow Rights: The Role of Lawyers and Courts in the Lesbian and Gay Civil Rights Movement*. Boulder, CO: Westview Press, 2000.

Murdoch, Joyce and Deb Price (editors), *Courting Justice*. New York: Basic Books, 2001.

Stychin, Carl and Didi Herman (editors), *Law and Sexuality*. Minneapolis: University of Minnesota Press, 2001.

Useful websites:

www.aclu.org/issues/gay
American Civil Liberties Union lesbian and gay rights.
www.ngltf.org
National Gay and Lesbian Task Force.

www.ibiblio.org/gaylaw
National Journal of Sexual Orientation Law.

The following debates in the Pro/Con series may also be of interest:

In this volume:

Topic 5 Should gay men and women be allowed to marry?

Topic 8 Should people have to obey unjust laws?

SHOULD THE CONSTITUTIONAL "RIGHT TO PRIVACY" PROTECT HOMOSEXUAL CONDUCT?

YES: Society and government still treat the gay community unfairly and thus propagate prejudice

YES: Freedom is an innate right, and as such the right to practice homosexuality is covered

DISCRIMINATION
Is society prejudiced against homosexuals?

CONSTITUTION
Does the Bill of Rights cover homosexuality?

NO: We live in a liberal democracy, and there are enough gay people in the public eye to alleviate prejudice. It is only a tiny minority who remain prejudiced against this group, and that is because of ignorance.

NO: Homosexuality is not condoned by the church or by society at large; thus the Constitution does not cover this subject

SHOULD THE CONSTITU-TIONAL "RIGHT TO PRIVACY" PROTECT HOMOSEXUAL CONDUCT? KEY POINTS

YES: People in positions of power lay themselves open to blackmail and extortion if they keep such secrets about their sexuality—the right to privacy just encourages lies and abuses

YES: By implication the Constitution acknowledges privacy as an important right

PRIVACY
Does the right to privacy encourage lying?

INDIVIDUAL RIGHTS
Is there a right to privacy?

NO: Society has quite strong privacy laws in place. Everyone should have a basic right to privacy, particularly about such personal matters as sexuality, and that shouldn't lead to lies.

NO: The Constitution does not explicitly guarantee privacy. To do so might allow criminal acts done in private to go unpunished.

Topic 5
SHOULD GAY MEN AND WOMEN BE ALLOWED TO MARRY?

YES

"GAY MARRIAGE: SHOULD LESBIAN AND GAY COUPLES BE ALLOWED TO MARRY"?
ACLU ANSWERS, JUNE 1998
AMERICAN CIVIL LIBERTIES UNION

NO

"A CRITICAL ANALYSIS OF CONSTITUTIONAL CLAIMS FOR SAME-SEX MARRIAGE"
BRIGHAM YOUNG UNIVERSITY LAW REVIEW
LYNN D. WARDLE

INTRODUCTION

The issue of whether same-sex couples should have the right to marry has been debated for more than 30 years. In the last few years the debate has become more heated as civil rights groups, gay activist groups, the church, and antigay organizations, among others, have argued both in and out of court on the ethical, legal, and moral implications of allowing same-sex couples to marry. For many people who view marriage as a heterosexual institution, primarily for the procreation of children, same-sex marriage is irrelevant. For advocates of same-sex marriage, however, the issue is about providing equal rights to the gay community. These rights would not only allow same-sex couples engaged in loving relationships to legally commit to each other. They would also enable them to have the same legal and societal rights as heterosexual couples. These rights can be very significant, particularly with regard to such issues as entitlement to various welfare or pension benefits, the ability to adopt children, and so on.

Supporters of same-sex relationships often use the civil rights campaign as the basis of their argument. They argue that homosexuality is comparable to race: It is genetically determined. Just as bans on interracial marriages were declared unconstitutional in 1967, bans on same-sex marriage should be similarly overturned. Opponents, however, argue that unlike race, homosexuality is a behavioral choice.

The debate about same-sex marriage poses particular religious and legal dilemmas. For many people it is a largely semantic question that hinges on the precise meaning of the word "marriage." In legal and biblical terms marriage is defined as a union between a man and a woman, and the call for same-sex marriage has stirred great debate in religious groups reluctant to change that definition. Marriage in Western society is perceived as a

Christian tradition with Christian values and mores, and homosexuality is not an act recognized or condoned by Western faiths. Several churches, such as the Presbyterian Church, have voted to ban any same-sex ceremony. Gay advocates such as the American Civil Liberties Union (ACLU) and its British equivalent, Stonewall, have been campaigning for same-sex marriage since 1977. They argue that marriage rites have differed throughout time; even within the Christian tradition marriage has meant different things at different times.

> *"Such as are in the institution [of marriage] wish to get out and such as are out wish to get in."*
>
> —RALPH WALDO EMERSON, AUTHOR AND PHILOSOPHER

In Hawaii the legalization of same-sex marriage was approved by a state court in 1996. In 1999, however, the Hawaii Supreme Court ruled that the original case was moot, and marriage was officially limited to heterosexual couples. In June 1999 the Dutch Cabinet made the landmark decision to authorize the introduction of bills that allow marriage and adoption by same-sex couples. Although same-sex adoption was already legal in Denmark, some U.S. states, and some provinces in Canada, marriage between same-sex couples is treated very differently.

There does not seem to be great public support for same-sex marriage.

In 1998, 62 percent of voters in the United States approved of a proposal to amend the Constitution to state that marriage can exist only between a man and a woman. That same year bills banning same-sex marriage were passed in 25 states, though they were blocked in a further 24.

In April 2000 Vermont authorized a new law that provided same-sex couples with a "civil union" license. This legitimized their right to receive benefits as a domestic couple. The bill permits a marriagelike union, and gay partners now enjoy all the state law protections available to their heterosexual peers, such as the right to change surnames, eligibility for the housing opportunity allowance, and the right to make medical decisions for partners. The move caused uproar among those opposed to same-sex marriage and only limited celebration among the gay community because the law still does not give same-sex partners the same tax or immigration benefits allowed to heterosexual couples under federal law.

The two articles that follow examine both sides of the argument. The ACLU argues that marriage is a basic human right that should not be denied to anyone. Denying gay and lesbians the right to marry, it says, denies them basic dignity and has practical costs, too.

Lynn D. Wardle examines the question from a legal point of view, explicitly the question of whether same-sex marriage is a right under the Constitution. He concludes that it is not and argues that there is no legal precedent for allowing same-sex marriage. While not denying gay men and women the right to have loving relationships, he argues that the essential meaning of marriage in the U.S. tradition is heterosexual.

GAY MARRIAGE
American Civil Liberties Union

Civil marriage is the primary institution in our society for recognizing our most intimate, committed relationships. It is also the device our society uses to identify our partners for a range of rights and responsibilities— everything from retirement programs to hospital visitations.

For years, lesbians and gay men across the country have been fighting for the freedom to marry in order to secure those same rights and recognition. But recently, spurred by a court case in Hawaii, the battle has moved center stage to become one of the burning issues of our time.

The Hawaii case

In December 1996, a trial court in Hawaii ruled that the state's ban on same-sex marriages violates the equal protection clause of the Hawaii constitution. The case was brought by two lesbian couples and one gay male couple who were denied marriage licenses in 1991.

The trial court ruling—the first of its kind in the nation's history—held that Hawaii had failed to meet its burden under a Hawaii Supreme Court decision to offer a "compelling" reason to maintain a discriminatory practice. That earlier decision by the Hawaii Supreme Court had held that the state's refusal to honor same-sex marriages may violate the Hawaii constitution's ban on sex discrimination, just as laws banning marriages between people of different races would violate race anti-discrimination laws.

The trial court ruling was appealed to the Hawaii Supreme Court, which has not yet rendered its final decision. Meanwhile, in November 1998, Hawaii's citizens will vote on whether the legislature should be instructed to amend the state's constitution to prohibit same-sex marriage.

The Hawaii Supreme Court ruled in 1999 that the original case was moot. That was because in 1998 opponents of same-sex marriage had voted for an amendment to the state Constitution restricting marriage to heterosexual couples.

Reaction in the mainland

There is a strong possibility that the lawsuit will compel Hawaii to begin allowing lesbians and gay men to marry. If that happens, other states will have to decide how to treat those legally married couples if they move to another state, or visit another state. The issue will also arise if a couple from another state goes to Hawaii to get married.

But opponents are not waiting for Hawaii to actually permit same-sex marriage. In the past couple of years, bills banning same-sex marriage were introduced in most states. Although many of these bills have been defeated, more than half the states have enacted discriminatory laws.

In addition, the federal government has stepped in and passed the so-called "Defense of Marriage Act" designed to ban federal recognition of lesbian and gay couples, and allow state governments to ignore same-sex marriages performed in other states.

Talking points

Gays and lesbians are currently denied the opportunity to marry in all 50 states. Yet, marriage is a basic human right that should not be denied to anyone. If a lesbian or gay couple wants to marry and commit themselves to each other, why should anyone interfere?

Marriage is also the device our society uses to identify our partners for an enormous range of practical situations. But because the committed relationships of lesbians and gay men are not recognized by law, they are denied the basic rights and protections that married couples enjoy. A gay couple who has been together for decades should have the right to visit a partner in a hospital, designate an heir, or take bereavement or sick leave.

Marriage is a personal decision that belongs to the two consenting adults in a relationship, not the government. The state should not be in the position of arranging [gay peoples'] marriages.

The ACLU position

The ACLU supports legal recognition of lesbian and gay relationships, including the right to marry. Such recognition is imperative for the complete legal equality of lesbian and gay individuals.
—ACLU Policy No. 264

The ACLU has also endorsed the "marriage resolution" developed by a coalition of groups working for the right of lesbians and gay men to marry. It states:

Because marriage is a basic human right and an individual personal choice, RESOLVED, the State should not interfere with same-gender couples who choose to marry and share fully and equally in the rights, responsibilities, and commitment of civil marriage.

In 2001, 36 states had laws prohibiting recognition of marriage between same-sex couples.

The Defense of Marriage Act was signed into law in 1996. It excludes same-sex couples from receiving any of the federal protections, rights, and responsibilities of marriage.

For more information on the "marriage resolution" see the Legal Defense and Education Fund (LAMDA) website at www.lamdalegal.org/cgi-bin/pages.

Rights denied to gay Americans

Denying lesbians and gay men the right to marry denies them simple, basic dignity and has serious practical costs as well. Among the practical consequences unique to marriage are the rights to:

- visit a partner or a partner's child in a hospital;
- inherit from your partner if she or he doesn't have a valid will;
- obtain joint health, home, and auto insurance policies;
- enter joint rental agreements;
- make medical decisions on a partner's behalf in event of illness;
- take bereavement or sick leave to care for a partner or a partner's child;
- choose a final resting place for a deceased partner;
- obtain wrongful death benefits for a surviving partner and children;
- get an equitable division of property in a divorce;
- have joint child custody, visitation, adoption, and foster care;
- determine child custody and support in a divorce;
- have a spouse covered under Social Security and Medicare;
- file joint tax returns;
- obtain veterans' discounts on medical care, education, and home loans;
- apply for immigration and residency for partners from other countries; and
- obtain domestic violence protective orders.

Marriage is a personal decision—not the government's

"Marriage is a basic human right. You cannot tell people they cannot fall in love," Dr. Martin Luther King, Jr. used to say when people talked about interracial marriage, and I quote, "Races do not fall in love and get married. Individuals fall in love and get married."
—Testimony of Rep. John Lewis of Georgia before Congress on the Defense of Marriage Act, 7/1/96

The issue is civil marriages

It will be up to each church to determine whether or not to conduct these marriages. This is a very different question than whether or not there are civil or State sponsored same-gender marriages. Regardless of the outcome of the court case, no church or clergy

COMMENTARY: Recognizing gay partnerships

Currently, gay and lesbian couples cannot legally marry anywhere in the United States. In the state of Vermont they can obtain a civil union certificate, which grants many of the protections, benefits, and responsibilities of marriage—but only in Vermont. Some religious faiths will bless a same-sex partnership in a religious ceremony, but that does not grant any legal protections or responsibilities. Same-sex couples can have a commitment ceremony in any state, but it has no legal significance.

The situation is somewhat different in other parts of the world. Although same-sex marriages are not legal in Canada, in 1999 the Supreme Court of Canada ruled that protections under law to "spouses" must also apply to gay and lesbian couples. A number of provinces now offer domestic partner benefits to gay and lesbian couples. In June 2001 Nova Scotia issued certificates formally recognizing same-sex couples as domestic partners. This gives these couples the same status as married heterosexual couples in the province, such as the provision of full spousal benefits and pensions.

Dutch first

In April 2001 the Netherlands became the first country to permit same-sex couples to marry and receive all the rights, protections, and benefits that heterosexual couples enjoy. For instance, gay and lesbian couples can take their partner's last name, jointly adopt children, and claim death benefits when one partner dies. Denmark, Greenland, Iceland, Norway, and Sweden have passed laws that permit same-sex couples to obtain "registered partnerships." These laws provide some but not all of the benefits of marriage—for example, couples cannot adopt each other's children.

Other countries have recognized gay and lesbian couples for the purposes of immigration. These countries include: Australia, Belgium, Canada, Denmark, Finland, France, Iceland, Israel, the Netherlands, New Zealand, Norway, South Africa, Spain, Sweden, and the United Kingdom.

will be forced to perform or to recognize same-gender marriages.
—Clergy Coalition and the Coalition for Equality and Diversity, Christianity, and Same-Gender Marriage, 8/96

Marriage is not just about procreation
"Marriage is not premised on procreation."
—1965 U.S. Supreme Court ruling in *Griswold v. Connecticut*
Besides, many married couples do not or cannot have children, and many lesbian and gay couples do have and raise children.

A CRITICAL ANALYSIS OF CONSTITUTIONAL CLAIMS FOR SAME-SEX MARRIAGE
Lynn D. Wardle

NO

X The proposed legalization of same-sex marriage is one of the most significant issues in contemporary American family law. Presently, it is one of the most vigorously advocated reforms discussed in law reviews, one of the most explosive political questions facing lawmakers, and one of the most provocative issues looming before American courts. If same-sex marriage is legalized, it could be one of the most revolutionary policy decisions in the history of American family law. The potential consequences, positive or negative, for children, parents, same-sex couples, families, social structure, social mores, public health, and the status of women are enormous.

The main purpose of this article is to stimulate and inform the exchange of legal analysis and policy perspectives regarding proposals to legalize same-sex marriage by critically analysing their leading constitutional arguments. The bulk of this article explains why no sound basis exists for constitutionalizing the same-sex marriage issue, either in fundamental rights doctrine or in equal protection doctrine.

Not a constitutional right

Despite some fine scholarship attempting to make the case, the claim that same-sex marriage is a part of the fundamental right to marry does not comport with our nation's history or traditions, which have long condemned homosexual behavior and have never allowed same-sex marriage. Likewise, the claim that same-sex sexual relations are "implicit in the concept of ordered liberty" is implausible. Thus, none of the established criteria for identifying special constitutional rights is satisfied by same-sex marriage claims.

Apart from the lack of proof of historical and conceptual validity, the precedents deny the constitutional rights claim, and all the rights arguments, for same-sex marriage. For example, in his landmark opinion in *Poe v. Ullman*, Justice Harlan explicitly linked the confining of sexual activity to

Supporters of same-sex marriage argue that there was resistance to women securing the vote and interracial marriage, yet these rights have now been enshrined in law.

marriage to the prohibition of homosexual activity, and concluded that both confinement of sexual activity to marriage and restriction of homosexual behavior were so deeply imbedded in the values and consciousness of the nation that they were both integral to "any Constitutional doctrine in this area."

… The most important precedent, however, is *Bowers v. Hardwick*. In *Bowers*, the Court upheld the constitutionality of a Georgia statute forbidding sodomy in a suit brought by a homosexual who had been charged with violating the law by engaging in consensual sexual behavior with another adult in the privacy of his own home. In reaching its decision, the Supreme Court directly considered, thoroughly examined, and unequivocally rejected the claim that the Constitution or the Supreme Court's interpretation of any of its provisions shelters any right to engage in, or provides any special protection for, homosexual behavior. The Supreme Court thus rejected any claim that homosexual behavior is constitutionally protected as part of a general category of constitutional privacy, as part of a right of intimate sexual conduct among consenting adults, or as part of a right to be free from governmental intrusion within a certain zone, namely, the home….The specific claim that the constitutionally protected right of marriage encompasses same-sex marriage was rejected when the Court explicitly concluded that "[n]o connection between family, marriage, or procreation on the one hand and homosexual activity on the other has been demonstrated."

> Should the Supreme Court have any say about individuals' private lives?

… Unless *Bowers* is overruled, the rights argument does not provide a plausible foundation for a constitutional claim for legalizing same-sex marriage. Therefore, it comes as no surprise to learn that every state court that has considered the issue, including the Hawaii Supreme Court in Baehr, has flatly rejected the claim that homosexuals have a federal or state constitutional right to marry each other.

For more information on the Hawaii Supreme Court case see pages 61–63 in this volume.

The nature and meaning of marriage

Another central flaw in the claim that same-sex marriage is protected as part of the constitutional right to marry concerns the nature and meaning of marriage. The relationship called marriage that has received special solicitude and protection by the Supreme Court for so many years has never included homosexual relations and has always involved or been defined as only heterosexual lifetime-commitment relationships. Likewise, all state and federal courts that have considered the issue have consistently held that marriage does not encompass same-sex relations.

Consistently in our legal tradition, the very nature and essential meaning of marriage is heterosexual.

> *Much of the author's argument here is based on the premise that only heterosexual unions can produce children. Supporters of same-sex marriage, however, argue that not all heterosexual couples can, or want to, have children.*

The heterosexual dimension of the relationship is at the very core of what makes marriage a unique union and is the reason why marriage is so valuable to individuals and to society. The concept of marriage is founded on the fact that the union of two persons of different genders creates a relationship of unique potential strength and inimitable potential value to society. The essence of marriage is the integration of a universe of gender differences (profound and subtle, biological and cultural, psychological and genetic) associated with sexual identity. In the same way that "separate but equal" was a false premise and that racial segregation is not equivalent to racial integration, same-sex marriage is not equivalent to heterosexual marriage.

Thus, the definition of marriage as a cross-gender union is not merely a matter of arbitrary definition or semantic wordplay; it is fundamental to the concept and nature of marriage itself. A same-sex relationship is something else; it may have many good partnership qualities, even some similar-to-marriage qualities, but it does not possess the unique nature of the cross-gender union that is marriage….

Rights to privacy v. public approval

Many constitutional rights arguments to legalize same-sex marriage assert zonal privacy claims. However … proponents of same-sex marriage fail to recognize the difference between public non-interference with private homosexual behavior and public approval or endorsement of homosexual behavior. As a matter of both modern and historical jurisprudence, there is a legally recognized and profound difference between the state not punishing private homosexual behavior between consenting adults and the state endorsing or recognizing a public right to engage in such behavior. The difference is that between privacy and rights….

Legislative rejection of same-sex marriage is unanimous in the United States. In the quarter century since the gay-rights movement in America began in earnest, no legislature in any American state has legalized same-sex marriage. Nor has Congress enacted any legislation promoting the legalization of same-sex marriage. Administrative acceptance of same-sex marriage also is virtually nil.

Race and sexuality are not analogous

… Same-sex marriage advocates argue that the illegality of same-sex marriage is analogous to the antiquated prohibition of marriage between races. This argument is often called the "Loving analogy...."

From the perspective of legitimate marriage policy, race is not a relevant consideration. In *Loving*, the Supreme Court found that interracial marriages and same-race marriages are functionally equal. The classification scheme in the Virginia antimiscegenation laws was logically unrelated to the subject of regulation, marriage. "There is patently no legitimate overriding purpose independent of invidious racial discrimination which justifies this classification." By comparison, the claim that same-sex relationships are equal to or fungible with conventional heterosexual marriage relationships is strained at best. The court in *Loving* emphasized the uniqueness of conventional marriage: "Marriage is ... fundamental to our very existence and survival." Surely, the "very existence and survival" of our society does not depend upon same-sex unions.

Furthermore, race is an inherent condition, but homosexual behavior is chosen behavior. Race is passive, homosexual behavior is active. Race is undeniably an immutable, biologically determined condition, which homosexual behavior has not been shown to be. Intuitively, there is a distinction between immutable racial classifications, which are logically irrelevant to legitimate legal policies, and personal sexual behavior choices, which are of substantial social concern, especially regarding marriage....

In Loving v. Virginia *(1967) the Supreme Court invalidated Virginia's laws forbidding and punishing interracial marriage. This was a landmark decision in legalizing interracial marriages in the United States.*

What recent scientific evidence can you find to question the idea that "homosexual behavior is chosen behavior"?

Formulating policy

The failure of the constitutional claims for legalization of same-sex marriage means that state and other lawmakers are not required under the Constitution to legalize same-sex marriage, although they may voluntarily choose to do so. Thus, this article establishes that legal scholars and lawmakers are free to fully consider, debate, and decide whether, as a matter of sound public policy, same-sex marriage should be legalized. If permitted to look beyond the coercive politics of constitutionalization, one may discover that committed, lifelong unions of a man and a woman are uniquely beneficial to individuals and uniquely essential to the health and well-being of civilized society. It is to that important policy issue that advocates and opponents of same-sex marriage should devote their research and analytical skills, and upon which the public discussion should focus, rather than pursuing strained and diversionary claims that the Constitution of the United States mandates the legalization of same-sex marriage. Let the policy debate begin.

Summary

Throughout the debate on same-sex marriage several questions arise. What is marriage? What is its role in society? Do domestic partnerships of any kind warrant the same rights as a marriage? How is the institution of marriage changing? In the first article the ACLU insists that same-sex marriage is a right and lists the ways in which people engaged in a same-sex relationship are currently excluded from very basic rights. It quotes the 1965 U.S. ruling in *Griswold v. Connecticut*: "Marriage is not premised on procreation. Besides, many married couples do not or cannot have children, and many lesbian and gay couples do have and raise children." Marriage, it argues, is a personal decision that belongs to two consenting adults, not to the government. It is a basic human right that should not be denied to anyone.

Lynn D. Wardle, in the second article, examines whether there is any Constitutional basis for same-sex marriages. Wardle uses several recent court cases to support his argument that no sound basis exists for sanctioning same-sex marriage. There is no legal precedent for it, he says, and neither is there any basis for legalizing it on constitutional grounds, either in fundamental rights doctrine or in equal protection doctrine. The diagram on the opposite page sums up the key points in the debate.

FURTHER INFORMATION:

Books:
Baird, Robert M. and Stuart E. Rosenbaum (editors), *Same-sex Marriage: The Moral and Legal Debate*. Amhurst, NY: Prometheus Books, 1997.
Eskridge Jr., William N, *The Case for Same-sex Marriage*. Glencoe, IL: Free Press, 1996.
Graff, E. J. *What Is Marriage For?*. Boston: Beacon Press, 2000.
Sullivan, Andrew & Joseph Landau (editors), *Same-sex Marriage: Pro and Con*. New York: Vintage Books, 1997.

Articles:
Marco, Anton N., "Same-sex 'Marriage': Should America Allow 'Gay Rights' Activists to Cross the Last Cultural Frontier"? 1999, Christian Leadership Ministries, www.leaderu.com/marco/marriage.

Useful websites:
www.aclu.org/issues/gay/hmgl.html
ACLU's Lesbian and Gay Rights Project.
www.hrc.org
Human Rights Campaign, working for lesbian, gay, bisexual, and transgender equal rights.
www.iglhrc.org
International Gay and Lesbian Human Rights Commission.
www.marriageequality.com
Marriage Equality, committed to securing the right to civil marriage for same-sex couples.
www.stonewall.org.uk
Stonewall, promoting equality for gays and lesbians.

The following debates in the Pro/Con series may also be of interest:

In this volume:
Topic 4 Should the constitutional "right to privacy" protect homosexual conduct?

Topic 8 Should people have to obey unjust laws?

SHOULD GAY MEN AND WOMEN BE ALLOWED TO MARRY?

YES: People should not be judged on their sexuality, just as race or gender are irrelevant. Gay people should have the same rights, including marriage, as other members of society.

YES: Love is not just a heterosexual option—gay and lesbian couples should have the right to legally commit if they want to

EQUAL RIGHTS
Should gay people have the same civil rights as other people in society?

LOVE
Marriage is a symbol of love between people— surely gay and lesbian couples should have this right?

NO: Marriage is for procreation—gay and lesbian couples cannot reproduce, so why should they enjoy this right?

NO: Marriage is historically a heterosexual institution and has no relevance to gay and lesbian couples. It could even be seen as repressive to their distinctive identity.

SHOULD GAY MEN AND WOMEN BE ALLOWED TO MARRY?

KEY POINTS

YES: At the moment, if a gay person dies, his or her partner has few if any rights compared to those of a legally married heterosexual partner

YES Allowing gay people this right will allow them to have a more equal legal status in affairs that have a direct bearing on the reality of their lives

LEGAL RIGHTS
Should people in gay marriages be entitled to the same legal rights as their heterosexual peers?

NO: Marriage is a defined relationship between a man and a woman and their potential offspring, and the legal rights that exist are based on the particular nature of this relationship

NO: Heterosexual marriages provide a greater benefit to society as a whole than gay marriages, so their legal rights should reflect this

Topic 6
SHOULD AFFIRMATIVE ACTION CONTINUE?

YES
"GIVE AFFIRMATIVE ACTION TIME TO ACT"
THE CHRONICLE OF HIGHER EDUCATION, DECEMBER 1, 2000
WILLIAM DARITY, JR.

NO
"DON'T ENCOURAGE INEQUALITY"
ALEX BRAITHWAITE

INTRODUCTION

Affirmative action is a set of public policies and initiatives designed to help eliminate past and present discrimination based on race, color, gender, and religion. Affirmative action has been a subject for debate for over 20 years. Advocates of the system argue that it has helped the United States become a more egalitarian, less discriminatory country in which people can get access to education and job opportunities regardless of their minority status.

Opponents reply that affirmative action, or "positive discrimination," as it is also known, is discriminatory by its nature, and further that it awards people for their minority status rather than for personal merit.

Discrimination has always been a popular topic of discussion. Accusations of unfair practices in the employment arena and in education are not uncommon. With this in mind and against the background of the civil rights movement, in March 1961

President John F. Kennedy issued Executive Order 10925, which established the president's Committee on Equal Employment Opportunity. The order required every federal contract to include the pledge that the contractor would not discriminate and would "take affirmative action to ensure that applicants are employed, and that employees are treated during employment, without regard to their race, creed, color, or national origin." The goal, as Kennedy stated, was "equal opportunity employment."

In 1965 President Lyndon B. Johnson went further by stating in his commencement address to Howard University that "it is not enough just to open the gates of opportunity. All our citizens must have the ability to walk through these gates … we seek not just equality as a right and a theory, but equality as a fact and equality as a result." Subsequent executive orders, including Johnson's Order 11246, established affirmative action goals for all federally funded programs and moved monitoring and enforcement to the Labor Department.

Affirmative action is practiced in many parts of American society, and hiring and recruiting practices have helped war veterans, women, ethnic minorities, and people with disabilities, among other groups. The policies have allowed large numbers of people, who in the past might have been overlooked for jobs or courses, to become more equally integrated into society and the business sectors.

"Mend it,
but don't end it."
—BILL CLINTON, 42ND
U.S. PRESIDENT, ON AFFIRMATIVE
ACTION, JANUARY 1996

Although the system has had a lot of support in the past, there is an increasingly powerful group of people who argue that affirmative action policies are now outdated, irrelevant, and discriminatory. They argue that while perhaps affirmative action was necessary in the past, it now means that white people are being punished for the injustices of the past and that the economy has suffered because the best people are not necessarily getting the university places or jobs they deserve. Thus affirmative action could be seen as an affront to civil liberties.

Historically, employers have hired people not just on their test scores, but on personal appearance, family and personal connections, and on race/gender/minority preferences.

Affirmative action, advocates argue, means that while the person with the best test score may not get the job at the end of the day, an eminently suitable person, capable of doing the job, will still be hired.

Other arguments against affirmative action assert that such policies have only benefited the people who need help the least—the middle classes or well-off—while the indigent still languish at the bottom of the education and employment piles. There have also been claims that affirmative action policies lower the self-esteem of the people they benefit. There is little or no statistical evidence to support such assertions. But it is possible that when a person is admitted into a university or given a job in a business that has positive discrimination policies, he or she may question whether it was personal merit or affirmative action that won him or her the position.

In recent years some American universities have begun to adopt policies by which they allow students to be awarded places on merit rather than on minority status. This has led to calls of discrimination from some sectors of society. Similarly, businesses and federal bodies are arguing that the time for affirmative action has long gone and that the United States is an integrated society.

The following articles examine many of the issues in the debate. William Darity, Jr., looks at the case of African Americans and argues that affirmative action policies are necessary since discrimination still exists. Former radical black campaigner Alex Braithwaite, however, argues that affirmative action is nothing more than a quota system and is as discriminatory as the policies it has sought to replace.

GIVE AFFIRMATIVE ACTION TIME TO ACT
William Darity, Jr.

A standard objection to affirmative action and other race-based programs designed to remedy economic disadvantage is the observation that living white Americans are not responsible for past injustices visited upon black Americans. No living white American has owned slaves; no living white American voted for laws that established Jim Crow practices in the South. Why, then, should living white Americans have to bear the cost of compensation for those injustices to living black Americans? Furthermore, opponents of affirmative action argue, black Americans today do not live under the crippling segregation that previous generations faced. Therefore, now is the time to get rid of race-conscious policies and move toward the ideal of a colorblind society.

"Jim Crow" describes the legally sanctioned racism that prevailed until overruled by the civil rights activism of the 1960s.

Affirmative action or assimilation?

The apex of that argument is the proposal that blacks should give up their attachment to blackness. The call for blacks to cease being black is oddly unilateral, seldom accompanied by a call for whites to cease being white. The subordinate group is to surrender an identity that helps shield its members from the power of the dominant group, while the dominant group does not need to surrender an identity that confers racial privilege upon its members. The foundation of that philosophical position is the view that the past is irrelevant in explaining black–white relations in the United States today.

The author criticizes opponents who, in abandoning any legal differentiation between black and white, would expose blacks to the inherent racism that, he goes on to point out, persists in U.S. society.

To believe that only the present matters is to deny the continued economic subordination of blacks. Yet as we enter the 21st century, black Americans' income per capita is only 59 percent of that for white Americans—the same percentage that the economists Richard Vedder, Lowell Gallaway, and David C. Klingaman estimate was the case in 1880. The continued subordination of blacks is due in significant measure to persistent discrimination against them at all stages of the employment process, from recruitment to interview, job offer, and promotion. Studies conducted in the 1990s by the Urban Institute in Chicago, San Diego, and Washington, and by the Fair Employment Council of Greater Washington Inc. in the Washington metropolitan area, show significant levels of discrimination in the labor market

Do you find this level of disparity surprising?

against black and Hispanic job applicants. Patrick Mason, an economist at Florida State University, and I recently reviewed the statistical research for the past 25 years and found that current discrimination in the labor market causes black men to earn 12 to 15 percent less than white men.

Discrimination

The discrimination that previous generations of blacks experienced in the labor market also harms modern blacks' employment prospects. For a paper in *The American Journal of Economics and Sociology* Jason Dietrich, David Guilkey, and I looked at census data for various ethnic and racial groups from 1880 to 1990. We controlled for variables like the individual's age, years of schooling, marital status, and whether he or she was born in the United States. We found astonishingly strong correlations between, on the one hand, the occupational status of American men and women in the 1980 and 1990 censuses, and, on the other, whether their ethnic or racial group had experienced discrimination a century ago. A crucial mechanism for the transmission of discrimination's effects across generations is the transfer of wealth. Indeed, the sharpest economic gap between blacks

---

"I support what I call 'affirmative access'—not quotas, not double standards ... but access—a fair shot for everyone."

—GEORGE W. BUSH, 43RD U.S. PRESIDENT

---

and whites in the United States today is the gap in wealth. Unlike income or earnings, wealth is a measure of what an individual owns, like a home or stocks. Ngina Chiteji and Frank Stafford have ... concluded—in a article published in *The American Economic Review* in May 1999—that the median white household wealth exceeds $10,000, while the median black household wealth is near zero.

The sociologists Melvin Oliver and Thomas Shapiro have shown in *Black Wealth/White Wealth* that access to wealth affects people in many ways: whether they go to college, and where; how well they can survive emergencies, like the loss of a job; whether they are self-employed; whether they own

Is economic discrimination as serious as political discrimination?

A protester expresses her views on the Supreme Court case of Allan Bakke, who claimed he was denied admission to the University of California Medical School because of affirmative action.

their homes; what they can leave to their children. Moreover, a study by Dalton Conley, another sociologist, concludes that the difference in wealth among racial groups is one of the most powerful factors explaining racial differences in performance on standardized tests. Today, as Francine Blau and John Graham documented in a 1990 article in *The Quarterly Journal of Economics*, the major source of wealth is inheritance. Although at all income levels blacks save more of their money than whites do, black families now have comparatively less wealth than whites do, because black parents had less to bestow upon their children.

Affirmative action can address continuing discrimination, but it cannot address the racial gap in wealth. Michael Steman and other policymakers have proposed class-based measures to redistribute assets—for example, supplementing the savings of poor people with matching funds from the government. We should also consider race-based policies—for instance, having the government pay blacks' college tuition. The social construct that we call race has a powerful impact on a person's opportunities in life. Because that impact persists over generations, policies like affirmative action may have to be applied for a century to have a significant effect.

The author proposes federal financial support for African Americans to redress the wealth gap between black and white.

The case of Kerala, South India

The case of India is instructive here. Soon after the nation became independent, the government adopted a national system of preferences for members of the untouchable Hindu castes and certain tribal groups, to erode disparities that the caste system had produced.

In the state of Kerala, the Ezhava caste, once a despised group, has displayed considerable upward mobility in recent years, to the point at which some younger members of the caste question whether they still need the preferences. But there is more to the story. The system of preferences has been in place at the national level since 1950, but Kerala, a politically progressive state, had initiated the preferences on behalf of the lower castes half a century earlier. Thus, the Ezhava have benefited from preferences for close to 100 years, or about four generations.

In what ways does the situation in India, where the caste system has for centuries upheld social divisions, parallel that in the United States?

Affirmative action in the United States, conducted on a much narrower scale than the Indian system, has been in effect for only a quarter of a century, and today it is being rolled back rapidly. Instead of pretending that racism and its effects no longer exist, we need to strengthen affirmative action and devise a new set of policies that directly tackle the racial gap in wealth.

DON'T ENCOURAGE INEQUALITY
Alex Braithwaite

NO

Affirmative action, sometimes referred to as "positive discrimination," was established to reduce the racial, ethnic, and gender discrimination prevalent in U.S. society. The term "affirmative action" originated in an executive order on nondiscrimination in federal hiring, signed by John F. Kennedy shortly after he became president. In 1965 Lyndon B. Johnson issued a second executive order using the term and created the Department of Labor to enforce affirmative action policies. But affirmative action crept into national life without a public consensus behind it. Government agencies, universities, and businesses created affirmative action programs of their own, most voluntarily, some under pressure from the federal government.

The original purpose of affirmative action was to rectify the injustices of the past by ensuring that certain groups—usually minority groups—were given additional advantages in order to compete for jobs or university places for which they would probably otherwise have been overlooked. However, affirmative action policies were only meant to exist until minority groups were treated fairly and were judged equally on meritocratic grounds. The tide, however, has turned. The United States has now reached that stage Yet these policies are still in place, and opposition to affirmative action is on the increase. Why? Because affirmative action is seen as an outdated, unfair quota system that gives a small minority unfair advantages. It is discrimination under another name.

The author asserts that there is now a level playing field of opportunity in the United States. Do you agree? If not, why not?

Preferential treatment

Preferential treatment perpetuates a discriminatory policy all of its own. In an article written for *The Washington Post* in 1995 William Raspberry argued that out of 248,000 teenagers surveyed nine out of ten opposed affirmative action in hiring and college admissions. Advocates of affirmative action would most probably argue that this figure just confirms that a large percentage of the teenage population is ignorant of discriminatory practices. However, Raspberry's research shows that affirmative action policies are not only outdated but are actually actively resented. Similarly, *Illiberal Education* author Dinesh D'Souza gives several examples of white or Asian students denied admission to colleges and universities even though their SAT scores were higher than some of their successful competitors—often African-Americans. D'Souza argues that this proves that affirmative action "depreciate[s] the importance of merit criteria in admissions."

The case of California

In the early 1990s two California academics began promoting the idea of a ballot initiative to abolish affirmative action. They identified the initiative with the Civil Rights Act of 1964, naming it instead the California Civil Rights Initiative, and actually paraphrased the 1964 Act to campaign for the banning of policies that were racially discriminatory. However, it was not until 1994, in the aftermath of the Republican congressional landslide, that the issue really gained any credence. In the early months of 1995 affirmative action became a popular obsession. California in particular was against the continuance of affirmative action policies, and on June 2, 1995, California Governor Pete Wilson signed an executive order abolishing a range of affirmative action programs affecting hiring and contracting in state agencies. He also abolished 118 boards and commissions created to advise state agencies on ethnic and gender diversity issues.

Public support for ending affirmative action led President Bill Clinton to establish a White House committee to review affirmative action. On July 20, 1995, President Clinton made

What effect does a climate of affirmative action programs have on your own attitude to scholastic merit and achievement?

See box on page 80 on California's Proposition 209.

"If affirmative action means programs that provide equal opportunity, then I am all for it. If it leads to preferential treatment or helps those that no longer need help, I am opposed."

—COLIN POWELL, U.S. SECRETARY OF STATE

---

the findings of the report public. He concluded that "the job of ending discrimination in this country is not done....We should reaffirm the principle of affirmative action and fix the practices. We should have a simple slogan: Mend it, but don't end it." The following day the University of California regents voted 14 to 10 to end race-based admissions at its campuses.

In 1997 California passed a referendum banning the use of

You can read the full report at clinton4.nara.gov/ textonly/WH/ EOP/OP/html/aa/ aa-lett.html.

COMMENTARY: California's Proposition 209

Of the many challenges to affirmative action during recent years, one of the most notorious was Proposition 209. This briefly worded initiative was adopted on November 5, 1996, by a 54 to 46 percent vote. On August 28, 1997, it became Section 31 of Article I of the California Constitution.

The first clause of Proposition 209 ordains that "The state shall not discriminate against, or grant preferential treatment to, any individual or group on the basis of race, sex, color, ethnicity, or national origin in the operation of public employment, public education, or public contracting." The words closely mirror those enshrined in Executive Order 10925 of 1961, an instrument by which the Kennedy administration sought to eradicate racism from U.S. society. At face evidence the new law appears to uphold Martin Luther King's "dream" of equality, and yet its critics—who include Rosa Parks, an important figure in the 1960s civil rights movement—have denounced Proposition 209 as a worrying step backward for minorities.

Proposition 209 began life in 1991 as the California Civil Rights Initiative (CCRI), the brainchild of Glynn Custred and Thomas Wood, two cofounders of CADAP (Californians Against Discrimination and Preferences). This group played a major role in oiling the progress of Proposition 209 through the courts and in defending it from attacks by the likes of the American Civil Liberties Union, the Coalition for Economic Equity, and civil rights leader Jesse Jackson. CADAP argued that the process of admitting a student or hiring an employee on the basis of skin color, not by personal merit, is by definition discriminatory, however praiseworthy its goal. Affirmative action, it claimed, rolls back all the progress made by civil rights groups.

In response, opponents of Proposition 209 claimed it would send the wrong message to minority candidates. The 1997 enrollment figures of first-year law students at UCLA seemed to support their fears: White enrollment was up 30 percent in 1996, while African American was down 50 percent.

An about-turn in education

Proposition 209 came hot on the heels of the 1995 vote, by the regents of the University of California, to adopt Resolutions SP-1 and SP-2. These resolutions abolished all affirmative action programs in student admissions and hiring of faculty. Taking effect from 1997–1998, their adoption met with stiff, if not universal, opposition from students and propelled the state's education system into a nationwide political debate. The situation was defused six years later when, on May 16, 2001, the board of regents voted to rescind both SP-1 and SP-2. Although supporters of affirmative action welcomed the rescindment, they acknowledged it to be a largely symbolic gesture, since Resolution 209 still held sway in California. Both on campus and in society at large, accusations of reverse discrimination continue to dog policies of affirmative action.

race and ethnicity in public college admissions; similarly in Texas a Federal court outlawed the consideration of race in higher-education admissions. As a result, by March 1998, 7 percent more black and 21 percent more Mexican-American applicants were eligible for enrollment in Texas than under the old affirmative action guidelines, and because of these changes more white high-school graduates had access to public education than under the old system. This illustrates that affirmative action policies were failing to work in Texas.

Discrimination and stigma

By its nature affirmative action creates quotas, bias, and discrimination. It is an unfair system that actively promotes the hiring of less skilled or educated workers and students at the cost of those better qualified for jobs or courses. For example, in 1993 Duke University adopted a resolution requiring each department to hire at least one new black for a faculty position. Affirmative action also promotes "reverse" discrimination. Some advocates argue that affirmative action is a way of making up for the past; however, discrimination against any group is wrong. This is not what … civil rights bodies fought for.

"Reverse discrimination" is said to occur when minorities (such as women, African Americans, or Hispanics) are favored in hirings or admissions to the disadvantage of majorities (i.e., whites).

A major consequence of affirmative action is that it places a stigma on the individuals or groups who are seen to receive preferential treatment. This unfairly disadvantages those people who have earned their position or place on a course due to ability or merit. This exacerbates existing problems.

Affirmative action has also led to an increase in racial tensions between whites and blacks at campuses. At colleges in North Carolina, for example, black students stated that they were treated like affirmative action cases even if they were not. Professors, seeking to help, asked them if they needed tutoring or other assistance, already assuming their lack of qualifications.

In *Reaching Beyond Race* academics Paul Sniderman and Edward Carmines conducted a "mere mention" test to discover what kind of reaction the words "affirmative action" got. Their results showed the power of affirmative action "to sharpen hostility toward blacks."

If affirmative action redresses some social ills but introduces others, is it worth it?

Affirmative action was originally constructed as a policy to help end racial and gender inequality in the workplace and in education. However, times have changed, and it is time to [adjust] Bill Clinton's words [to] "End it, not mend it." While injustice and inequality still exist in the United States, affirmative action polices are counterproductive and if anything exacerbate existing problems and tensions.

Summary

In his article supporting the continuation of affirmative action William Darity, Jr., writes that he and his colleagues examined census data on various ethnic and racial groups from 1880 to 1990 and found strong links between the occupational status of American men and women in the 1980 and 1990 censuses and the discrimination that their ethnic and racial groups experienced in 1880. This evidence of continued racism, Darity argues, shows the need for affirmative action policies. Alex Braithwaite, however, argues that those policies are discriminatory, mean that the best person doesn't get the job, and exacerbate existing prejudices, since inevitably those people who are suitably qualified for jobs or courses end up resenting the candidates who get them on grounds of minority status rather than meritocracy.

FURTHER INFORMATION:

Books:

Ezorsky, G., *Racism and Justice: The Case for Affirmative Action*. Ithaca, NY: Cornell University Press, 1991.

Useful websites:

www.affirmativeaction.org/
Site of the American Association for Affirmative Action.
www.aad.english.ucsb.edu/
A comprehensive research resource on affirmative action that is maintained by the University of Santa Barbara in California.
www.aad.enlish.ucsb.edu/docs/Cahn.html
Stephen Kahn on the history of affirmative action.
www.aad.enlish.ucsb.edu/docs/Novaa.html
Jose Novoa, excerpts from "At times the problem is economics, not racism."
clinton4.nara.gov/textonly/WH/EOP/OP/html/aa-index.html
A 1995 presidential review of affirmative action programs.
www.puaf.umd.edu/ippp/tqq.htm
A resource page of the Maryland School of Public Affairs.
www.frontpagemag.com/columnists/perazzo/jp08-13-01.htm
J. Perazzo, "The Ugly Face of Affirmative Action," *Frontpage Magazine*, August 13, 2001. A critique of affirmative action.

www.now.org/nnt/08-95/affirmhs.html
Marquita Sykes, "The Origins of Affirmative Action."
www.inmotionmagazine.com/idaa/geg2.html
"Eliminating Affirmative Action Is Resegregating Higher Education," an interview with Graciela E. Geyer.
www.feminist.org/other/ccri/aafact1.html
A history of affirmative action for women.
www.ncpa.org/pd/affirm.html
National Center for Policy Analysis site disseminating views on government policy on affirmative action.
www.nationalcenter.org/AA.html
An affirmative action resource site provided by the National Center for Public Policy Research.
www.socialpsychology.org/affirm.htm
S. Plous, "Ten Myths about Affirmative Action."

The following debates in the Pro/Con series may also be of interest:

In this volume:

Topic 2 Is it possible to live in a nonracist society?

Topic 14 Should society make reparations to the descendants of slaves?

SHOULD AFFIRMATIVE ACTION CONTINUE?

YES: Even if society itself is now integrated, affirmative action has an important role in taking that integration into the working and educational environments

YES: Martin Luther King, John F. Kennedy, and Lyndon Johnson worked to end racism, but it is still institutionalized in American society today

BETTER RELATIONS
Does affirmative action improve relations between mainstream society and minorities?

DEFINITIONS
Does the 1960s interpretation of discrimination remain true today?

NO: People resent the beneficiaries of these policies, and that can exacerbate prejudice

NO: The 1964 Civil Rights Act was a tool for eradicating morally repugnant racial attitudes. Today discrimination has been redefined de facto by affirmative action programs in which even the most progressive company, lacking any racist intent, can face a lawsuit for not meeting diversity goals.

SHOULD AFFIRMATIVE ACTION CONTINUE?

KEY POINTS

YES: There are still too few minorities in senior societal roles, and still too wide a salary gap between black and white

YES: There are still glaring inequalities in wealth between black and white Americans; redistribution is needed

PAYBACK TIME
Is it unjust to make the current generation pay for the faults and sins of earlier generations?

NO: The Civil Rights Act of 1964 struck at discrimination against Americans of any color, creed, or sex to make a level playing field of opportunity; affirmative action reintroduces preferential treatment and is thus racist

NO: It is unjust to make the current generation pay for the faults and sins of earlier generations

NO: Employers and educational establishments should recruit or promote on merit alone, not on any basis of color or gender

AFFIRMATIVE ACTION POLICIES

Activism in the 1960s marked a turning point in the rights of ethnic minorities and women. Presidents Kennedy and Johnson both sponsored landmark legislation that established and defended affirmative action programs (see pages 72–83). Later, however, court cases tested the practicality of the new laws, and the century's close saw serious challenges to existing policies in California and Florida.

1961 President John F. Kennedy issues Executive Order (E.O.) 10925. It uses the term affirmative action for the first time. The Committee on Equal Employment Opportunity is also created.

1964 The Civil Rights Act prohibits discrimination by employers of over 15 employees. The Equal Employment Opportunity Commission (EEOC) is founded.

1965 President Lyndon B. Johnson issues E.O. 11246. It requires all federal contractors and subcontractors to take affirmative action to expand job opportunities for minorities. It establishes the Office of Federal Contract Compliance (OFCC) in the Department of Labor to administer the order.

1967 Johnson amends E.O. 11246 to include affirmative action for women.

1970 The Labor Department, under President Richard M. Nixon, issues Order No. 4, which authorizes flexible goals and timetables to correct "underutilization" of minorities by federal contractors.

1971 Nixon issues E.O. 11625, directing federal agencies to develop a national Minority Business Enterprise (MBE) contracting program.

1973 Nixon issues "Memorandum— Permissible Goals and Timetables in State and Local Government Employment Practices," distinguishing between proper goals and timetables and impermissible quotas.

1978 The Supreme Court in *Regents of the University of California v. Bakke* uphold the use of race as one factor in choosing among qualified applicants for admission, but rules against the practice of reserving 18 seats for minority students in each entering class of 100 in the university's medical school.

1979 President Jimmy Carter issues E.O. 12138, which creates a National Women's Business Enterprise Policy and requires each agency to take affirmative action to support women's business enterprises. The Supreme Court rules in *United Steel Workers of America, AFL–CIO v. Weber* that race-conscious affirmative action efforts are permissible if they are temporary and do not violate the rights of white employees.

1983 President Ronald Reagan issues E.O. 12432. Every federal agency with substantial procurement or grant-making authority is now required to have a Minority Business Enterprise (MBE) development plan.

1987 The Supreme Court rules in *Johnson v. Transportation Agency, Santa Clara County, CA*, that severe underrepresentation of women and minorities justifies the use of race or sex as "one factor" in choosing among qualified candidates.

1989 In *City of Richmond v. J.A. Croson Co.* the Supreme Court finds Richmond's minority contracting program unconstitutional.

1994 In *Adarand Constructors, Inc., v. Pena* the Supreme Court holds that a federal affirmative action program remains constitutional when fighting discrimination.

1995 President Bill Clinton reviews affirmative action guidelines by federal agencies and declares support for affirmative action with a "Mend it, don't end it" policy.

1995 Senator Robert Dole and Representative Charles Canady introduce the Equal Opportunity Act in Congress. It is intended to prohibit race- or gender-based affirmative action in all federal programs. The regents of the University of California vote to end affirmative action programs on all university campuses. The bipartisan Glass Ceiling Commission releases a report on barriers that deny women and minorities access to decision-making positions.

November 1996 California's Resolution 209 is passed. It abolishes public-sector affirmative action programs in employment, education, and contracting.

1996 In *Hopwood v. Texas* the Court of Appeals for the Fifth Circuit rules that the consideration of race in admissions of the law school of the University of Texas violates the Constitution's equal-protection guarantee.

1997 Voters in Houston reject an initiative to ban affirmative action policies in city contracting and hiring. California's Proposition 209 comes into effect. The House Judiciary Committee votes 17-9 on a bipartisan basis to defeat legislation aimed at dismantling federal affirmative action programs for women and minorities.

1998 The House of Representatives and the Senate reject amendments to abolish the Disadvantaged Business Enterprise program funded through the Transportation Bill. The House also rejects an attempt to eliminate affirmative action in admissions in higher education programs funded through the Higher Education Act. The ban on affirmative action in admissions at the University of California begins. UC Berkeley suffers a 61 percent drop in minority admissions, UCLA a 36 percent decline. Washington State voters face a ballot initiative, Proposition 200, similar to California's Proposition 209, to ban all state affirmative action programs for women and minorities in education, contracting, and employment. It is opposed by many corporations. Consequently, Chinese-American Governor Gary Locke warns that Proposition 200 is "full of hidden consequence" and "will hurt real people."

Early 1999 Businessman Ward Connerly pushes for the elimination of all of Florida's affirmative-action programs. Connerly, a former University of California regent, led the campaign behind California Proposition 209, which ended affirmative action in that state's public colleges.

November 1999 Florida Governor Jeb Bush ends affirmative action programs in the awarding of state contracts and admissions to Florida universities. A media poll shows that Florida voters, by a margin of more than two to one, would ban public race and gender preferences. At California's Stanford Medical School minority enrollment drops from 20 percent in 1998 to 14 percent in 1999.

May 2001 The regents of the University of California rescind their antiaffirmative action policies of 1995, though Resolution 209 remains in place.

Topic 7
SHOULD ENGLISH BE THE OFFICIAL LANGUAGE IN THE UNITED STATES?

YES
BILINGUAL EDUCATION: A CRITIQUE
WWW-HOOVER.STANFORD.EDU/PUBLICATIONS/HE/22/22D.HTML
PETER DUIGNAN

NO
"ENGLISH ONLY"
ACLU BRIEFING PAPER, 1996
AMERICAN CIVIL LIBERTIES UNION

INTRODUCTION

An estimated 1.5 billion people communicate with each other in English around the world. Out of that group the cultural body the British Council estimates that around 375 million are native English speakers, a similar number speak English as a second language in their own countries, and around 750 million speak it as a foreign language altogether. English is the most commonly used language of commerce, science, the airways, and the Internet, and it is the official language in around 75 nations, including some Asian and African countries that have many native languages of their own.

In the United States every aspect of official life, whether it be schooling or work, already necessitates that citizens communicate in English. And yet there is a strong movement formally to make English the official or authorized language of the country.

Advocates of an official English policy, including organizations such as U.S.

English, argue that the United States needs to make a legal stand on language. They say that large-scale Asian, East European, and Hispanic immigration in the 1990s has led substantial segments of the population to speak English poorly or not at all.

Critics, however, argue that multiculturalism is important to any society, and that an English only policy would just be another indication of the inherent racism prevalent in the United States. They assert that many immigrants, especially from Asian and East European countries, speak and write English well—a fact verified by the 1990 census. They also contend that the children of immigrant parents rapidly learn English with or without an official English policy, and that the English that immigrant groups use is of a higher standard than the "American English" used by most people in the United States who claim to speak English as a first language.

The 2000 census found that there are more than 35 million people of Hispanic or Latino origin in the United States, representing 12.5 percent of the total population. According to the same census, there are around 10 million Asians, or 3.6 percent of the population. The numbers of people who speak English as a second language have been growing at a much faster rate than the size of the native American-English speaking population. For example, in the 1980s the numbers of people speaking a language other than English at home increased by 38 percent, whereas there was only a 6 percent increase in monolingual American-English speakers. The Hispanic population is projected to become the largest U.S. minority group by 2005.

> *"Even American English is a local dialect of global English now."*
>
> —DAVID CRYSTAL, AUTHOR OF *ENGLISH AS A GLOBAL LANGUAGE*

Some American people feel threatened by the dramatic growth of immigrant populations in the United States and point to the fact that George W. Bush is the first Spanish-speaking president in U.S. history. As a result the issue of whether English should be the only official language has become political.

In the past politicians like Theodore Roosevelt stressed the importance of English in uniting a country full of immigrants. Roosevelt stated: "We have room for but one language here, and that is the English language, for we intend to see that the crucible turns our people out as Americans, of American nationality, and not as dwellers in a polyglot boarding house." With such important people emphasizing the importance of the English language, it is hardly surprising that English-only groups grew in strength.

In 1981 Senator S. I. Hayakawa, a longtime critic of bilingual education and bilingual ballots, introduced in the U.S. Senate a constitutional amendment to make English the official language. It was unsuccessful. However, Hayakawa went on to form U.S. English, with John Tanton, to promote English as the official language in the United States. U.S. English has received a lot of support, and former board members include the writer and broadcaster Alistair Cooke and former CBS news anchor Walter Cronkite.

Official English initiatives were passed in California in 1986 and by Arkansas, Mississippi, and four other states in 1987, followed by Colorado, Florida, and Arizona in 1988 and Alabama in 1990. Similarly, H.R. 123, better known as the Emerson Bill, was passed in the U.S. House of Representatives in 1986 and specifies that English is the official language of the government. However, there is a strong U.S. pro-bilingualism and multiculturalism lobby, including the American Civil Liberties Union (ACLU), which fights such policies.

The authors of the following two articles—Peter Duignan and the American Civil Liberties Union respectively—highlight the main arguments in the debate over whether English should be the official language in the United States.

BILINGUAL EDUCATION: A CRITIQUE
Peter Duignan

YES

Some members of the education bureaucracy, guided by the principle of "cultural maintenance," want Hispanic-surnamed children to continue to be taught Spanish language and culture and English only as a second language. The extremists among them even want Spanish to be a second national language. The Center for Equal Opportunity's president and CEO, Linda Chavez, accuses these advocates of bilingual education of being politicized and manipulated by cultural activists. The programs they favor, she claims, have failed and have undermined the future of the Latino children they were meant to help. Chavez's criticisms are supported by the evidence. Latinos, Hispanics, or Chicanos [Americans of Mexican descent] taught in bilingual programs test behind peers taught in English-only classrooms, drop out of school at a high rate, and are trapped in low-skilled, low-paying jobs.

The author quickly establishes his main point, that bilingual education actually harms the people it is supposed to help.

History of bilingual education
As noted earlier, the problem began in 1974 when the Supreme Court in *Lau v. Nichols* ignored 200 years of English-only instruction in America's schools and said that students who did not speak English must receive special treatment from local schools. This allowed an enormous expansion of bilingual education. Advocates of bilingual education in the U.S. Office for Civil Rights had begun a small program in 1968 to educate Mexican American children, but by 1996 it had expanded from a $7.5 million to an $8 billion a year industry. The initial objective to teach English to Spanish speakers for one or two years was perverted into a program to Hispanicize, not Americanize, Spanish speakers. The federal program insists that 75 percent of education tax dollars be spent on bilingual education, that is, long-term native-language programs, not English as a second language. Asians, Africans, and Europeans are all in mainstream classes and receive extra training in English-as-a-second-language programs for a few hours a day. Hispanic students, in contrast, are taught in Spanish 70 to 80 percent of the time. New York is especially irresponsible in this regard, forcing children with Spanish surnames, even those who speak no Spanish at home, to take Spanish and to spend at least 40 percent of the

What do you think Duignan means by his distinction between Americanization and Hispanicization?

class time in Spanish classes. New England schools are about as bad, forcing Spanish- and Portuguese-surnamed children to take Spanish or Crioulo!

Crioulu is a mix of Portuguese and West African dialects.

The linguistic divide

Some critics of bilingualism claim that the vast majority of Spanish speakers want their children to be taught in English, not Spanish, and do not want the U.S. government to keep up Hispanic culture and language. The bilingual bureaucracy at local and federal levels wants to Hispanicize and to capture federal funds for schools. Meanwhile, other ethnic groups achieve higher academic scores, in part because they are not wasting time on bilingual classes and culture and failing to master the language of the marketplace and higher education—English. Since there are seldom enough bilingual teachers, Arab, Asian, and European students go right into classes with English-speaking students. They achieve higher scores and more of them graduate than the bilingually taught. The Center for Equal Opportunity in its reports shows the dangers of bilingualism and demands its reform. Otherwise the United States will become deeply divided linguistically and be stuck with a Latino underclass that cannot meet the needs of a high-tech workplace because its English is poor.

Why might Arab, Asian, and European students get better results when they are taught in English rather than in bilingual classes?

Since Latino immigration—legal or illegal—is likely to continue in the future and since Latino fertility levels are high, the Latino population will grow. According to Hoover economist Edward Lazear, the economic costs of not adequately educating Hispanics will be great, and their economic well-being will be lower than if they were to stay in school longer and focus on English, not on bilingualism. Lazear argues that much of the anti-immigrant rhetoric in America is generated by government policies that reduce the incentives to become assimilated and emphasize the differences among ethnic groups in the population. Examples are bilingual education and unbalanced immigration policies that bring in large numbers of Asians and Hispanics who move into large and stable ghettos.

Do you agree that antiimmigrant feelings in the United States are sometimes strengthened by government bilingual education policies?

Advantages of English-only education

Rosalie Pedolino Porter, a bilingual education teacher for more than twenty years, is convinced that all limited-English-proficiency students can learn English well enough for regular classroom work in one to three years, if given some help. The old total immersion system still works best; the longer students stay in segregated bilingual programs, the less successful they are in school. Even after twenty-eight years of bilingual programs, the dropout rate for Latinos is the highest in the country. In Los Angeles the Latino students dropped out at double the state average (44 percent over four years of high school). Special English-language instruction from day one gets better results than Spanish-language instruction for most of the day.

Latino activists now call for limited recognition to be accorded to Spanish—inglés y más ("English and more") runs the slogan. (Official documents of various kinds are now printed in Spanish and other languages as well as English. At the Democratic convention of 1996 speeches were given in Spanish as well as English.) If this course continues, the demand for recognition of Spanish will inevitably change into a demand for recognition of Spanish as an official language. Such a transformation would give great benefits to Spanish speakers in public employment but leave others at a disadvantage. Bilingualism, or multilingualism, imposes economic transaction costs; the political costs are even higher. I do not wish to see the United States become a bilingual country like Canada or Belgium, which both suffer from divisiveness occasioned by the language issue.

Would the situation change if Spanish was an official language? Isn't the United States in many ways already a bilingual country?

Immigration and cultural assimilation

I also would like to insist on a higher degree of proficiency in English than is at present required by applicants for naturalization in the United States. A citizen should be able to read all electoral literature in English—no more foreign-language ballots! For similar reasons, I oppose those educators in publicly funded high schools who believe that their task is to maintain the immigrant's cultural heritage. Such endeavors should be left to parents, churches, "Saturday schools," and the extended family. The role of the public schoolteacher is to instruct students in English and American culture and political values. English plays a crucial role in cultural assimilation, a proposition evident also to minority people. (In Brooklyn, for example, the Bushwick Parents Organization went to court in 1996 to oppose the Spanish-English education of Hispanics in the local public schools, arguing that this instruction would leave their children badly disadvantaged when they graduated.) As Ruth Wisse, herself a distinguished educator, puts it, before we encourage ethnic-language revivals in the European manner, "we should recall what millions of immigrants instinctively grasped: that English is the most fundamental pathway to America's equal opportunities." (The European experience is likewise clear. "In general, mother-tongue education is unrealistic and

Would this proposal deprive some citizens of their electoral rights?

Do you agree that public teachers should instruct students only in American culture and political values?

unsuccessful. The children of immigrant parents rapidly acquire the language of their country of residence, and are often less comfortable and successful in their parents' mother-tongue.")

Anyone can learn English

Knowledge of English is an acquired, not an inherent, skill—anyone, white, black, or brown, can learn English. Immigrants line up to learn English because they believe that learning English will improve their prospects—and it does, significantly. English is the most widely used language in history. English is the language of science, technology, diplomacy, international trade, and commerce. Half of Europe's business is carried out in English, and more than 66 percent of the world's scientists read English. Eighty percent of the world's electronically stored information is in English. The world's forty million Internet users mostly communicate in English. Experts conclude that one-third of mankind speaks or understands some English. Selecting immigrants on the basis of some command of the language therefore cannot be discriminatory.

Grouping related facts in a list makes for a powerful impact.

How might U.S. history have been different if immigrants had been admitted only if they could speak English?

Failure of bilingual education

Bilingual education in California is a vast industry—about 1.3 million children attend bilingual classes at a cost of more than $5 billion a year. (In the United States 2.6 million students are enrolled in bilingual classes. There is, therefore, a financial incentive to keeping the system.) Schools that provide bilingual education are able to get numerous federal and state grants. Yet bilingual education is a bizarre and unsuccessful program. Only about 5 percent of children in bilingual classes ever make it into English-speaking classes each year. And large numbers of children, mostly Spanish speakers, leave school unable to read or write English, the official language of their adopted country. Shockingly, the federal legislation calling for bilingual education "expired a decade ago," yet bilingual education persists.

To strengthen the conclusion to his argument, Duignan points out that even some people who favor bilingual education agree that it does not work in practice.

Advocates of bilingual education reluctantly concede the system does not work. But political infighting in the California legislature has prevented rational reform. Large numbers of children each year are forced into bilingual classes even if their parents don't want it. Bilingual teachers, moreover, are in short supply, so some teachers are hired who have no teacher training but speak Spanish or some language other than English. This results in poor teaching and little or no English-language teaching.

ENGLISH ONLY
American Civil Liberties Union

NO

Q: What is an "English Only" law?

A: "English Only" laws vary. Some state statutes simply declare English as the "official" language of the state. Other state and local edicts limit or bar government's provision of non-English language assistance and services. For example, some restrict bilingual education programs, prohibit multilingual ballots, or forbid non-English government services in general—including such services as courtroom translation or multilingual emergency police lines.

Q: Where have such laws been enacted?

A: Sixteen states have "English Only" laws, and many others are considering such laws. In some states, the laws were passed decades ago during upsurges of nativism, but most were passed within the last few years. The "English Only" states are Arizona, Arkansas, California, Colorado, Florida, Georgia, Illinois, Indiana, Kentucky, Mississippi, Nebraska, North Carolina, North Dakota, South Carolina, Tennessee, and Virginia.

Q: What are the consequences of "English Only" laws?

A: Some versions of the proposed English Language Amendment would void almost all state and federal laws that require the government to provide services in languages other than English. The services affected would include: health, education and social welfare services, job training, translation assistance to crime victims and witnesses in court and administrative proceedings; voting assistance and ballots, drivers' licensing exams, and AIDS-prevention education. Passage of an "English Only" ordinance by Florida's Dade County in 1980, barring public funding of activities that involved the use of languages other than English, resulted in the cancellation of all multicultural events and bilingual services, ranging from directional signs in the public transit system to medical services at the county hospital.

Where basic human needs are met by bilingual or multilingual services, the consequences of their elimination could be dire. For example, the Washington Times reported in 1987 that a 911 emergency dispatcher was able to save the

The American Civil Liberties Union has adopted a question-and-answer format to make its views more accessible to the general reader.

In order to add weight to its argument, the Union describes a specific case in which the provision of bilingual services was vital.

life of a Salvadoran woman's baby son, who had stopped breathing, by coaching the mother in Spanish over the telephone to administer mouth-to-mouth and cardio-pulmonary resuscitation until the paramedics arrived.

Q: Do "English Only" laws affect only government services and programs?

A: "English Only" laws apply primarily to government programs. However, such laws can also affect private businesses. For example, several Southern California cities have passed ordinances that forbid or restrict the use of foreign languages on private business signs.

Some "English Only" advocates have opposed a telephone company's use of multilingual operators and multilingual directories, Federal Communications Commission licensing of Spanish-language radio stations, and bilingual menus at fast food restaurants.

Q: Who is affected by "English Only" laws?

A: "English Only" campaigns target primarily Latinos and Asians, who make up the majority of recent immigrants. Most language minority residents are Spanish-speaking, a result of the sharp rise in immigration from Latin America during the mid-1960s.

While the overwhelming majority of U.S. residents—96 percent—are fluent, approximately ten million residents are not fluent in English, according to the most recent census.

Q: How do "English Only" laws deprive people of their rights?

A: The ACLU [American Civil Liberties Union] believes that "English Only" laws are inconsistent with the Equal Protection Clause of the Fourteenth Amendment. For example, laws that have the effect of eliminating courtroom translation severely jeopardize the ability of people on trial to follow and comprehend the proceedings. "English Only" laws interfere with the right to vote by banning bilingual ballots, or with a child's right to education by restricting bilingual instruction. Such laws also interfere with the right of workers to be free of discrimination in workplaces where employers have imposed "speak English only" rules.

In 1987, the ACLU adopted a national policy opposing "English Only" laws or laws that would "characterize English as the official language in the United States ... to the extent that [they] would mandate or encourage the erosion" of the rights of language minority persons.

The ACLU points out that "English Only" laws affect private companies as well as government agencies. Might the laws infringe the rights of businesses and consumers as a result?

Do you agree that English-only policies are illegal according to the Fourteenth Amendment? Read the full text of the Amendment at www.access.gpo.gov/congress/senate/constitution/conart.html.

Q: What kinds of language policies were adopted with regard to past generations of immigrants?

A: Our nation was tolerant of linguistic diversity until the late 1800s, when an influx of Eastern and Southern Europeans, as well as Asians, aroused nativist sentiments and prompted the enactment of restrictive language laws. In order to "Americanize" the immigrants and exclude people thought to be of the lower classes and undesirable, English literacy requirements were established for public employment, naturalization, immigration and suffrage. The New York State Constitution was amended to disfranchise over one million Yiddish-speaking citizens. The California Constitution was similarly amended to disfranchise Chinese, who were seen as a threat to the "purity of the ballot box."

Here the Union argues that in the past American language policies were discriminatory. Does it follow that the policies were also racist?

Ironically, during the same period, the government sought to "Americanize" Native American Indian children by taking them from their families and forcing them to attend English-language boarding schools, where they were punished for speaking their indigenous languages.

The intense anti-German sentiment that accompanied the outbreak of World War I prompted several states, where bilingual schools had been commonplace, to enact extreme language laws. For example, Nebraska passed a law in 1919 prohibiting the use of any other language than English through the eighth grade. The Supreme Court subsequently declared the law an unconstitutional violation of due process.

At this stage in the debate the authors include a brief paragraph that summarizes their argument so far.

Today, as in the past, "English Only" laws in the U.S. are founded on false stereotypes of immigrant groups. Such laws do not simply disparage the immigrants' native languages but assault the rights of the people who speak the languages.

Q: Why are bilingual ballots needed since citizenship is required to vote, English literacy is required for citizenship, and political campaigns are largely conducted in English?

A: Naturalization for U. S. citizenship does not require English literacy for people over 50, and/or who have been in the U. S. for 20 years or more. Thus, there are many elderly immigrant citizens whose ability to read English is limited, and who cannot exercise their right to vote without bilingual ballots. Moreover, bilingual campaign materials and ballots foster a better informed electorate by increasing the information available to people who lack English proficiency.

Q: Doesn't bilingual education slow immigrant children's learning of English, in contrast to the "sink or swim" method that was used in the past?

A: The primary purpose of bilingual programs in elementary and secondary schools, which use both English and a child's native language to teach all subjects, is to develop proficiency in English and, thus, facilitate the child's transition to all-English instruction.

Although debate about this approach continues, the latest studies show that bilingual education definitely enhances a child's ability to acquire the second language. Some studies even show that the more extensive the native language instruction, the better students perform all around, and that the bilingual method engenders a positive self-image and self-respect by validating the child's native language and culture.

The "sink or swim" experience of past immigrants left more of them underwater than not. In 1911, the U. S. Immigration Service found that 77 percent of Italian, 60 percent of Russian, and 51 percent of German immigrant children were one or more grade levels behind in school compared to 28 percent of American-born white children. Moreover, those immigrants who did manage to "swim" unaided in the past, when agricultural and factory jobs were plentiful, might not do so well in today's "high-tech" economy, with its more rigorous educational requirements.

The authors make good use of statistics to back up their arguments.

Q: But won't "English Only" laws speed up the assimilation of today's immigrants into our society and prevent their isolation?

A: In fact, contrary to what "English Only" advocates assume, the vast majority of today's Asian and Latino immigrants are acquiring English proficiency and assimilating as fast as did earlier generations of Italian, Russian and German immigrants. For example, research studies show that over 95 percent of first generation Mexican Americans are English proficient, and that more than 50 percent of second generation Mexican Americans have lost their native tongue entirely.

In addition, census data reveal that nearly 90 percent of Latinos five years old or older speak English in their households. And 98 percent of Latinos surveyed said they felt it is "essential" that their children learn to read and write English "perfectly."

The best insurance against social isolation of those who immigrate to our nation is acceptance—and celebration—of the differences that exist within our ethnically diverse citizenry. The bond that unites our nation is not linguistic or ethnic homogeneity but a shared commitment to democracy, liberty, and equality.

Summary

The issue of whether English should be made the official U.S. language has caused much heated debate. Peter Duignan, in "Bilingual Education: A Critique," argues that bilingual education is so expensive that it is prohibitive, and that the bilingual programs that currently exist do not work. He further argues that the role of the schoolteacher is to enforce U.S. values and language and not to help preserve the cultural identity of the student—that, Duignan says, is up to the student's church and family. Duignan also argues that immigration, legal or not, has helped add to the expense of providing proficient English-language education to those who need it. The American Civil Liberties Union, however, argues that English-only laws are inconsistent with the Fourteenth Amendment and that they infringe on the civil rights of nonnative English speakers. It also argues that such laws promote and propagate false stereotypes about immigrants, their proficiency in English, and the way in which they interact in U.S. society.

FURTHER INFORMATION:

Books:

Bryson, Bill, *Mother Tongue: English and How It Got That Way*. New York: Avon Books, 1996.

Crystal, David, *English as a Global Language*. Cambridge, U.K.: Cambridge University Press, 1998.

Useful websites:

www.us-english.com
Official site of the U.S. English organization.

www.ourworld.compuserve.com/homepages/
JWCRAWFORD/Englishonly.htm
Page that discusses the English-only movement and highlights important legislation and groups.

www.wire.ap.org/APpackages/english/english1.htm
Ted Anthony, "English: 1 Tongue for the New Global Village," with links to other articles on the English language in the global economy.

www.wire.ap.org/APpackages/english/vacuum.htm
Ted Anthony, "English Sweeps Round the World."

www.theatlantic.com/issues/97apr/english.htm
Robert D. King, "Should English Be the Law"?
at *The Atlantic Monthly* site.

www.theatlantic.com/issues/2000/11/wallraff.htm
Barbara Wallraff, "What Global Language?"
at *The Atlantic Monthly* site. Includes links to other articles on the subject by Wallraff.

The following debates in the Pro/Con series may also be of interest:

In this volume:

Topic 1 Is inequality a problem?

Topic 2 Is it possible to live in a nonracist society?

Part 2: Social responsibility in a civil society, pages 98–99

Topic 8 Should people have to obey unjust laws?

Topic 11 Is hate speech a right?

In Government:

Topic 2 Are all human beings created equal?

SHOULD ENGLISH BE THE OFFICIAL LANGUAGE IN THE UNITED STATES?

YES: An English-only policy can and has been perceived as racist and does not reflect the multiethnic population in the United States

YES: Many first- and second-generation Americans do not speak the language of their parents

IMMIGRATION
Is an official English policy unfair to the substantial immigrant population?

ASSIMILATION
Would an official English policy encourage assimilation of cultures?

NO: English is a global language, and given the size of the United States and the different ethnic groups living there, it is important to make sure that everyone can communicate adequately

NO: Studies have shown that most children of immigrant parents rapidly learn English anyway, so need no encouragement to assimilate

SHOULD ENGLISH BE THE OFFICIAL LANGUAGE IN THE UNITED STATES?

KEY POINTS

YES: The United States is tied by geography to Central and Latin America, so it is important to learn both Spanish and English

YES: The Hispanic population is very large, and this should be reflected in the country's official language

BILINGUALISM
Should the United States be a bilingual country?

NO: This would just be divisive and create further tensions in a country already rife with racial problems

NO: Studies have shown that bilingual students end up being proficient in two languages but excelling in neither

SOCIAL RESPONSIBILITY IN A CIVIL SOCIETY

INTRODUCTION

The Latin term *civilis societas*, or "civil society," originally referred to communities that followed norms above and beyond the laws set by the state. Those norms might be a set of moral or religious values, a sense of duty or responsibility, or so on. But because its foundations were built on something other than simply the laws of the state, civil society was perceived as something that served to check the power of the state.

Today the United Nations Development Fund (UNDP) defines civil society as "the sphere in which social movements become organized" and observes that it represents many diverse and sometimes contradictory social interests. The relationship between those different groups determines how civil society works. It in turn is directed by the social behavior and responsibility of the individuals within it.

Social responsibility

Not everyone agrees with the idea of civil society. The 19th-century German philosopher Friedrich Nietzsche argued that without laws society would collapse. Individuals, he believed, only act in their own self-interest. Any act that benefits another party is either self-interested at heart or benefits them by accident rather than design.

Civil society still has many supporters, however, who see in it a possible way to counter a perceived social breakdown that is manifested in crime, violence, and disrespect.

Organizations such as the Massachusetts-based Educators for Social Responsibility work to foster social responsibility among young adults by stressing how important it is for the individual to: commit to the well-being of themselves and the people around them, resolve conflicts in a peaceful manner, solve problems in cooperation with their peers, value diversity and cultural differences, counter bias and confront prejudice, think critically and creatively, and make responsible, or thought-out, decisions. The basis of such an approach to society is the subject of the second section of this volume.

The law

The Bill of Rights protects Americans' rights to free speech, privacy, and religious freedom, among other things. Laws help enforce those rights. However, in some cases laws that protect the rights of some citizens disempower other groups in the same society, leading to social unrest.

Topic 8 asks whether people should have to obey unjust laws. It looks particularly at the U.S. civil rights movement, during which a group of white Alabama clergymen called for antisegregationist protesters to obey the law. The reply from Dr. Martin Luther King, Jr., outlines the reasons why people were disobeying existing laws. Topic 9 also looks at the individual's right to disobey laws, particularly on religious grounds, using the Amish community as an example. Topic 10 also examines the rights of the individual and the law, debating whether violent protest is ever justified. Alex Braithwaite argues that sometimes it is the only option and uses the civil rights

The Bill of Rights is also quoted in defense of gun ownership. Advocates cite the Second Amendment's "right to bear arms" as justification for private gun ownership. Critics, however, argue that this is a wilful misinterpretation of the Constitution. This issue is debated in Topic 12.

The criminal justice system that enforces the law is the subject of Topic 13, which asks if the death penalty is justifiable. It draws on a classic 19th-century speech by the political theorist John Stuart Mill to defend execution and the ACLU to oppose it.

By now we know that peace and prosperity cannot be achieved without partnerships involving governments, international organizations, the business community and civil society. In today's world, we depend on each other."
—KOFI ANNAN, UN SECRETARY GENERAL

---

movement and Apartheid in South Africa to support her case. Mahatma Gandhi, the most influential advocate of nonviolent protest, takes the contrary view that change through violence causes more harm than good.

Hatred and violence

Most societies work to eradicate hatred and violence. Topic 11 deals with the issue of hate speech in U.S. society, asking if it is an individual right. Free speech advocates argue that it is a right protected by the First Amendment. Critics argue that hate speech is dangerous, pervasive, and unwelcome, and that in extreme cases it results in violence and death.

Individuals often look to past events in order to make informed decisions concerning the future. One of the dark episodes in U.S. history is slavery. Modern descendants of slaves argue that they should receive reparations for the treatment of their ancestors. This issue is debated in Topic 14.

Another important moral issue is abortion and whether women have the right to choose whether or not to have a baby. Topic 15 looks at the moral, philosophical, religious, and gender implications of abortion, and asks if it is a woman's right. The last topic in this section deals with the related issue of surrogate motherhood and asks if it is morally and socially wrong.

Topic 8
SHOULD PEOPLE HAVE TO OBEY UNJUST LAWS?

YES

STATEMENT BY EIGHT ALABAMA CLERGYMEN, APRIL 12, 1963
WWW.DU.EDU/~AIRVINE/TEACHING/MLK/PUBLIC_STATEMENT.HTM

NO

LETTER FROM A BIRMINGHAM JAIL, APRIL 16, 1963
MARTIN LUTHER KING ESTATE
MARTIN LUTHER KING, JR.

INTRODUCTION

Laws are necessary to enforce social order. Without laws society would likely descend into chaos. Citizens in a country or a state have a duty to accept the laws of the society in which they live. If they break the law, they are punished. However, in modern democracies laws themselves also have a duty. They must be seen to be just and nondiscriminatory, so that they apply equally to all citizens. Laws are not always fair and unbiased, however. In such cases are people within their rights to disobey them? Or must they avoid challenging the social order?

The question is a difficult one that has occupied lawmakers and moralists for centuries. In ancient Greece it was tackled by the philosopher Socrates and in medieval Europe by the religious thinker Thomas Aquinas. It remains the subject of debate today. At its heart is a fundamental question: Who should decide whether a law is just or not?

Does the simple fact that a person disagrees with a law constitute a valid reason to ignore or disobey it? The vast majority of Americans today accept laws that make slavery illegal, but there is a minority who do not believe that such laws are unjust. Most people believe that drunk-driving laws save lives, but others object strongly to what they see as a constraint on their freedom. What if everyone who disagreed with an aspect of state or federal spending disobeyed the laws that make them pay their taxes?

Throughout U.S. history there have been numerous instances of laws that are now widely perceived as unjust, from those that deprived Native Americans of their land to those that forbade women the vote or those that made black Americans second-class citizens.

For more than 70 years in the United States organizations such as the American Civil Liberties Union (ACLU) have fought against laws they perceive as infringing individuals' civil rights. The ACLU has a lot of support, boasting some 1.5 million members, and every year it spends more than $35 million fighting what it sees as legal injustice across the country. Its influence in helping change U.S. legislation and educate people to think differently has been extensive. Such organizations have their critics, however. They have been criticized for going against laws accepted by the majority, which is the basis of U.S. government and its legislative power.

---

*"An order has
the force of law
only when it is just."*

—THOMAS AQUINAS, THEOLOGIAN
AND PHILOSOPHER

The 19th-century German philosopher Immanuel Kant said, "All resistance against the supreme legislative power is the greatest and most powerful crime … for it destroys its very foundations." Kant's implication is that the citizen's duty is to support the state, no matter how unjust its laws, because the alternative would be the breakdown of society.

However, those who believe in challenging unjust laws argue that governments can be flawed or corrupt and can make bad laws. They point out cases in which laws deprive objectors of their right to protest, as in South Africa's racist apartheid laws. They draw on historical examples to show what can happen if people do not protest against unfair laws. One example is that of Nazi Germany after 1933, when Adolf Hitler's government imposed anti-Semitic legislation that prevented millions of Jews from holding public office and deprived them of many rights. Although some Germans protested, most went along with the new laws. Critics see such laws as the first step toward making possible the "final solution," the mass murder of Jews and other groups.

The civil rights movement of the 1960s is a leading example of Americans taking a stand against laws they saw as unjust. Laws supported the segregation of black Americans and their exclusion from many rights enjoyed by whites. Civil rights leaders such as Martin Luther King, Jr., and Malcolm X encouraged black Americans to object to these laws, some through nonviolent resistance, others through a more violent approach.

The following extracts come from two letters of the time. The first is a statement by eight Alabama clergymen objecting to demonstrations organized by black civil rights leaders. They argue that any change in the law should happen through the law courts, and that the decisions of the courts should be peacefully obeyed, even the segregation laws. Even peaceful actions that incite hatred and violence, they say, do not resolve problems.

The second extract is a reply to the clergymen's statement by Martin Luther King, Jr. Written while he was in jail for a civil rights protest, it completely rejects the churchmen's logic. Any law that degrades the human personality, King says, is unjust. Unjust laws are those that are out of harmony with moral laws. Since segregation is morally wrong and sinful, he argues, the segregation ordinances should be disobeyed, particularly since they are inflicted on a minority that had no part in their making.

STATEMENT BY ALABAMA CLERGYMEN

☑ **The following statement by eight white Alabama clergymen, reprinted by the American Friends Service Committee, prompted King's "Letter from Birmingham Jail."**

We the undersigned clergymen are among those who, in January, issued "An Appeal for Law and Order and Common Sense" in dealing with racial problems in Alabama. We expressed understanding that honest convictions in racial matters could properly be pursued in the courts, but urged that decisions of those courts should in the meantime be peacefully obeyed.

Since that time there had been some evidence of increased forbearance and a willingness to face facts. Responsible citizens have undertaken to work on various problems that cause racial friction and unrest. In Birmingham, recent public events have given indication that we will have opportunity for a new constructive and realistic approach to racial problems.

However, we are now confronted by a series of demonstrations by some of our Negro citizens, directed and led in part by outsiders. We recognize the natural impatience of people who feel that their hopes are slow in being realized. But we are convinced that these demonstrations are unwise and untimely.

King's reply to this part of the letter is that justice too long delayed is justice denied. See page 106.

We agree rather with certain local Negro leadership that has called for honest and open negotiation of racial issues in our area. And we believe this kind of facing of issues can best be accomplished by citizens of our own metropolitan area, white and Negro, meeting with their knowledge and experience of the local situation. All of us need to face that responsibility and find proper channels for its accomplishment.

What ways might there be to ensure that people face this "responsibility"?

Just as we formerly pointed out that "hatred and violence have no sanction in our religious and political traditions," we also point out that such actions as incite to hatred and violence, however technically peaceful those actions may be, have not contributed to the resolution of our local problems. We do not believe that these days of new hope are days when extreme measures are justified in Birmingham.

We commend the community as a whole, and the local news media and law enforcement officials in particular, on the calm manner in which these demonstrations have

A vigil is held in 1968 for Black Panther fugitive Eldridge Cleaver, who was on the run after a police shoot out. The Panthers advocated direct, sometimes violent action to support civil rights.

COMMENTARY: Martin Luther King, Jr.

Martin Luther King, Jr., a principal leader of the black civil rights movement, advocated using nonviolent methods for social change.

Born in Atlanta, Georgia, on January 15, 1929, Martin Luther King, Jr., was part of a family that had strong African American Baptist Church roots. Both his grandfather and his father were pastors, and King himself became pastor of Dexter Avenue Baptist Church in Montgomery, Alabama.

In December 1955 a black woman, Rosa Parks, refused to obey the segregation rules of Montgomery, which required her to give up her seat on a bus to a white person. At the time, African Americans in some Southern states were not allowed to sit up front on buses with white passengers but had to sit in back. Parks was arrested, and five days later King organized a boycott of the Montgomery bus system.

King was arrested and charged with violating the state laws of Alabama regarding protest marching. King was essentially protesting about segregation, which had been made illegal, at least in schools, in 1954. In December 1956 the Montgomery buses were desegregated after the U.S. Supreme Court declared Alabama's segregation laws to be unconstitutional.

During 1959 King toured India, where he learned more about Mahatma Gandhi's strategies of nonviolent protest (see Topic 10 *Is Violent Protest Ever Justified?* on pages 138–139 in this volume). King was criticized by some black activists, who were impatient for change and saw his call for nonviolent action as too moderate and cautious to bring about real social change.

In spring 1963 King led demonstrations in Birmingham, Alabama, which led to violent clashes between black demonstrators and white police officers using dogs and fire hoses to disperse the crowd. More than 250,000 protesters marched on Washington, D.C., in August 1963, where King delivered his famous "I have a dream" speech. He was awarded the Nobel Peace Prize in 1964. King faced many challenges to his leadership. Many northern blacks, for instance, saw the message of black nationalism expressed by Malcolm X (1927–1965) as more representative of their views. King was assassinated on April 4, 1968. Today he remains an important—if controversial for some—symbol of the black civil rights movement.

been handled. We urge the public to continue to show restraint should the demonstrations continue, and the law enforcement officials to remain calm and continue to protect our city from violence.

We further strongly urge our own Negro community to withdraw support from these demonstrations, and to unite locally in working peacefully for a better Birmingham. When rights are consistently denied, a cause should be pressed in the courts and in negotiations among local leaders, and not in the streets. We appeal to both our white and Negro citizenry to observe the principles of law and order and common sense.

For a discussion about violent protest see Topic 10 Is Violent Protest Ever Justified? on pages 126–137 in this volume.

Signed by:
C. C. J. Carpenter, D.D., LL.D., Bishop of Alabama
Joseph A. Durick, D.D., Auxiliary Bishop, Diocese of Mobile–Birmingham
Rabbi Milton L. Grafman, Temple Emanu-El, Birmingham, Alabama
Bishop Paul Hardin, Bishop of the Alabama–West Florida Conference of the Methodist Church
Bishop Nolan B. Harmon, Bishop of the North Alabama Conference of the Methodist Church
George M. Murray, D.D., LL.D., Bishop Coadjutor, Episcopal Diocese of Alabama
Edward V. Ramage, Moderator, Synod of the Alabama Presbyterian Church in the United States
Earl Stallings, Pastor, First Baptist Church, Birmingham, Alabama

LETTER FROM A BIRMINGHAM JAIL
Martin Luther King, Jr.

NO

My dear fellow Clergymen

Do you agree that King's position gives him authority to protest in Birmingham?

… I think I should give the reason for my being in Birmingham, since you have been influenced by the argument of "outsiders coming in." I have the honor of serving as president of the Southern Christian Leadership Conference, an organization operating in every Southern state, with headquarters in Atlanta, Georgia. We have some 85 affiliate organizations all across the South—one being the Alabama Christian Movement for Human Rights. Whenever necessary and possible we share staff, educational and financial resources with our affiliates. Several months ago our local affiliate here in Birmingham invited us to be on call to engage in a nonviolent direct action program if such were deemed necessary. We readily consented, and when the hour came we lived up to our promises. So I am here, along with several members of my staff, because I have basic organizational ties here.

Beyond this, I am in Birmingham because injustice is here. … Injustice anywhere is a threat to justice everywhere. … Anyone who lives inside the United States can never be considered an outsider anywhere in this country.

You deplore the demonstrations that are presently taking place in Birmingham. … [I]t is unfortunate that so-called demonstrations are taking place in Birmingham at this time, but I would say in more emphatic terms that it is even more unfortunate that the white power structure of this city left the Negro community with no other alternative.

King drew on many cultural traditions for his ideas about nonviolent protest, particularly the philosophy of the Indian leader Mahatma Gandhi.

In any nonviolent campaign there are four basic steps: 1) Collection of the facts to determine whether injustices are alive. 2) Negotiation. 3) Self-purification and 4) Direct action. We have gone through all of these steps in Birmingham. There can be no gainsaying of the fact that racial injustice engulfs this community.

Birmingham is probably the most thoroughly segregated city in the United States. Its ugly record of police brutality is known in every section of this country. Its unjust treatment of Negroes in the courts is a notorious reality. There have been more unsolved bombings of Negro homes and churches in Birmingham than any city in this nation. These are the hard, brutal, and unbelievable facts. On the basis of these conditions, Negro leaders sought to negotiate with the city fathers. But the political leaders consistently refused to engage in good faith negotiation. ... After this we felt that direct action could be delayed no longer.

You may well ask: "Why direct action? Why sit-ins, marches, etc.? Isn't negotiation a better path?" You are exactly right in your call for negotiation. Indeed, this is the purpose of direct action. Nonviolent direct action seeks to create such a crisis and establish such creative tension that a community that has constantly refused to negotiate is forced to confront the issue. It seeks so to dramatize the issue that it can no longer be ignored. I just referred to the creation of tension as a part of the work of the nonviolent resister. This may sound rather shocking. But I must confess that I am not afraid of the word tension. I have earnestly worked and preached against violent tension, but there is a type of constructive nonviolent tension that is necessary for growth. Just as Socrates felt that it was necessary to create a tension in the mind so that individuals could rise from the bondage of myths and half-truths to the unfettered realm of creative analysis and objective appraisal, we must see the need of having nonviolent gadflies to create the kind of tension in society that will help men to rise from the dark depths of prejudice and racism to the majestic heights of understanding and brotherhood. So the purpose of the direct action is to create a situation so crisis-packed that it will inevitably open the door to negotiation. We, therefore, concur with you in your call for negotiation. Too long has our beloved Southland been bogged down in the tragic attempt to live in monologue rather than dialogue. ...

Do you agree that without protest society sometimes avoids confronting an issue?

We have waited for more than 340 years for our constitutional and God-given rights. The nations of Asia and Africa are moving with jet-like speed toward the goal of political independence, and we still creep at horse and buggy pace toward the gaining of a cup of coffee at a lunch counter. I guess it is easy for those who have never felt the stinging darts of segregation to say, "Wait." But when you have seen vicious mobs lynch your mothers and fathers at will and drown your sisters and brothers at whim; when you have seen hate-filled policemen curse, kick, brutalize, and even kill your black brothers and sisters with impunity; when you see the vast majority of your twenty million Negro brothers smothering in an airtight cage of poverty in the midst of an affluent society; when you suddenly find your tongue twisted and your speech stammering as you seek to explain to your six-year-old daughter why she can't go to the public

The sit-in movement began in 1960 when a black student was refused service at a Woolworth's lunch counter.

Building a long list of repetitious phrases is a powerful debating technique.

amusement park that has just been advertised on television, and see tears welling up in her eyes when she is told that Funtown is closed to colored children, and see the depressing clouds of inferiority begin to form in her little mental sky, and see her begin to distort her little personality by unconsciously developing a bitterness toward white people; when you have to concoct an answer for a five-year-old son asking in agonizing pathos: "Daddy, why do white people treat colored people so mean?"; when you take a cross-country drive and find it necessary to sleep night after night in the uncomfortable corners of your automobile because no motel will accept you; when you are humiliated day in and day out by nagging signs reading "white" and "colored"; when your first name becomes "nigger," your middle name becomes "boy" (however old you are), and your last name becomes "John," and your wife and mother are never given the respected title "Mrs."; when you are harried by day and haunted by night by the fact that you are a Negro, living constantly at tip-toe stance never quite knowing what to expect next, and plagued with inner fears and outer resentments; when you are forever fighting a degenerating sense of "nobodiness"; then you will understand why we find it difficult to wait. There comes a time when the cup of endurance runs over, and men are no longer willing to be plunged into an abyss of despair. I hope, sirs, you can understand our legitimate and unavoidable impatience.

You express a great deal of anxiety over our willingness to break laws. This is certainly a legitimate concern. Since we so diligently urge people to obey the Supreme Court's decision of 1954 outlawing segregation in the public schools, it is rather strange and paradoxical to find us consciously breaking laws. One may well ask: "How can you advocate breaking some laws and obeying others?" The answer is found in the fact that there are two types of laws: There are just and there are unjust laws. I would agree with Saint Augustine that "An unjust law is no law at all."

Now, what is the difference between the two? How does one determine when a law is just or unjust? A just law is a man-made code that squares with the moral law or the law of God. An unjust law is a code that is out of harmony with the moral law. To put it in the terms of Saint Thomas Aquinas, an unjust law is a human law that is not rooted in eternal and natural law. Any law that uplifts human personality is just. Any law that degrades human personality is unjust. All segregation statutes are unjust because segregation distorts the soul and damages the personality. It gives the segregator a false sense

Although in theory segregation had been made illegal in the 1950s, many states in the South still segregated black and white people into the 1960s.

Having laid out his evidence, King makes a direct appeal to his audience.

King spends the rest of his argument trying to define "unjust" laws. Why is this so important to his argument?

of superiority, and the segregated a false sense of inferiority. To use the words of Martin Buber, the Jewish philosopher, segregation substitutes an "I-it" relationship for an "I-thou" relationship, and ends up relegating persons to the status of things. So segregation is not only politically, economically, and sociologically unsound, but it is morally wrong and sinful. Paul Tillich has said that sin is separation. Isn't segregation an existential expression of man's tragic separation, an expression of his awful estrangement, his terrible sinfulness? So I can urge men to disobey segregation ordinances because they are morally wrong.

Let us turn to a more concrete example of just and unjust laws. An unjust law is a code that a majority inflicts on a minority that is not binding on itself. This is difference made legal. On the other hand a just law is a code that a majority compels a minority to follow that it is willing to follow itself. This is sameness made legal.

Let me give another explanation. An unjust law is a code inflicted upon a minority which that minority had no part in enacting or creating because they did not have the unhampered right to vote. Who can say that the legislature of Alabama which set up the segregation laws was democratically elected? Throughout the state of Alabama all types of conniving methods are used to prevent Negroes from becoming registered voters and there are some counties without a single Negro registered to vote despite the fact that the Negro constitutes a majority of the population. Can any law set up in such a state be considered democratically structured?

Until 1965 states could use devices such as literacy tests to prevent black people from registering to vote.

These are just a few examples of unjust and just laws. There are some instances when a law is just on its face and unjust in its application. For instance, I was arrested Friday on a charge of parading without a permit. Now there is nothing wrong with an ordinance which requires a permit for a parade, but when the ordinance is used to preserve segregation and to deny citizens the First-Amendment privilege of peaceful assembly and peaceful protest, then it becomes unjust.

I hope you can see the distinction I am trying to point out. In no sense do I advocate evading or defying the law as the rabid segregationist would do. This would lead to anarchy. One who breaks an unjust law must do it openly, lovingly … and with a willingness to accept the penalty. I submit that an individual who breaks a law that conscience tells him is unjust, and willingly accepts the penalty by staying in jail to arouse the conscience of the community over its injustice, is in reality expressing the very highest respect for law.

Summary

The issue of whether citizens should obey unjust laws is a complex one. The two extracts illustrate the moral complexities of the issue. In the "Statement by Alabama Clergymen" the authors argue that any injustices must be changed legally, through the law courts, and not through mass demonstrations. They assert that "such actions as incite to hatred and violence, however technically peaceful those actions may be, have not contributed to the resolution of our local problems."

The statement prompted Martin Luther King, Jr., to reply in "Letter from a Birmingham Jail." King quotes Saint Augustine, stating that "an unjust law is no law at all." He argues that nonviolent direct action is negotiation and that it is necessary to change unjust and unfair conditions under which black Americans live. The white power structure leaves the black community no alternative, he says, while political leaders have refused to engage in good-faith negotiation. According to King, history is a long and tragic story of the fact that privileged groups seldom give up their privileges voluntarily. He defines an unjust law as one that is immoral or that degrades the human personality. Another definition of an unjust law is a law that a majority has inflicted on a minority that is not binding on itself, particularly one that the minority had no say in creating. He reminds his audience that at the time, most states in the South employed methods such as literacy tests to prevent black voters from registering. The main points in the debate are summarized in the diagram on the opposite page.

FURTHER INFORMATION:

Books:

Bass, Jonathan S., *Blessed Are the Peacemakers: Martin Luther King, Jr., Eight White Religious Leaders, and the "Letter from a Birmingham Jail."* Baton Rouge: Louisiana State University Press, 2001.

Bay, Christian and Charles Walker, *Civil Disobedience: Theory and Practice*. Tonawanda, NY: Black Rose Books Ltd, 1996.

Carson, Clayborne, *The Eyes on the Prize: Civil Rights Reader: Documents, Speeches, and Firsthand Accounts from the Black Freedom Struggle, 1954–1990*. New York: Penguin, 1991.

Joseph, Jennifer (editor), *The Civil Disobedience Handbook: A Brief History and Practical Advice for the Politically Disenchanted*. San Francisco: Manic D Press, 2001.

Terkel, Susan Neuberg, *People Power: A Look at Nonviolent Action and Defense*. Birmingham, AL: Lodestar Books, 1996.

Useful websites:

www.civilrights.org
The Social Justice Network site has information and articles relating to civil rights.

The following debates in the Pro/Con series may also be of interest:

In this volume:

Topic 9 Should there be a right to violate laws for religious reasons?

Topic 10 Is violent protest ever justified?

SHOULD PEOPLE HAVE TO OBEY UNJUST LAWS?

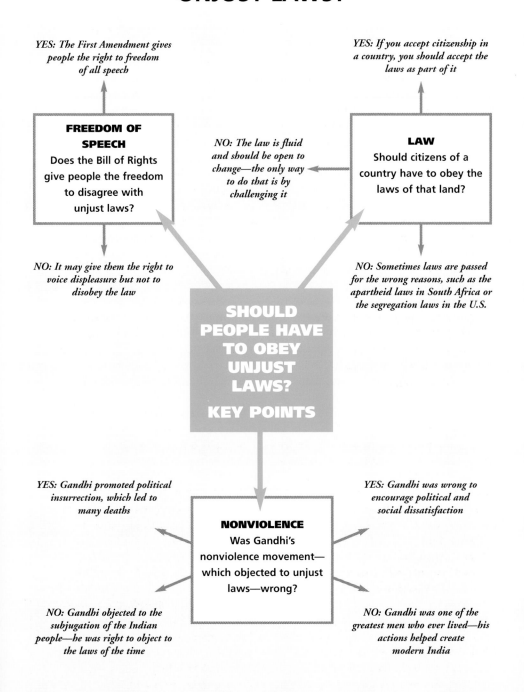

YES: The First Amendment gives people the right to freedom of all speech

YES: If you accept citizenship in a country, you should accept the laws as part of it

FREEDOM OF SPEECH
Does the Bill of Rights give people the freedom to disagree with unjust laws?

NO: The law is fluid and should be open to change—the only way to do that is by challenging it

LAW
Should citizens of a country have to obey the laws of that land?

NO: It may give them the right to voice displeasure but not to disobey the law

NO: Sometimes laws are passed for the wrong reasons, such as the apartheid laws in South Africa or the segregation laws in the U.S.

SHOULD PEOPLE HAVE TO OBEY UNJUST LAWS?

KEY POINTS

YES: Gandhi promoted political insurrection, which led to many deaths

YES: Gandhi was wrong to encourage political and social dissatisfaction

NONVIOLENCE
Was Gandhi's nonviolence movement— which objected to unjust laws—wrong?

NO: Gandhi objected to the subjugation of the Indian people—he was right to object to the laws of the time

NO: Gandhi was one of the greatest men who ever lived—his actions helped create modern India

THE VALUE OF DEBATE

Since the first intercollegiate debate between Harvard and Yale Universities in 1892, hundreds of thousands of American students have participated in academic debate. Several notable presidents, including John F. Kennedy and Bill Clinton, were school/college debaters. Debating skills are important since they can be used in every facet of everyday life.

"Freedom is hammered out on the anvil of discussion, dissent, and debate."

—HUBERT H. HUMPHREY, POLITICIAN

Why debate?

In modern democracies the right to debate is an invaluable asset. Orderly, rational debate, in which the speakers argue for the acceptance of various ideas or answers to a specific question (as in the *Pro/Con* series), is seen on a daily basis in parliaments and congresses around the world. Debate is one of the oldest activities of civilization. Ancient monarchs used councils of noblemen to give them advice, and the process of debate helped in decision-making.

In the United States there are various methods by which a speaker can propose a new solution to a problem or question. One way is to put a petition together to put a proposal on the ballot in an election. The proponents then speak to the voters on behalf of the proposal in the hope that their proposal might be voted into law. If there are opponents to the measure, it is important that both sides know how to debate the issue properly, calmly, and in an orderly fashion.

Formal debating is done by legislative bodies in the United States, such as the Senate or House of Representatives. In these places elaborate rules are laid down to make sure that two cornerstones of debate are followed:

1. That one issue is presented at a time;
2. That there's provision for equal representation of each point of view.

Every situation that asks you to compare alternatives is a situation forcing you to debate the merits and disadvantages of those alternatives. Sometimes the debating is conducted in your mind, such as when you have to weigh the pros and cons of going to college, taking a particular job, wearing certain clothes—sometimes it's done in your presence for you, by a judge in court, by a teacher in a schoolroom, or by a sales person on your doorstep.

Occasionally, you may be called on to argue for or against a situation yourself, and it is important that you know how to do this. Thus the debating skills you develop now can be of benefit to you throughout your life.

SEVEN TALENTS NEEDED IN DEBATING

Good debaters are people who secure support for the ideas they propose even in the face of analytical, organized opposition. The following seven skills are necessary to debate with success:

• Ability to research, collate, and organize ideas
You may need to sift through large amounts of material to build up your argument. You will need to collate this information in an organized manner. See *Research Skills* in the *Government* volume, pages 58–59.

• Ability to subordinate ideas
During a debate you may hear up to 5,000 words during one round. You need to be able to sort out what the major ideas are in your opponent's argument, and remember them and repeat them if necessary in your own speech.

• Ability to evaluate evidence
Not every idea or statement in a debate is worth refuting or replying to. You need to be able to realize what is important and what isn't.

• Ability to see logical connections
So much material is presented during a debate that it is likely to cause confusion. Aristotle once commented that the mark of genius is the ability to see similar things among the dissimilar. That is also the mark of a good debater.

• Ability to think and speak in outline terms
The ability to think clearly and have a mind map, if you like, of your argument is important. However, it is essential to be able to translate it to your audience. Clarity is a key factor in a good debate argument.

• Ability to pitch your ideas correctly to different audiences
It is important to believe your argument; but in order to win, you must convince your audience too. Different audiences react in different ways, and a good debater can judge the level at which he or she must pitch his or her argument.

• Ability to adapt to new ideas
A debate is a fluid situation in which an exchange of ideas occurs. Both parties must be able to engage in a dialogue and adapt their thoughts and arguments accordingly. A good debater must be able to react very quickly to whatever situation arises.

If you follow these seven steps, they should help you become a better debater.

Topic 9

SHOULD THERE BE A RIGHT TO VIOLATE LAWS FOR RELIGIOUS REASONS?

YES

WISCONSIN V. YODER
CHIEF JUSTICE WARREN BURGER

NO

"THE IMPORTANCE OF BEING AMISH"
FROM *IN DEFENSE OF LIBERAL DEMOCRACY*
WALTER BERNS

INTRODUCTION

The First Amendment to the U.S. Constitution provides that "Congress shall make no law respecting an establishment of religion, or prohibiting the free exercise thereof." Religious freedom is the first and most fundamental of the liberties enjoyed by citizens of free societies, so it is fitting that it has pride of place in the Bill of Rights, ratified in 1791.

The idea of religious freedom includes both freedom to practice one's own religion without the supervision of the state ("free exercise") and freedom from the religious tyranny of those who would impose an orthodoxy on all citizens (no "establishment of religion"). These two aspects of religious freedom are in many cases reverse sides of the same coin: Free exercise is perhaps possible only where there is no establishment of a favored religion.

In this topic we consider one of the most hotly debated questions about the meaning of "free exercise" of religion. From time to time, generally applicable state laws that are not targeted at religion will nevertheless have difficult consequences for the practice of some religion. Does "free exercise" of religion require the state to exempt religious citizens in such cases from the ordinary duty to obey the law?

Suppose that a state law bans drug use, and that peyote is included on the list of forbidden drugs. Suppose, too, that the sacramental use of peyote is an ordinary religious practice of a Native American religious community. Should the law, which was passed out of a concern about drug use but which imposes a burden on the free exercise of religion, be applied to forbid the sacramental religious use of peyote? Or should the Native American religious community receive an exemption from this otherwise unobjectionable law, even though the law was not targeted at religious practice? If the religious community is given an exemption, is it merely a permissible accommodation of free exercise of religion? Or is it an impermissible favoritism for religion in general or for a particular religion?

> *"Difference of religion breeds more quarrels than difference of politics."*
>
> —WENDELL PHILLIPS,
>
> REFORMER AND ORATOR

In this particular case (*Employment Division v. Smith*, 1990) the Supreme Court refused to grant the Native American religious community an exemption from a state statute prohibiting peyote use. Free exercise, said the court, means freedom of belief and profession but not the freedom to perform acts, even as part of worship, that are otherwise unlawful. Free exercise cannot excuse the religious from their obligation to obey the law if the law is genuinely neutral (that is, if it is not targeted at religion).

Many years earlier the court had upheld the conviction of a Mormon man for bigamy despite his claim to free exercise of his religion. And in a case involving a Sunday closing law, the court had rejected a similar free exercise argument. *Employment Division v. Smith* went further than these earlier decisions, and it was very controversial. To some it seemed that the court had abandoned another older rule, established in *Wisconsin v. Yoder* (discussed in both articles in this topic), which recognized a religious exemption from a Wisconsin compulsory education law.

In *Yoder* the court considered the case of a member of the Old Order Amish religious community who refused to permit his daughter to attend school beyond eighth grade, in violation of Wisconsin's compulsory education law, on the grounds that public school attendance would be contrary to the Amish religion. The Supreme Court held that a conviction under this state statute would violate the free exercise clause of the First Amendment.

The question was whether an exemption from an otherwise valid state law was necessary in order for the Amish to preserve their right under the Constitution to free exercise of religion. Chief Justice Burger argued that universal compulsory education was by no means absolute to the exclusion or subordination of all other interests. By exposing the Amish to worldly influences, and by interfering with a child's religious development and his or her integration into the Amish way of life at the crucial adolescent stage, Burger argued, compulsory secondary education contravenes the basic religious practice of the Amish faith. The compulsory-attendance law also carries an objective danger to the First Amendment's free exercise of religion clause, he said, by posing a very real threat of undermining the Amish community and religious practice.

Walter Berns makes the case that the Supreme Court's decision in *Wisconsin v. Yoder* is dangerous. He argues that if one is entitled to disobey a law that is contrary to one's own religious beliefs, and is entitled also to define one's religious beliefs, there will be a proliferation of sects, such as drug cultists and snake worshipers.

WISCONSIN V. YODER
Chief Justice Warren Burger

✓ There is no doubt as to the power of a State, having a high responsibility for education of its citizens, to impose reasonable regulations for the control and duration of basic education. [But], a State's interest in universal education, however highly we rank it, is not totally free from a balancing process when it impinges on fundamental rights and interests, such as those specifically protected by the Free Exercise Clause of the First Amendment, and the traditional interest of parents with respect to the religious upbringing of their children so long as they, in the words of Pierce, "prepare [them] for additional obligations."

> *The case being discussed here dates from 1972.*

The free exercise of religion

It follows that in order for Wisconsin to compel school attendance beyond the eighth grade against a claim that such attendance interferes with the practice of a legitimate religious belief, it must appear either that the State does not deny the free exercise of religious belief by its requirement, or that there is a State interest of sufficient magnitude to override the interest claiming protection under the Free Exercise Clause. Long before there was general acknowledgment of the need for universal formal education, the Religion Clauses had specifically and firmly fixed the right to free exercise of religious beliefs, and buttressing this fundamental right was an equally firm, even if less explicit, prohibition against the establishment of any religion by government. The values underlying these two provisions relating to religion have been zealously protected, sometimes even at the expense of other interests of admittedly high social importance.

> *Do you think that the fact that the Religion Clauses were passed before many others means that they are still more important?*

The essence of all that has been said and written on the subject is that only those interests of the highest order and those not otherwise served can overbalance legitimate claims to the free exercise of religion. We can accept it as settled, therefore, that, however strong the State's interest in universal compulsory education, it is by no means absolute to the exclusion or subordination of all other interests.

We come then to the quality of the claims of the respondents concerning the alleged encroachment of

Wisconsin's compulsory school-attendance statute on their rights and the rights of their children to the free exercise of the religious beliefs they and their forebears have adhered to for almost three centuries. In evaluating those claims we must be careful to determine whether the Amish religious faith and their mode of life are, as they claim, inseparable and interdependent. A way of life, however virtuous and admirable, may not be interposed as a barrier to reasonable State regulation of education if it is based on purely secular considerations; to have the protection of the Religion Clauses, the claims must be rooted in religious belief. Although a determination of what is a "religious" belief or practice entitled to constitutional protection may present a most delicate question, the very concept of ordered liberty precludes allowing every person to make his own standards on matters of conduct in which society as a whole has important interests. Thus, if the Amish asserted their claims because of their subjective evaluation and rejection of the contemporary secular values accepted by the majority, much as Thoreau rejected the social values of his time and isolated himself at Walden Pond, their claims would not rest on a religious basis. Thoreau's choice was philosophical and personal rather than religious, and such belief does not rise to the demands of the Religion Clauses.

Henry David Thoreau (1817–1862), an American naturalist and writer, is best known for his Walden experiment. He lived as a recluse in the woods of Walden near Concord, Massachusetts, in 1845–1846.

Way of life and religious conviction

Giving no weight to such secular considerations, however, we see that the record in this case abundantly supports the claim that the traditional way of life of the Amish is not merely a matter of personal preference, but one of deep religious conviction, shared by an organized group, and intimately related to daily living. That the Old Order Amish daily life and religious practice stem from their faith is shown by the fact that it is in response to their literal interpretation of the biblical injunction from the Epistle of Paul to the Romans, "be not conformed to this world...." This command is fundamental to the Amish faith. Moreover, for the Old Order Amish, religion is not simply a matter of theocratic belief. As the expert witnesses explained, the Old Order Amish religion pervades and determines virtually their entire way of life, regulating it with the detail of the Talmudic diet through the strictly enforced rules of the church community.

What criteria could you use to define a religion from, say, a philosophical attitude toward life?

The record shows that the respondents' religious beliefs and attitude toward life, family, and home have remained constant—perhaps some would say static—in a period of unparalleled progress in human knowledge generally and

The simple, unworldly Amish way of life was portrayed in the movie Witness (1985), starring Harrison Ford.

great changes in education. The respondents freely concede, and indeed assert as an article of faith, that their religious beliefs and what we would today call "life style" have not altered in fundamentals for centuries. Their way of life in a church-oriented community, separated from the outside world and "worldly" influences, their attachment to nature and the soil, is a way inherently simple and uncomplicated, albeit difficult to preserve against the pressure to conform. Their rejection of telephones, automobiles, radios, and television, their mode of dress, of speech, their habits of manual work do indeed set them apart from much of contemporary society; these customs are both symbolic and practical.

Conflict between traditional and modern society

As the society around the Amish has become more populous, urban, industrialized, and complex, particularly in this century, government regulation of human affairs has correspondingly become more detailed and pervasive. The Amish mode of life has thus come into conflict increasingly with requirements of contemporary society exerting a hydraulic insistence on conformity to majoritarian standards. So long as compulsory education laws were confined to eight grades of elementary basic education imparted in a nearby rural schoolhouse, with a large proportion of students of the Amish faith, the Old Order Amish had little basis to fear that school attendance would expose their children to the worldly influence they reject. But modern compulsory secondary education in rural areas is now largely carried on in a consolidated school, often remote from the student's home and alien to his daily home life. As the record so strongly shows, the values and programs of the modern secondary school are in sharp conflict with the fundamental mode of life mandated by the Amish religion; modern laws requiring compulsory secondary education have accordingly engendered great concern and conflict. The conclusion is inescapable that secondary schooling, by exposing Amish children to worldly influences in terms of attitudes, goals, and values contrary to beliefs, and by interfering with the religious development of the Amish child and his integration into the [Amish] way of life at the crucial adolescent stage, contravenes the religious tenets and practice of the Amish faith, both as to the parent and the child.

The impact of the compulsory-attendance law on respondents' practice of the Amish religion is not only severe, but inescapable, for the Wisconsin law affirmatively compels them, under threat of criminal sanction, to perform acts

COMMENTARY: Religious Freedom in America

During the late 1980s the trend in the U.S. Supreme Court was to allow governments to restrict religious freedom as long as the limitations applied equally to all faiths. More than 60 religious organizations and civil liberties groups combined to form the Coalition for the Free Exercise of Religion to fight this trend. Today the group has expanded to include 72 very different organizations that often have opposite views on almost every topic. The group promoted the federal Religious Freedom Restoration Act (RFRA), which required governments to refrain from limiting religious freedom unless they have a compelling societal reason for doing so, and if they do need to restrict religious freedom, to choose the least intrusive way to achieve their goal.

The bill was signed into law in 1993. Since then there have been many cases that have made use of it. In other lawsuits, however, the act was found to be unconstitutional, and in 1997 the U.S. Supreme Court declared the law to be unconstitutional. A number of state laws have been modeled on RFRA. A bill to replace RFRA, the Religious Liberty Protection Act, did not pass the Senate. However, a pared-down bill, the Religious Land Use and Institutionalized Persons Act, was signed into law in 2000. It restricts governments from interfering with the religious use of land and also guarantees religious freedom to inmates of institutions.

undeniably at odds with fundamental tenets of their religious beliefs.... Nor is the impact of the compulsory-attendance law confined to grave interference with important Amish religious tenets from a subjective point of view. It carries with it precisely the kind of objective danger to the free exercise of religion that the First Amendment was designed to prevent. As the record shows, compulsory school attendance to age 16 for Amish children carries with it a very real threat of undermining the Amish community and religious practice as they exist today; they must either abandon belief and be assimilated into society at large, or be forced to migrate to some other and more tolerant region.

Burger clearly summarizes the three bases on which he has made his decision.

In sum, the unchallenged testimony of acknowledged experts in education and religious history, almost 300 years of consistent practice, and strong evidence of a sustained faith pervading and regulating respondents' entire mode of life support the claim that enforcement of the State's requirement of compulsory formal education after the eighth grade would gravely endanger if not destroy the free exercise of respondents' religious beliefs.

THE IMPORTANCE OF BEING AMISH
Walter Berns

NO

X The Amish have won from the Supreme Court of the United States a special exemption allowing them, and so far only them, to ignore an otherwise valid statute. It is not part of my purpose here to speculate about the reasons for their unprecedented success—and it is unprecedented, for although many groups have tried, none before the Amish has ever succeeded. But if it were my purpose, I would attribute their success to the fact that when it comes to culture there is no group more counter than the Amish, and in this day of bourgeois diffidence, that sort of thing matters.

The Court would have us believe that there is nothing novel about the decision or the rule on which it rests. As Burger put it in his opinion, only state interests "of the highest order … can overbalance legitimate claims to the free exercise of religion"; or again, while "religiously grounded conduct must often be subject to the broad police power of the State [this] is not to deny that there are areas of conduct protected by the Free Exercise Clause of the First Amendment and thus beyond the power of the State to control, even under regulations of general applicability." But this is not the rule that had been applied in earlier cases, including the ones Burger cites; and it surely is not the rule of the case most apposite to *Yoder's*, the second flag-salute case (1943), which he does not even deign to mention.

Quoting an opposing argument in order to challenge it can be highly effective.

The flag-salute case

West Virginia required school children to salute the flag and recite the pledge of allegiance. Children who refused to comply were expelled and treated as delinquents; and their parents were made liable to prosecution and, upon conviction, a fine and jail sentence. Jehovah's Witnesses refused to salute the flag, on the ground that to do so would constitute worship of a graven image, and their parents brought suit to enjoin enforcement of the regulation.

Find out some of the other beliefs of Jehovah's Witnesses. Which other laws might conflict with their beliefs?

Here, in every material sense, is the compulsory school attendance case: in each case children and their parents are being compelled, by a statute carrying criminal penalties, to perform acts contrary to their religious beliefs. The court ruled in favor of the Jehovah's Witnesses, but it was very careful to avoid making them the special beneficiaries of its decision. The flag-salute requirement was held to be unconstitutional, a violation not, however, of the free exercise of religion clause of the First Amendment but of the free speech provision. Stated otherwise, the court held that no one, pious sectarian or militant atheist could be required to salute the flag. In the school attendance case, on the other hand, the court held that the statute was constitutional, except as applied to Yoder and the other Amish.

Dangerous law

The court has never before held that one's religious convictions entitle him to an exemption from the requirements of a valid criminal statute. This is new law, and of a dangerous sort. It is dangerous because if one is entitled to disobey a law that is contrary to his religious beliefs, and entitled as well to define his own religious beliefs, the proliferation of sects and of forms of worship will be wonderful to behold: drug cultists, snake worshippers, income-tax haters—why, in Shelley's words, the sense faints picturing them all. But there will be no stopping this religious revival (or what, for legal purposes, will be labeled a religious revival), short of permitting public officials, and ultimately the judges, to do precisely what the Supreme Court has insisted they may not do, namely, get in the business of distinguishing the honest from the dishonest, the genuine from the spurious. The principle was stated best by Justice Robert Jackson in the second flag-salute case: "If there is any fixed star in our constitutional constellation, it is that no official, high or petty, can prescribe what shall be orthodox in ... religion, or other matters of opinion or force citizens to confess by word or act their faith therein."

But in Yoder's case the court took the first step in this heretofore prohibited direction by drawing a line between the religious and the secular; it did this by emphasizing that the exemption being carved out for this religious group could not be claimed by other kinds of groups, "however virtuous and admirable" may be their "way of life." No assertion of "secular values" will do, chief Justice Burger insisted in his opinion. Even Thoreau, who, like the Amish, "rejected the social values of his time and isolated himself at Walden Pond," would not have been entitled to the privilege, because, unlike the Amish, his "choice was philosophical and personal rather than religious."

This, inevitably and with very good reason, proved too much for Justice Douglas. He agreed that the Amish could not

In fact, in the case of Sherbert vs. Verner (1963) the U.S. Supreme Court ruled that the South Carolina Unemployment Compensation Act violated the right to free exercise of religion by refusing an application because of religious beliefs.

Do you believe that "religious" considerations are more important than "secular" ones?

An Amish man in the 1950s shown wearing the traditional clothing that symbolizes Amish nonconformity to modern society.

be compelled to go to high school, but he insisted that the privilege could not be restricted to those whose objection to a law rests on religious belief in a formal sense. So what's wrong with Thoreau's philosophical position? he wanted to know. And the "philosophy" of the conscientious objector who figured it out for himself that "human life is valuable in and of itself?" Douglas wants it known that he adheres to "these exalted views of 'religion,'" and we can expect him to send battalions of his favorite cultists—flag-burners, not-this-war-I-won'ters, and the like—through the gap that will inevitably be blown in that line.

Finally, is it not strange to be told now—after eighteen years of effort to integrate the public schools, when one of the principal political issues appears to be whether there shall be busing to achieve a balance between races; when the decision that gave rise to all this in 1954 held that "education is perhaps the most important function of state and local governments," that "compulsory school attendance laws … demonstrate our recognition of the importance of education to our democratic society," that, indeed, it is "the very foundation of good citizenship," that, in the famous statement that so troubled the logicians, "separate facilities are inherently unequal"—is it not strange to be told now that it is unconstitutional for a state to require children (or, at least, some children) even to go to high school? Is it not strange that they be permitted to segregate themselves from the rest of the American community? That they cannot be forced to attend other schools or, presumably, to accept other children in their schools? Is this not inconsistent with the law of school integration? Or shall we see the day when a suburban school district, asked to show cause why it should not be integrated with an inner-city school district, will reply with the following words:

> *Said counsel for schools suburbanish:*
> *"Sure, we admit that we're clannish;*
> *But there's no use your fussing for court-ordered busing,*
> *'Cause there's no one out here but us Amish."*

Berns compiles a whole list of similar phrases to underline his point.

Summary

Should one's religious beliefs give one the right to violate certain laws? In the first article Chief Justice Burger, arguing for the majority of the U.S. Supreme Court, concedes that it is within the power of the state to impose compulsory education laws. However, this state interest in universal education cannot override the fundamental rights of citizens. He argues that the right to free exercise of religion is so deeply embedded in the nation's constitutional traditions that even legislation of "high social importance" must give way to the extent that it conflicts with free exercise. And in this instance it is clear that the traditional Amish way of life, which is founded on deep religious conviction, rejects "contemporary secular values accepted by the majority." In order to preserve their religious community from worldly influences that would tend to "destroy" it, the Amish are entitled to an exemption from Wisconsin's compulsory education law, Burger argues.

Walter Berns, in an essay criticizing the Supreme Court's decision in *Wisconsin v. Yoder*, argues that if religious communities are entitled to special exemptions, does that not require the courts to enter into the dangerous business of determining what is real religion and what is not? Or, if courts refuse to decide what counts as true religion, will there not be a proliferation of bizarre religions, each claiming special privileges as "free exercise of religion," such as drug cultists and snake worshipers? Chief Justice Burger had argued that Thoreau would not have been entitled to the exemption conferred on the Amish because Thoreau did not act on the basis of religious convictions. However, is this distinction between religious objection and other forms of conscientious objection (say, to the obligation to fight in a war) fair or tenable? The key points of this debate are summarized in the diagram on the opposite page.

FURTHER INFORMATION:

Books:

Goldstein, Robert Justin, *Flag Burning and Free Speech: The Case of Texas v. Johnson*. Lawrence, KS: University Press of Kansas, 2000.

Long, Carolyn N., *Religious Freedom and Indian Rights: The Case of Oregon v. Smith*. Lawrence, KS: University Press of Kansas, 2000.

Smith, Steven D., *Foreordained Failure: The Quest for a Constitutional Principle of Religious Freedom*. New York: Oxford University Press, 1999.

Useful websites:

www.beliefnet.com

A multifaith religious website, promoting tolerance.

www.religioustolerance.org

Ontario Consultants on Religious Tolerance website.

The following debates in the Pro/Con series may also be of interest:

In this volume:

Topic 8 Should people have to obey unjust laws?

The Value of Debate, pages 112–113

SHOULD THERE BE A RIGHT TO VIOLATE LAWS FOR RELIGIOUS REASONS?

YES: The United States is made up of immigrants who have all had to assimilate to a certain degree

YES: It is a basic and fundamental right protected by the Bill of Rights

NO: The Bill of Rights gives the individual freedom of speech; and if the law violates a person's rights in any way, he or she has the power to complain or disagree

RELIGIOUS FREEDOM
Does the First Amendment protect religious freedom?

LAW
Is every community obliged to obey the laws of the place in which they live?

NO: It has to be judged within reason, otherwise it would give anyone the right to behave in any way in the name of religion

NO: The law is not infallible, and because of the size of the United States it sometimes has laws in place that benefit the majority and not minorities

SHOULD THERE BE A RIGHT TO VIOLATE LAWS FOR RELIGIOUS REASONS?

KEY POINTS

YES: If a minority group is treated differently on matters such as the draft, for example, it will inevitably cause friction

YES: You cannot have one rule for one group and another for everyone else without it causing discrimination

PREJUDICE
Could allowing certain religious groups exemption from certain laws lead to discrimination?

NO: Certain people are prejudiced regardless of circumstances

Topic 10

IS VIOLENT PROTEST EVER JUSTIFIED?

YES

THE CASE OF THE CIVIL RIGHTS MOVEMENT AND APARTHEID
ALEX BRAITHWAITE

NO

VIOLENCE AND TERRORISM
WWW.MKGANDHI.ORG/NONVIOLENCE/PHIL7.HTM
MAHATMA GANDHI

INTRODUCTION

Throughout history people have turned to violence as a means of trying to bring about social or political change in society. It is, however, a fundamental necessity of social organization that people living in a certain society abide by its rules. Those rules inevitably condemn the use of violence. But when a particular group feels that it is powerless to change a social order that is unfair, must it simply accept the situation, or should it turn to violence?

These questions have led to much debate and discussion. In many parts of the world violent protest is common, or has been in the relatively recent past. In South Africa black activists used violence to protest against the apartheid policy of the white minority government. In the United States in the 1960s the Black Panthers advocated violence in support of civil rights. In Britain, Spain, Sri Lanka, Indonesia, Russia, and many other nations terrorist groups use violence to express their opposition to the government.

Throughout history various groups have protested against governments.

The protesters are sometimes a majority group, as in South Africa, and sometimes a minority, as with the Basque separatists in Spain. The government can be a tyranny or a small, privileged elite, but in some cases it has been elected by a democratic majority. Sometimes protesters are objecting to their own government, at others to governments they see as representing foreign oppressors.

Violence most often occurs when particular groups feel that they have no other way in which to protest against a regime. Slaves in the ancient Roman Empire had few rights, for example; in the first century B.C. thousands expressed their frustration by joining an uprising led by the Thracian slave Spartacus. After a two-year military campaign against their Roman rulers the slaves were ultimately defeated.

Later, when Europeans established empires throughout the world from the 15th to the 19th centuries, they imposed political systems that often gave no civil or political rights to the majority of their subjects. Again, they were subject to violent protests that often took the form of full-scale war. In the United States in the 19th century John Brown turned to violence to support his campaign for the abolition of slavery. Radical labor groups such as the Molly Maguires took up violence to try to win better wages and conditions for workers. In the decades following the Civil War violence was a standard tactic in the campaign of the Ku Klux Klan against black Americans.

"Nonviolence is the greatest force at the disposal of mankind. It is mightier than the mightiest weapon of destruction devised by the ingenuity of man."

—MAHATMA GANDHI, INDIAN CIVIL RIGHTS LEADER

There are, however, many protesters and activists who have opposed the use of violence. Chief among them in the 20th century was the Indian leader Mohandas Gandhi, called Mahatma or "Great Soul."

Living under British rule in South Africa and his homeland, India, Gandhi found himself deprived of his rights. He developed a philosophy of resistance to British rule based on nonviolence. It became known as "Satyagraha"—a combination of two Sanskrit words, "satya" meaning "truth" and "agraha" meaning "pursuit of." Gandhi said, "We must be the change we wish to see," meaning that in order to turn the British away from violent oppression, the protesters must themselves adopt peaceful means. Gandhi advocated noncooperation and peaceful demonstrations through sit-ins and marches. His policies helped change the treatment of Asians and Africans in South Africa and eventually won independence for India. Gandhi's philosophy influenced other leaders, such as Martin Luther King Jr. in the United States and Aung San Suu Kyi in Myanmar (Burma). The latter uses nonviolent tactics to protest against the military dictatorship in Myanmar.

There are those, however, who argue that nonviolence does not work. While Martin Luther King advocated peaceful means in the struggle for civil rights, young militants, frustrated at the lack of progress, formed the Black Panthers. The Panthers, who claimed 5,000 members, advocated armed struggle in support of their aims. They adopted guerrilla uniforms, brandished firearms, and were involved in numerous violent confrontations with the police.

The following two articles discuss the issues of violence and nonviolence from highly contrasting viewpoints. The author of the first, Alex Braithwaite, was herself a Black Panther but is now an academic. She considers the history of violent protest in the civil rights movement in the United States and in South Africa during apartheid. She argues that in both cases violence succeeded where nonviolent demonstrations failed.

The second article comes from the works of Gandhi. Writing over 50 years ago, he expresses his philosophy of nonviolence and his belief that victories won by violence are temporary and do more harm than good.

THE CASE OF THE CIVIL RIGHTS MOVEMENT AND APARTHEID
Alex Braithwaite

YES

Throughout our long and often-controversial history the use of violence has been one of the most persuasive tools of change—used by religious, sovereign, and hegemonic regimes to conquer, subjugate, and control aspects of daily life. Yet, whenever violence is used against the self-same system of authority it is perceived as unnecessary and abhorrent in a world where reason and justice purportedly serve to rectify any wrongs. However, attitudes to the use of violence differ and depend very much on what the society in question perceives to be a "wrong," and, for the purpose of this discussion, whether or not the "wrong" in any way infringes on the beliefs or doctrines of the individual or body that governs that society. However, if a certain political or social group reaches a consensus that deprives an individual or group of individuals of essential civil rights that other groups in that society enjoy, that can be perceived as an injustice or "wrong."

In most societies there is some course for redress for that kind of inequality. However, what happens if the targeted group lacks both the fundamental right to object and the means or agency to resolve its exclusion? If it has no voice, what action can it possibly use to rectify the imbalance? In extreme circumstances violent action is the only way to achieve social change. It is most often not the preferred method of change, but the last resort.

In the following article I will examine the role of violent protest in the Civil Rights movement in the United States and Anti-apartheid in South Africa. Both movements arose out of discriminatory practices and racial intolerance that prompted the outbreak of violence in the struggle for equality and civil liberty when no other course was left.

Look at www.aclu.org, the site of the American Civil Liberties Union. Make a list of issues that are currently under debate.

At the start of your argument it can help to state clearly what you intend to discuss.

Background

Between 1492 and 1870 around 10 million native Africans were forceably taken from their homes and brought to one of several Atlantic ports to work on tobacco, sugar, coffee, and cotton plantations or in mines or in the houses of the ruling colonial elite. From the beginning slaves were treated like a different species. Their living and social conditions were far inferior to those of their white "masters."

As early as 1670 George Fox, founder of the Quakers, denounced slavery as inhumane. In the 1700s Quakers on both sides of the Atlantic followed suit. Under extreme opposition from the abolitionist movement Britain abolished the slave trade in 1807; British abolitionists then turned their attention to America. The American Civil War (1861–1865) was partly the culmination of that interest. Although the war was primarily about secession, the southern or Confederate states wanted to maintain state rights on certain issues, including the right to maintain slaves, whereas the northern or Union states wanted to maintain the union and argued for slave emancipation as a secondary issue. After the war slavery became illegal, but the majority of blacks still worked and lived under slave conditions, subsisting on poor wages, although a small minority benefited during Reconstruction.

The two world wars brought great political and social change. Increasingly, previously oppressed groups of people began to rally for equal rights and political power in their own countries.

Nonviolent protest and the United States
In South Africa and later India a young Indian lawyer, Mohandas (Mahatma) K. Gandhi became a major political force, advocating equal rights and promoting change through peaceful means rather than violence. Gandhi soon became an international figure and his influence can still be seen in movements advocating social change.

In 1942 in Chicago, Illinois, an interracial group of students, deeply influenced by Gandhi's teachings of nonviolent resistance, founded the Congress of Racial Equality (CORE). The group pioneered nonviolent direct action in the United States and organized sit-ins, jail-ins, and Freedom Rides, one of which was the 1955 Montgomery bus boycott in Alabama. The protest was initially intended to be a one-day boycott to coincide with the trial of Rosa Parks, a young black woman arrested for refusing to give up her seat to a white man on a Montgomery bus.

The peaceful demonstration, backed by 50 black leaders and one white minister, ended in chaos as both police officials and white supremacists harassed the demonstrators, proving to the black community that peaceful resistance could not work in a society used to violence and aggression.

The Christian Quaker movement, or Society of Friends, was founded in 1650 by George Fox. It rejects the sacraments, ritual, and formal ministry, and allows its members to speak at meetings. Quakers have promoted social reform.

See www.home. att.net/~reniqua/the ology.htm for more details of the boycott.

Malcolm X and Black Power

In 1952 Malcolm Little was released from prison. Little renamed himself Malcolm X in repudiation of the "white man's name." Malcolm X had studied the teachings of Elijah Muhammad, the Nation of Islam (NOI) leader and after his release from prison he quickly rose within the ranks of the NOI organization. His commitment to raising racial consciousness began to influence many of the blacks in the United States in the late 1960s.

Malcolm argued that "blacks should focus on improving their own communities rather than striving for complete integration" and that blacks had the right to retaliate against violent assaults. His statements rang true with a number of black people who saw the noncooperation movement as a failure, and so Black Power, a political and social movement that represented both a conclusion to the decade's Civil Rights movement and a reaction against the racism and imperialism that still persisted in the United States, began to gain strength.

Black Panther Party (BPP)

The author uses a quotation to imply that violence is inherent in U.S. society. Do you agree?

H. Rap Brown, a national spokesman for Black Power, drew much criticism from the white establishment when he stated that "violence is as American as apple pie," and opposition to Black Power subsequently intensified. However the party had gained the support of a more prominent and militant black political group, the Black Panther Party (BPP), which drew its name from an animal that is not naturally aggressive, but will fight to the death when under attack.

The organization was founded in Oakland, California, in 1966 by two students—Huey Newton, who had studied law and was a staunch defender of civil rights and Bobby Seale. It was set up for the sole purpose of encouraging individuals to defend themselves. The party went on to establish patrols in black communities in order to monitor police activities as well as to protect residents from police brutality. Their revolutionary tactics and often violent protest marches, resulted in constant harassment by the local authorities and condemnation by the white society at large. However, the violent protest of groups such as the BPP had the effect of bringing world attention to U.S. racism and inequality. The political parties that formed and used violence to protest and to protect themselves and their communities from state and right-wing abuse brought social change to the country. Under their aegis black children were allowed to attend the same schools and have the same rights as other children. Today, the

United States still has a racial problem but the effect of violence was to facilitate a needed change that arguably would not have occurred otherwise. In this case violent protest was both the only and final option for an oppressed group of people and worked where noncooperation failed.

Apartheid and South Africa

Another example of violent protest bringing about social and political change can be seen in apartheid in South Africa. "Apartheid" comes from the Dutch word expressing "apartness," and basically meant that the white and black populations lived separately, to the denigration of the latter group. Apartheid was officially imposed on South Africa in the mid-20th century, although it had been an unofficial policy in the country's history for almost 300 years prior to that. In 1912 a group composed of mostly educated, bourgeois blacks, the African National Congress, began to organize systems of reform through petitions and other legal channels. However, little if anything was achieved as the authorities who imposed apartheid on the black population were openly aggressive and violent. The Sharpeville massacre—which began as a nonviolent protest—resulted in 69 deaths and every one of them was an unarmed protester. The response to this outrage encouraged the ANC to meet government violence with armed resistance. In 1976 primary and secondary students organized the Soweto uprising. It was a nonviolent protest but resulted in 575 deaths of unarmed children. Soweto marked the revival of mass violent resistance in South Africa and consolidated the ANC's standing throughout the South African nations. By the 1980s, the actions of the ANC had helped to direct international attention to South Africa and world economic sanctions, entertainment boycotts, and political pressure eventually led to its end in 1990.

See www.anc.org.za for more information on the African National Congress.

Do you think that economic sanctions are an effective tool for forcing governments to change their policies? Can you think of occasions when sanctions have failed?

Conclusion

In both the Civil Rights movement and the Anti-apartheid struggle violence was only advocated when all else failed. The prevailing authorities failed to defend the civil and legislative rights of all its citizens, using force to try and quell any rebellion. This brought about retaliatory action and resulted in violent protest by the oppressed groups. As Mahatma Gandhi once said, "If there is an outbreak of violence, it would not be without cause. We are yet far from the independence of our dream." This statement, in my opinion, is as true today as it was when the Mahatma first uttered them.

VIOLENCE AND TERRORISM
Mahatma Gandhi

NO

X MY EXPERIENCE teaches me that truth can never be propagated by doing violence. Those who believe in the justice of their cause have need to possess boundless patience and those alone are fit to offer civil disobedience who are above committing criminal disobedience or doing violence.

Popular violence

If I can have nothing to do with the organized violence of the Government, I can have less to do with the unorganized violence of the people. I would prefer to be crushed between the two.

What do you think Gandhi means when he says that he can overcome government violence more easily than popular violence?

For me popular violence is as much an obstruction in our path as the Government violence. Indeed, I can combat the Government violence more successfully than the popular. For one thing, in combating the latter, I should not have the same support as in the former.

I make bold to say that violence is the creed of no religion and that, whereas non-violence in most cases is obligatory in all, violence is merely permissible in some cases. But I have not put before India the final form of non-violence.

I object to violence because, when it appears to do good, the good is only temporary; the evil it does is permanent.

No faith in violence

To illustrate his point that violence is not only wrong but futile, Gandhi gives a specific example of when the use of violence would fail to solve a problem.

It is an unshakable faith with me that a cause suffers exactly to the extent that it is supported by violence. I say this in spite of appearances to the contrary. If I kill a man who obstructs me, I may experience a sense of false security. But the security will be short-lived. For I shall not have dealt with the root cause. In due course, other men will surely rise to obstruct me. My business, therefore, is not to kill the man or men who obstruct me, but to discover the cause that impels them to obstruct me and deal with it.

I do not believe in armed risings. They are a remedy worse than the disease sought to be cured. They are a token of the spirit of revenge and impatience and anger. The method of violence cannot do good in the long run.

The revolutionary

I do not deny the revolutionary's heroism and sacrifice. But heroism and sacrifice in a bad cause are so much waste of splendid energy and hurt the good cause by drawing away attention from it by the glamour of the misused heroism and sacrifice in a bad cause.

I am not ashamed to stand erect before the heroic and self-sacrificing revolutionary because I am able to pit an equal measure of non-violent men's heroism and sacrifice untarnished by the blood of the innocent. Self-sacrifice of one innocent man is a million times more potent than the sacrifice of a million men who die in the act of killing others. The willing sacrifice of the innocent is the most powerful retort to tyranny that has yet been conceived by God or man.

Heroic patience

I invite the attention of the revolutionaries to the three great hindrances to Swaraj—the incomplete spread of the spinning wheel, the discord between Hindus and Mussalmans [Muslims] and the inhuman ban on the suppressed classes. I ask them patiently to take their due share in this work of patient construction. It may not be spectacular enough. But on that very account it requires all the heroic patience, silent and sustained effort and self-effacement of which the tallest among the revolutionaries is capable. Impatience will blur the revolutionary's vision and lead him astray.

Swaraj means "self-rule" and was one of Gandhi's four main aims and principles. The other three were Truth, Ahinsa (nonviolence), and Satyagraha (passive resistance).

Slow and inglorious self-imposed starvation among the starved masses is every time more heroic than the death on the scaffold under false exaltation.

Prevention of brutalization

I am more concerned in preventing the brutalization of human nature than in the preventing of the sufferings of my own people.... I know that people who voluntarily undergo a course of suffering raise themselves and the whole of humanity, but I also know that people, who become brutalized in their desperate efforts to get victory over their opponents or to exploit weaker nations or weaker men, not only drag down themselves but mankind also.

Gandhi suggests that martyrdom—dying for the cause—is in fact an easier option than a life of resistance. Do you agree?

There is no necessary charm about death on the gallows; often such death is easier than a life of drudgery and toil in malarious tracts.... I suggest to my friend the revolutionary that death on the gallows serves the country only when the victim is a "spotless lamb".

I do not condemn everything European. But I condemn for all climes and for all times secret murders and unfair methods even for a fair cause.... Armed conspiracies against something satanic is like matching Satans against Satan. But since one Satan is one too many for me, I would not multiply him....

Cowardice, whether philosophical or otherwise, I abhor. And if I could be persuaded that revolutionary activity has dispelled cowardice, it will go a long way to soften my abhorrence of the method, however much I may still oppose it on principle....

I do not regard killing or assassination or terrorism as good in any circumstances whatsoever. I do believe that ideas ripen quickly when nourished by the blood of martyrs. But a man who dies slowly of jungle fever in service bleeds as certainly as the one on the gallows. And if the one who dies on the gallows is not innocent of another's blood, he never had ideas that deserved to ripen.

Heroes of history

Gandhi lists various patriotic leaders from, respectively, India, the United States, Italy, and Russia.

To compare [revolutionaries'] activities with those of Guru Govind Singh or Washington or Garibaldi or Lenin would be most misleading and dangerous. But, by test of the theory of non-violence, I do not hesitate to say that it is highly likely that, had I lived as their contemporary and in the respective countries, I would have called every one of them a misguided patriot, even though a successful and brave warrior....

I disbelieve history so far as details of acts of heroes are concerned. I accept broad facts of history and draw my own lessons for my conduct. I do not want to repeat it in so far as the broad facts contradict the highest laws of life. But I positively refuse to judge men from the scanty material furnished to us by history. *De mortuis nil nisi bonum.*

Here Gandhi includes a Latin saying meaning "Of the dead speak kindly or not at all." This has the effect of adding weight to his argument.

Kemal Pasha and De Valera, too, I cannot judge. But, for me as a believer in non-violence out and out, they cannot be my guides in life in so far as their faith in war is concerned. I believe in Krishna. But my Krishna is the Lord of the Universe, the creator, preserver and destroyer of us all. He may destroy because He creates ....

I have not the qualifications for teaching my philosophy of life. I have barely qualifications for practising the philosophy I believe....The revolutionaries are at liberty to reject the whole of my philosophy.... But India is not like Turkey or Ireland or Russia and that revolutionary activity is suicidal at this stage of the country's life at any rate, if not for all time in a country so vast, so hopelessly divided and with the masses so deeply sunk in pauperism and so fearfully terror-struck.

The revolutionary destroys the body for the supposed benefit of the adversary's soul.... I do not know a single revolutionary who has even thought of the adversary's soul. His single aim has been to benefit the country, even though the adversary may perish body and soul.

I honour the anarchist for his love of the country. I honour him for his bravery in being willing to die for his country; but I ask him: Is killing honourable death? I deny it. I repeat my deliberate opinion that, whatever may be true of other countries, in India at least political murder can only harm the country.

The page of history is soiled red with the blood of those who have fought for freedom. I do not know an instance in which nations have attained their own without having to go through an incredible measure of travail. The dagger of the assassin, the poison bowl, the bullet of the rifle-man, the spear—and all these weapons and methods of destruction have been used up to now by what I consider blind lovers of liberty and freedom.... I hold no brief for the terrorist.

Let the revolutionary pray with and for me that I may soon become that [free from passions, wholly incapable of sin]. But, meanwhile, let him take with me the one step to it which I see as clearly as day-light, viz. to win India's freedom with strictly non-violent means.

Gandhi admits that those who take up arms against an unjust government are patriotic, but denies that they are honorable. In your opinion is this a fair distinction to make?

Summary

Violent protest has always caused great moral and ethical debate. Should individuals or groups have the right to organize and protest in a violent manner when all else fails? Alex Braithwaite argues they should and gives the cases of the civil rights movement and apartheid in South Africa as examples in which peaceful protest failed, sometimes with tragic results, and violent protest, although undesirable, facilitated political and social change. Braithwaite argues that violence is excusable when all else fails.

Mohandas K. Gandhi, famous for his stance on nonviolent protest as exemplified by Satyagraha, argues that violence is never the answer to a prevailing problem. He asserts that when it is used, it causes more problems than it solves and creates an unstable and often temporary balance. He argues that freedom can only be attained through nonviolent methods.

FURTHER INFORMATION:

Books:

Fischer, Louis (editor). *The Essential Gandhi: His Life, Work, and Ideas: An Anthology*. New York: Vintage Books, 1983.

Kloos, Peter. "The Struggle between the Lion and the Tiger" in Cora Govers and Hans Vermeulen (editors), *The Politics of Ethnic Consciousness*. London: Macmillan, 1997.

X, Malcolm, and Alex Haley. *The Autobiography of Malcolm X*. New York: Ballantine Books, 1992.

Useful websites:

www.nmaa-ryder.si.edu/collections/ exhibits/posters/mlk.htm
Short introduction to Martin Luther King's "I Have A Dream" speech, with audio links.
www.anc.org.za/un/reddy/struggle3.html
About "Spear of the Nation," the militant wing of ANC.
www.engagedpage.com/gandhi.html
Page on Mahatma Gandhi, including famous quotations.
www.cbu.edu/Gandhi/html/articles/html
Arun Gandhi, Gandhi's granddaughter, writes on the subject of "Nonviolence—21st century."
www.geocities.com/CapitolHill/7768/oppressor.html
Article on "Myanmar: the Oppressor and Oppressed." Looks at freedom movements in Myanmar (Burma) and South Africa.

www.casnws.scw.vu.nl/publicaties/kloos-jvp.html
Peter Kloos, "Violent Youth Movements in Sri Lanka."
www.geocities.com/CapitolHill/7768/activism.html
Article on the extent of activism in South Africa.
www.news.bbc.co.uk/hi/englihs/uk politics.newsid 1392000/1392004.stm
"Blair: Anarchists Will Not Stop Us." Article on the violent protests that marred the European Union summit in Gothenburg, Sweden, in June 2001.

The following debates in the Pro/Con series may also be of interest:

In this volume:

Topic 2 Is it possible to live in a nonracist society?

Topic 6 Should affirmative action continue?

Topic 8 Should people have to obey unjust laws?

Topic 11 Is hate speech a right?

IS VIOLENT PROTEST EVER JUSTIFIED?

YES: In certain regimes violence is the only way to overthrow oppressive political regimes

YES: Sometimes violence is the only way to gain international support for a problem, for example, in the case of apartheid in South Africa and civil rights in the United States

YES: Some political regimes, such as dictatorships, only relate to violence since it is the way that they maintain power

DISCRIMINATION
Is violent protest justified in the case of extreme discrimination?

JUSTICE
Does the end justify the means?

NO: As Gandhi taught, nonviolence can be as effective as violence

NO: Violence just perpetuates violence, and a new regime or movement born out of violence can only proceed in the same way

IS VIOLENT PROTEST EVER JUSTIFIED?
KEY POINTS

YES: Yes it is; for example, antiapartheid support grew out of world recognition of South Africa's oppressive, racist policy

INTERNATIONAL ATTENTION
Is violent protest or terrorism a way of gaining international credence for a cause?

NO: Terrorism and violence only bring international condemnation

NO: Violence makes it difficult to ascertain who is the perpetrator and who is the victim, and it just confuses matters in the end

Topic 11

IS HATE SPEECH A RIGHT?

YES

"HATE SPEECH ON CAMPUS"
ACLU BRIEFING PAPER, 1996
AMERICAN CIVIL LIBERTIES UNION

NO

"HATE SPEECH: THE SPEECH THAT KILLS"
INDEX ON CENSORSHIP, 1/98
URSULA OWEN

INTRODUCTION

The First Amendment (see quotation, right) is one of the cornerstones of American democracy. Consequently, the United States enjoys one of the most liberal policies on freedom of expression in the world, and free speech is seen as an essential, fundamental right. However, while the First Amendment undeniably protects the views and opinions of American citizens, it has also frequently been cited in the justification or defense of "hate speech." Hate speech has been defined as any expression that ridicules, degrades, or reviles a person, institution, or group on the basis of their race, creed, sexual orientation, religion, handicap, national origin, or economic condition.

Hate speech has parallels with other forms of expression that some individuals find undesirable, such as pornography, which is also protected by the First Amendment. However, some women find pornography offensive and degrading. So, should pornography therefore be censored

to protect the sensibilities of those it offends? (See page 145.)

The complex relationship between free speech, hate speech, and the First Amendment has been the focus of much heated debate. In the past individual states and local governments have taken legal action to restrict or censor speech and the media in general—although the Fourteenth Amendment, as adopted in 1868, has limited such restrictive action by stating that: "No State shall make or enforce any law which shall abridge the privileges or immunities of citizens of the United States."

The most important cases involving hate speech have typically involved minority groups—the Ku Klux Klan, anti-Semites, the National Socialist Party of America (NSPA)—and their right to express their views freely, however subversive they may seem.

The right to free speech in any form was defended by Judge Learned Hand in 1917, when he stated that dissident speech was generally protected against government regulation. Since then the Supreme Court has mostly upheld the right to free speech even in controversial cases.

One of the most important hate/free speech trials in the history of the United States was the result of a proposed march of the National Socialist Party of America in Skokie, Illinois, in 1977 (see box on page 146). Village officials managed to get an injunction placed against the march, since the village had a large Jewish population made up predominantly of Holocaust survivors. However, in the ensuing legal battle the court decided that any attempt to restrict the people's "right to express any thought, free from government censorship" would be detrimental to the country's commitment to open debate.

The Skokie decision reaffirmed U.S. society's right to free speech whatever the content or opinion voiced, but the court did also add that there was provision in the First Amendment for the government to protect individuals or groups from offensive speech.

The increasing importance of the media in society has made the question of hate speech all the more important. The First Amendment affords individuals or groups the right to express their views in any medium— whether it be in newsprint, on the radio, in television, or film, and through the Internet—and any moves to prevent this through the introduction of restrictive legislation have, on the whole, been rejected.

In 1992, for example, a Minnesota statute attempting to ban "hate speech" was unanimously rejected by the United States Supreme Court as unconstitutional. Similarly, the introduction of speech codes at several university campuses in the United States has been severely criticized, and recent attempts to restrict the information available on the Internet have incensed anticensorship organizations. No Americans, it seems, want to live in a society in which censorship is an accepted practice.

> *"Congress shall make no law respecting an establishment of religion, or prohibiting the free exercise thereof; or abridging the freedom of speech, or of the press; or of the right of the people peaceably to assemble, and to petition the government for a redress of grievances."*
> —THE FIRST AMENDMENT

In the following two articles the arguments for and against hate speech are discussed. The ACLU briefing paper "Hate Speech on Campus" argues that everyone has a First Amendment right to freedom of speech, even if it is ugly and offensive to other people. It says that censoring speech is not the answer to fighting bigotry. On the other hand, in "Hate Speech: The Speech That Kills," Ursula Owen of the British organization Index on Censorship asserts that hate speech can incite violence, hatred, or discrimination, and in the worst scenario may even end in murder.

HATE SPEECH ON CAMPUS
American Civil Liberties Union

YES

Try summing up your argument at the very start. This makes your position clear to the audience.

✓ The First Amendment to the United States Constitution protects speech no matter how offensive [it is]. Speech codes adopted by government-financed state colleges and universities amount to government censorship, in violation of the Constitution. And the ACLU believes that all campuses should adhere to First Amendment principles because academic freedom is a bedrock of education in a free society.

You can tailor your argument to a specific audience. Universities are being addressed here because free speech is a vital issue on campuses.

Speech codes

Where racist, sexist, and homophobic speech is concerned, the ACLU believes that more speech—not less—is the best revenge. This is particularly true at universities, whose mission is to facilitate learning through open debate and study, and to enlighten. Speech codes are not the way to go on campuses, where all views are entitled to be heard, explored, supported, or refuted. Besides, when hate is out in the open, people can see the problem. Then they can organize effectively to counter bad attitudes, possibly change them, and forge solidarity against the forces of intolerance.

College administrators may find speech codes attractive as a quick fix, but as one critic put it: "Verbal purity is not social change." Codes that punish bigoted speech treat only the symptom: the problem itself is bigotry. The ACLU believes that instead of gestures that only appear to cure the disease, universities have to do the hard work of recruitment to increase faculty and student diversity; counseling to raise awareness about bigotry, and changing curricula to [incorporate] more inclusive approaches to all subject matter.

Asking clear and direct questions is an effective way of engaging with the opposing argument.

Questions

Q: I just can't understand why the ACLU defends free speech for racists, sexists, homophobes, and other bigots. Why tolerate the promotion of intolerance?

A: Free speech rights are indivisible. Restricting the speech of one group or individual jeopardizes everyone's rights because the same laws or regulations used to silence bigots can be used to silence you. Conversely, laws that defend free speech for bigots can be used to defend the rights of civil rights workers, antiwar protesters, lesbian and gay activists, and others fighting for justice. For example, in the 1949 case of *Terminiello v. Chicago* the ACLU successfully defended an ex-Catholic priest who had delivered a racist and anti-Semitic speech. The precedent set in that case became the basis for the ACLU's successful defense of civil rights demonstrators in the 1960s and '70s. The indivisibility principle was also illustrated in the case of neo-Nazis whose right to march in Skokie, Illinois, in 1979 was successfully defended by the ACLU. At the time, then ACLU executive director Aryeh Neier, whose relatives died in Hitler's concentration camps during World War II, commented: "Keeping a few Nazis off the streets of Skokie will serve Jews poorly if it means that the freedoms to speak, publish, or assemble any place in the United States are thereby weakened."

The authors cite legal evidence to back up their argument.

Q: Aren't some kinds of communication not protected under the First Amendment, like "fighting words?"
A: The U.S. Supreme Court did rule in 1942, in a case called *Chaplinsky v. New Hampshire*, that intimidating speech directed at a specific individual … amounts to "fighting words," and that the person engaging in such speech can be punished if "by their very utterance [the words] inflict injury or tend to incite an immediate breach of the peace." Say, a white student stops a black student … and utters a racial slur. In that one-on-one confrontation, which could easily come to blows, the offending student could be disciplined under the "fighting words" doctrine for racial harassment.

Over the past 50 years, however, the Court hasn't found the "fighting words" doctrine applicable in any of the hate speech cases that have come before it, since the incidents involved didn't meet the narrow criteria stated above. Ignoring that history, the folks who advocate campus speech codes try to stretch the doctrine's application to fit words or symbols that cause discomfort, offense, or emotional pain.

Why has the "fighting words" doctrine proved so ineffectual in hate speech cases?

Q: What about nonverbal symbols, like swastikas and burning crosses—are they constitutionally protected?
A: Symbols of hate are constitutionally protected if they're worn or displayed before a general audience in a public place —say, in a march or at a rally in a public park. But the First Amendment doesn't protect the use of nonverbal symbols to encroach upon, or desecrate, private property, such as burning a cross on someone's lawn or spray-painting a swastika on the wall of a synagogue or dorm. In its 1992 decision in *R.A.V. v. St. Paul*, the Supreme Court struck down as unconstitutional a city ordinance that prohibited

Why might nonverbal symbols need to be constitutionally protected?

cross-burnings based on their symbolism, which the ordinance said makes many people feel "anger, alarm, or resentment." Instead of prosecuting the cross-burner for the content of his act, the city government could have rightfully tried him under criminal trespass and/or harassment laws. The Supreme Court has ruled that symbolic expression, whether swastikas, burning crosses or, for that matter, peace signs, is protected by the First Amendment because it's "closely akin to 'pure speech.'" That phrase comes from a landmark 1969 decision in which the Court held that public school students could wear black armbands in school to protest the Vietnam War. And in another landmark ruling, in 1989, the Court upheld the right of an individual to burn the American flag in public as a symbolic expression of disagreement with government policies.

The authors point out that there are different ways to legally punish bigots other than censorship.

Q: Aren't speech codes on college campuses an effective way to combat bias against people of color, women, and gays?
A: Historically, defamation laws or codes have proven ineffective at best and counterproductive at worst. For one thing, depending on how they're interpreted and enforced, they can actually work against the interests of the people they were created to protect. Why? Because the ultimate power to decide what speech is offensive and to whom rests with the authorities—the government or a college administration—not with those who are the alleged victims of hate speech.

Who should decide what speech is offensive? The government? The victims?

Under a speech code in effect at the University of Michigan for 18 months, white students in 20 cases charged black students with offensive speech. One of the cases resulted in the punishment of a black student for using the term "white trash" in conversation with a white student. The code was struck down as unconstitutional in 1989, and to date the ACLU has brought successful legal challenges against speech codes at the universities of Connecticut, Michigan, and Wisconsin. These examples demonstrate that speech codes don't really serve the interests of persecuted groups. The First Amendment does. As one African American educator observed: "I have always felt as a minority person that we have to protect the rights of all because if we infringe on the rights of any persons, we'll be next."

Q: But don't speech codes send a strong message to campus bigots, telling them their views are unacceptable?
A: Bigoted speech is symptomatic of a huge problem in our country; it is not the problem itself. Everybody, when they come to college, brings with them the values, biases and

assumptions they learned while growing up in society, so it's unrealistic to think that punishing speech is going to rid campuses of the attitudes that gave rise to the speech in the first place. Banning bigoted speech won't end bigotry, even if it might chill some of the crudest expressions. The mindset that produced the speech lives on and may even reassert itself in more virulent forms. Speech codes, by simply deterring students from saying out loud what they'll continue to think in private, merely drive biases underground.

The authors reach the crucial issue of the debate. "Hate speech" must be distinguished from "hate thought." Banning the speech will not stop the thought behind it.

Q: Well, given that speech codes are a threat to the First Amendment, and given the importance of equal opportunity in education, what type of campus policy on hate speech would the ACLU support?
A: The ACLU believes that the best way to combat hate speech on campus is through an educational approach that includes counterspeech, workshops on bigotry and its role in American and world history, and real—not superficial— institutional change.

Rather than simply rejecting censorship, the authors put forward other ways to combat hate speech. Does this give their argument more weight?

Universities are obligated to create an environment that fosters tolerance and respect among the campus community, [and] in which all students can exercise their right to participate fully in campus life without being discriminated against. Campus administrators should, therefore:

- speak out loudly and clearly against expressions of racist, sexist, homophobic, and other bias, and react promptly to acts of discriminatory harassment;

- create forums to raise awareness and promote dialogue on issues of race, sex, and sexual orientation;

The ACLU states its alternatives to censorship clearly and logically.

- intensify their efforts to recruit members of racial minorities on student, faculty, and administrative levels;

- and reform their institutions' curricula to reflect the diversity of peoples and cultures that have contributed to human knowledge and society, in the United States and throughout the world.

The authors sum up with a quotation— that it is more important to educate people and foster tolerance than to impose restrictions.

ACLU Executive Director Ira Glasser stated: "There is no clash between the constitutional right of free speech and equality. Both are crucial to society. Universities ought to stop restricting speech and start teaching."

HATE SPEECH
Ursula Owen

NO

The author grabs
attention by
immediately
focusing on the
dramatic premise
of her central
argument: that
hate speech kills.

Hate speech, as Americans call it, is a troubling matter for people who believe in free speech. It is abusive, insulting, intimidating, and harassing. And it may lead to violence, hatred, or discrimination; and it kills. The United States, as the least censored society in the world, has held firmly to the First Amendment and to Article 19 of the Universal Declaration of Human Rights, which has meant that attempts to make provisions against hate speech have almost all been disallowed by the Supreme Court.

Legal inconsistencies

What countries do
you know of in
which expressions
of free speech are
regularly punished?

International law appears more contradictory. Article 19 of the International Covenant on Civil and Political Rights says that "everyone shall have the right to hold opinions without interference" and "everyone shall have the right to freedom of expression," though this is subject to restrictions necessary "for respect of the rights or reputations of others" or "for the protection of public order, or of public health or morals." But Article 20 of the same Covenant states that "any advocacy of national, racial, or religious hatred that constitutes incitement to discrimination, hostility, or violence must be prohibited."

None of these statements have stopped the fierce debate on that difficult borderline between free speech and equality of respect. Free speech is thought of as sacred to a democratic society, as the freedom upon which all others depend. But in a world where the effects of speech that fosters hatred are all too visible, there are two difficult questions that must be asked about the defense of free expression: At what cost? And at the expense of whose pain?

Owen asks two
crucial questions
that are central to
her argument.
What is the price of
hate speech, and at
whose expense?

Paying the price

Does allowing
any censorship
encourage all
censorship?

It is, of course, dangerous to suggest the possibility of more censorship. The slippery slope argument—if we can censor this, what is to stop someone else censoring that—is hard to argue against. Censorship can kill and maim, for when people draw a cloak of secrecy over their actions, gross abuse may happen with impunity. In the United States, hate speech is typically defended as the price society has decided to pay for safeguarding free expression. Historically, perhaps the most famous defense of the right to express hate occurred in the case of Skokie, Illinois, in 1977 when a U.S. neo-Nazi group tried to march on a public street in a community populated by many Holocaust survivors. The courts affirmed their right to do so, basing their judgment on the First Amendment. Such a ruling, they believed, was ultimately to the benefit of racial and other minorities, protecting their right to express their views freely.

Dangers of censorship

Nevertheless, hate speech and censorship continue to have a troubled relationship. Catherine MacKinnon and Andrea Dworkin's now-famous campaign to outlaw pornography was based on their view that pornography is in effect hate speech: it treats women as sexual objects and subordinates them in a vile way to men. Though they did not succeed in persuading the U.S. courts, the Canadian legislature did introduce a severe censorship law. But the first authors to be banned under the new Canadian statute were not those the feminists had in mind. They were prominent homosexual authors, a radical black feminist accused of stirring up race hatred against white people and, for a time, Andrea Dworkin herself. Liberals who had warned against the dangers of censorship felt vindicated.

MacKinnon and Dworkin are American feminist thinkers and writers.

Seductions of the right

In 1993, Umberto Eco was one of 40 European intellectuals who publicly called on all Europeans to be on their guard against the maneuvers of the extreme right. In an interview, he [said]: "In order to be tolerant, one must first set the boundaries of the intolerable." What, in his view, was intolerable? "I see nothing shocking," he went on, "in a serious and incontrovertible work of scholarship establishing that the figure for genocide of the Jews by the Nazis was not 6 million but 6.5 or 5.5 million. What is intolerable is when something which purports to be a work of research loses all value by becoming something quite other; when it becomes a message suggesting that 'if a few less Jews than we thought were killed, there was no crime.'"

An apt quotation, used in the right place, is a powerful debating tool.

What Eco and his fellow signatories were particularly disturbed by was the extent to which dangerous ideas on the right, including racism and xenophobia, were becoming commonplace—and newly seductive. And it is for just such reasons that it is essential to continue this difficult debate about hate speech. At the end of the Maastricht summit in December 1991 the European Union's Council of Ministers

Would specific examples help illustrate this point about racism and democracy?

issued a condemnation of racism and xenophobia, observing that "manifestations of fascism and xenophobia are steadily growing in Europe". The report also comments on a paradox of history: that racism increased as democracy spread through the post-Communist world.

Free speech advocates claim there is little connection between hate speech laws and the lessening of ethnic and racial violence or tension. They argue that what is needed is more, rather than less, attention to the ideas of racial and

COMMENTARY: Skokie's "march of hate"

The predominantly Jewish suburb of Skokie in Illinois was at the center of a controversial hate speech debate in 1977. At that time, one in six of Skokie's Jewish citizens was a survivor—or related to a survivor—of the Holocaust (the mass killing of European Jews by the Nazis during World War II). When a neo-Nazi group, the National Socialist Party of America (NSPA), announced its intention to parade there, the village won a court injunction against the march, arguing that it would offend its Jewish citizens.

NSPA founder Frank Collin (the son of a Holocaust survivor himself) stated his intention to intimidate Skokie's Jewish community: "We want to reach the good people—get the fierce anti-Semites who have to live among the Jews to come out of the woodwork and stand up for themselves. I hope [the Holocaust survivors] are terrified." Despite criticism, the American Civil Liberties Union (ACLU) defended the NSPA's right to free speech under the First Amendment, and the Supreme Court ruled in their favor.

In the end, the NSPA never did parade in Skokie. Collin and his followers marched in Chicago's Marquette Park instead. And the ACLU paid a high price for fighting the NSPA's case: 30,000 of its members left the organization. But the Skokie case highlighted the difficult issues surrounding freedom of speech. No matter how much you may disagree with what someone says, they still have a constitutional right to say it. As the French philosopher Voltaire said: "I detest what you say, but I will defend to the death your right to say it."

religious superiority; that they must be confronted to be understood; that dialogue and democracy are more effective tools in understanding the anatomy of hate than silence; and for that reason, freedom of expression is necessary. Though laudable in principle, it is arguable that these views lack force in the face of much 20th-century history. They perhaps require us to believe too simply in the power of democracy and decency and above all rationality; in the ability of a long, slow onslaught on racism to have an effect; to believe, in the face of so much evidence to the contrary, that there is always progress, however slow.

Culture of hatred

At the end of [the 20th] century, we have once again in Europe been faced with an outburst of hatred and destruction based on racial, political, and religious differences, which has all but destroyed a country—former Yugoslavia—at least temporarily. It is just half a century since the Holocaust. If that terrifying monument to the dark power of hate speech failed to alter consciousness constructively, what are we to say about the liberal belief in the human capacity to evolve morally? The most dangerous threat behind hate speech is surely that it can go beyond its immediate targets and create a culture of hate, a culture which makes it acceptable, respectable even, to hate on a far wider scale. Such a culture of hate is not easy to define, and does not necessarily have one trajectory, but its evolution is evident in the circumstances surrounding some events in recent history.

Earlier Owen referred to the slippery slope argument in terms of censorship. Here she uses it to highlight the equal dangers of not curbing hatred.

The U.S. philosopher and political scientist Sidney Hook set out starkly his experience of the workings of expressions of hate. "I believe any people in the world, when roused to a fury of nationalistic resentment, and convinced that some individual or group is responsible for their continued and extreme misfortunes, can be led to do or countenance the same things the Germans did. I believe that if conditions in the United States were ever to become as bad psychologically and economically as they were in Germany in the 1920s and 1930s, systematic racial persecution might break out. It could happen to the Blacks, but it could happen to the Jews too, or any targeted group."

Hook is referring to the conditions in Germany that led to Hitler's rise to power. He thinks that in a severe social and economic climate persecution can flourish anywhere.

Words can kill

Words can turn into bullets, hate speech can kill and maim, just as censorship can. So, as dedicated opponents of censorship and proponents of free speech, we are forced to ask: is there a moment where the quantitative consequences of hate speech change qualitatively the arguments about how we must deal with it? And is there no distinction to be made between the words of those whose hate speech is a matter of conviction, however ignorant, deluded, or prejudiced, and hate speech as propaganda, the calculated and systematic use of lies to sow fear, hate, and violence in a population at large?

Finishing the debate on a critical question makes for a memorable ending.

Summary

The ACLU briefing paper and the extract from Ursula Owen's article on hate speech present both sides of the argument clearly. The ACLU, which has historically opposed censorship of any kind, asserts that free speech—even hate speech—is a fundamental right under the First Amendment to the Constitution. It argues that the problem with hate speech lies not in the words themselves but in the inherent bigotry behind them, which cannot be treated by "quick fix" speech codes or with censorship of speech. Censorship of one group can be the thin end of the wedge, quickly leading to wider curtailment of freedom.

Ursula Owen, on the other hand, argues that society should be wary of hate speech since it is "abusive, insulting, intimidating and harassing; and it kills." Owen argues that hate speech can create an insidious "culture of hate" in which it becomes acceptable to express intolerance on a wide scale. She says that history, particularly in the 20th century, has shown that as democracy increases, so does hatred based on racial, religious, and political differences. Her essay quotes the example of the Nazi persecution of the Jews and raises fears that a similar situation could easily recur. Her argument rests on the premise that hate speech is wrong and as such should be subject to control. The key points of the arguments are summarized opposite.

FURTHER INFORMATION

Books:

Hentoff, Nat, *Free Speech for Me—But Not for Thee: How the American Left and Right Relentlessly Censor Each Other.* New York: Harper Perennial, 1993.

Lederer, Laura, *The Price We Pay: The Case against Racist Speech, Hate Propaganda, and Pornography.* New York: Hill and Wang, 1995.

MacKinnon, Catherine A., *Only Words.* Cambridge, MA: Harvard University Press, 1993.

Orr, Lisa, *Censorship: Opposing Viewpoints.* San Diego, CA: Greenhaven Press, 1990.

Smolla, Rodney A., *Free Speech in an Open Society.* New York: Vintage Books, 1993.

Walker, Samuel, *Hate Speech: The History of an American Controversy.* Lincoln, NE: University of Nebraska Press, 1994.

Articles:

Lee, Douglas, "Criminalizing Hate Shackles Everyone's Rights," October 30, 1998 (www.freedom forum.org).

Sorensen, Karen, "Silencing the Net," Human Rights Watch (www.cwrl.utexas. edu/-monitors/hrw).

Sunstein, Cass, "Is Violent Speech a Right?" 1992. *American Prospect* 6: 22.

"Cults, Hate Groups, Violent Gangs and 'Offensive Speech': Should We Kill" (www.frnew.com/archive/cults).

Useful websites:

www.freedomforum.org

News and views relating to First Amendment issues.

The following debates in the Pro/Con series may also be of interest:

In this volume:

Topic 2 Is it possible to live in a nonracist society?

Topic 10 Is violent protest ever justified?

IS HATE SPEECH A RIGHT?

YES: People are entitled to express their individuality through speech

YES: Freedom of speech is essential to the functioning of a truly democratic society

YES: Restricting the speech of one group or individual jeopardizes everyone's democratic rights

HUMAN RIGHTS
Is any form of free speech—including speech that is offensive to others—a human right?

DEMOCRACY
Freedom of expression is enshrined in the First Amendment. Is this right?

NO: Hate speech undermines the human rights of its targets

NO: Hate speech can damage, even kill, and lead to the destruction of democracy

IS HATE SPEECH A RIGHT?
KEY POINTS

YES: Censorship is not the answer to hate speech because it does not address the bigotry that lies behind the words

YES: Tolerance in the form of more open debate will challenge bigotry and is more likely to lead to enlightenment and reform

CENSORSHIP
Is it wrong to impose speech codes on university campuses to curb bigoted speech?

YES: More censorship means restrictions on speech for everybody—regardless of the views being expressed

MORE TOLERANCE
Will more tolerance toward hate speech fight the bigotry underlying it?

NO: Speech codes can prohibit outbursts of hatred toward others based on racial, political, and religious differences

NO: Hate speech creates a culture of hate in which intolerance can be expressed on a wider scale

NO: The argument that tolerance combats intolerance is weak in the face of the evidence of history

Topic 12
IS GUN CONTROL UNCONSTITUTIONAL?

YES
"TO PRESERVE LIBERTY—A LOOK AT THE RIGHT TO KEEP AND BEAR ARMS"
NORTHERN KENTUCKY LAW REVIEW 10
RICHARD E. GARDINER

NO
"THE SECOND AMENDMENT: WHAT IT REALLY MEANS"
SAN FRANCISCO BARRISTER, DECEMBER 1989
SARAH BRADY

INTRODUCTION

The United States remains one of the leading gun markets in the world. Private individuals are estimated to own around 200 million firearms, and around 60 million of them are handguns. Recent surveys have shown that some 40 percent of U.S. households own at least one gun, and that by 2003 handgun ownership will exceed car ownership. However, handgun control and ownership is a topical issue in the United States.

Why is handgun ownership such a controversial subject? At the center of the debate is the issue of the Second Amendment, which states that "A well regulated militia, being necessary to the security of a free State, the right of the people to keep and bear Arms, shall not be infringed." But what precisely does that mean? Advocates of handgun ownership argue that the "right to bear arms" protects the individual's right to protect himself or herself, especially in such times of rising crime. The anti-handgun lobby, however, asserts that the Second Amendment protects the "collective" right to bear arms and is intended mainly to assert the rights of states to maintain militias in order to protect and conserve freedom and security. It further argues that the situation in the United States is out of control; that there is an "eye for an eye" mentality in society and that legislation must be tightened to prevent tragedies such as the shootings at Columbine High in 1999 from happening again.

The National Rifle Association (NRA) insists that the only way for responsible Americans to protect their homes and families is through gun ownership, and the fact that around a third of the firearms owned privately are handguns supports the fact that many Americans agree with that organization. However, David Hemenway of the Harvard Injury Control Center argues that "If you want to understand the issue of benefits and costs of firearms you would have to know what is happening with suicides."

According to an article published in *The American Prospect*, in 1997 there were almost 18,000 gun suicides, compared to 13,000 gun homicides. In Colorado, for example, the gun suicide to gun homicide ratio is almost three to one. According to one recent study, most suicides are the result of impulsive behavior, and thus guns are a popular and effective way of committing suicide and can easily change a depressive bout into a tragedy.

> *"The national ACLU is neutral on the issue of gun control. We believe that the Constitution contains no barriers to reasonable regulations of gun ownership. If we can license and register cars, we can license and register guns."*
> —AMERICAN CIVIL LIBERTIES UNION ON GUN CONTROL

A dreadful example of this was when Bartholomew Stupak Jr.—the son of four-term Democratic Congressman Bart Stupak, who is an advocate of handgun ownership and member of the NRA—was found dead on Mother's Day 2000. According to police reports, Stupak used a family gun to commit suicide. This event prompted Republican Congresswoman Mary Bono to send an open letter to the NRA asking that they "inform parents, teens, and all gun owners of the potentially dangerous connection between the access to guns and suicide." The Centers for Disease Control and Prevention has estimated that every day 14 children aged 19 or under are killed in gun homicides, suicides, and accidental shootings, and that for every child killed a further four are wounded.

Recent debate has focused on the culpability of gun manufacturers. On July 1, 1993, Gian Luigi Ferri killed eight people and wounded six more in a law office in San Francisco with two TEC-DC9 semiautomatic pistols and a revolver. The relatives of the victims sued the manufacturer Navegar Inc., arguing that since TEC-DC9s are used by criminals, the company should have foreseen such a massacre. On August 6, 2001, however, the California Supreme Court ruled that gun manufacturers cannot be sued for crimes committed with their merchandise.

Private gun ownership has a lot of supporters in the United States— Hollywood veteran Charlton Heston among them. In July 2001 the NRA put U.S. Attorney General John Ashcroft on the cover of one of its magazines after he told CNN's Larry King that "Law-abiding citizens have a right under the Constitution to have firearms." He also wrote this in a letter that the NRA distributed to its members. His statement led the NRA Executive Director to state that this "dramatically reverses the 'collective right' theory held by the Clinton administration."

The following two articles examine in greater depth the issue of gun control and the Constitution. In the first article Richard E. Gardiner argues that the Second Amendment's purpose is "to secure to each individual the right to keep and bear arms." Sarah Brady conversely argues that the amendment "guarantees a state's right to maintain a militia—not an individual's right to own a handgun."

TO PRESERVE LIBERTY—A LOOK AT THE RIGHT TO KEEP AND BEAR ARMS
Richard E. Gardiner

In the last several decades, a vocal minority, popular with the major news media, has put forth a distorted interpretation of the Second Amendment to the United States Constitution for the avowed political purpose of removing an obstacle from the path leading toward their goal of depriving private citizens of some or all of their firearms. And, as with virtually all attempts to minimize those precious freedoms guaranteed each American by the Bill of Rights, that minority has twisted the original and plain meaning of the right to keep and bear arms....

The author suggests that proponents of gun control have misinterpreted the Second Amendment to suit their purpose.

The history of the Second Amendment

The history of the Second Amendment indicates that its purpose was to secure to each individual the right to keep and bear arms so that he could protect his absolute individual rights as well as carry out his obligation to assist in the common defense. The Framers did not intend to limit the right to keep and bear arms to members of a formal military body, but rather intended to ensure the continued existence of an "unorganized" armed citizenry prepared to assist in the common defense against a foreign invader or a domestic tyrant.

The Right is General. It may be supposed from the phraseology of this provision that the right to keep and bear arms was only guaranteed to the militia; but this would be an interpretation not warranted by the intent. The militia, as has been elsewhere explained, consists of those persons who, under the law, are liable to the performance of military duty, and are officered and enrolled for service when called upon. But the law may make provision for the enrollment of all who are fit to perform military duty or of a small number only, or it may wholly omit to make any provision at all; and if the right were limited to those enrolled, the purpose of this guarantee might be defeated altogether by the action or neglect to act of the government it was meant to hold in check. The meaning of the provision undoubtedly is, that the people, from whom the militia must be taken, shall have the

Gardiner believes that, despite the phraseology used in the Second Amendment, it is the people in general, and not just a formal militia, that have been granted the right to bear arms.

right to keep and bear arms, and they need no permission or regulation of law for that purpose.

Need for guns is unchanged

The passage of time has not altered the need for individuals to exercise their right to keep and bear arms, even in the context of the common defense. Indeed, one court has observed that individual marksmanship is an important skill even in the nuclear age. In the Second World War, moreover, the unorganized militia proved a successful substitute for the National Guard, which was federalized and activated for overseas duty. Members of the unorganized militia, many of whom belonged to gun clubs and whose ages varied from 16 to 65, served without pay and provided their own arms. In fact, it was necessary for the members of the unorganized militia to provide their own arms since the U.S. government not only could not supply sufficient arms to the militia but "turned out to be an Indian giver" by recalling rifles. The 15,000 volunteer Maryland Minute Men brought their own rifles, shotguns, and pistols to musters. And all over the country individuals armed themselves in anticipation of threatened invasion. Thus, a manual distributed en masse by the War Department recommended the keeping of "weapons which a guerrilla in civilian clothes can carry without attracting attention. They must be easily portable and easily concealed. First among these is the pistol."

In *United States v. Miller*, the only case in which the Supreme Court has had the opportunity to apply the Second Amendment to a federal firearms statute, the Court carefully avoided making an unconditional finding of the statute's constitutionality; it instead devised a test by which to measure the constitutionality of statutes relating to firearms. The holding of the Court in *Miller*, however, should be viewed as only a partial guide to the meaning of the Second Amendment, primarily because neither defense counsel nor defendants appeared before the Supreme Court, and no brief was filed on their behalf giving the Court the benefit of argument supporting the trial court's holding that Section 11 of the National Firearms Act was unconstitutional.

The Court's interpretation

The heart of the Court's decision is to be found in the following statement:

In the absence of any evidence tending to show that possession or use of a "shotgun having a barrel of less

In general terms the militia consists of all able-bodied male U.S. citizens between the ages of 17 and 45 and of female members of the National Guard. It is divided into two classes: the organized militia (the National Guard and the Naval Militia) and the unorganized militia, which consists of all other militia members.

The National Firearms Act was approved on June 26, 1934. Section 11 made unlawful the movement of a firearm between states unless the weapon had been properly registered or its transfer correctly applied for under the terms of the act.

COMMENTARY: National Rifle Association

The National Rifle Association (NRA) of America came into being in 1871. Colonel William C. Church and General George Wingate had been so disturbed by poor marksmanship among Union troops in the Civil War that they set up the organization to promote rifle shooting. The NRA's first practice facility was at Creedmoor, Long Island, but within around 20 years the association had moved to Sea Girt, New Jersey, and later a major range was constructed at Camp Perry, near Toledo, Ohio. The NRA's headquarters is situated in Fairfax, Virginia.

Defense of the Second Amendment

The NRA is concerned with marksmanship and firearms education and training, and its activities include holding shooting competitions, promoting youth programs, and running courses for hunters and law enforcement officers. The association has three publications, *The American Rifleman*, *The American Hunter*, and *The American Guardian*, aimed at the various interests within its four million membership. However, the association also sees itself as the principle defender of rights provided under the Second Amendment. In 1975 it set up its Institute for Legislative Action (ILA), whose area of operations includes informing the NRA membership of any proposed gun control legislation at the local, state, or federal level and lobbying on Second Amendment issues at these same levels of government.

than eighteen inches in length" at this time has some reasonable relationship to the preservation or efficiency of a well regulated militia, we cannot say that the Second Amendment guarantees the right to keep and bear such an instrument. Certainly it is not within judicial notice that this weapon is any part of the ordinary military equipment or that its use could contribute to the common defense....

One of the chief values of Miller is its discussion of the development and structure of the militia which, the Court pointed out, consisted of "all males physically capable of acting in concert for the common defense" and that "when called for service these men were expected to appear bearing arms supplied by themselves and of the kind in common use at the time." Miller is also significant for its implicit rejection of the view that the Second Amendment, in addition to guaranteeing the right to keep and bear only certain types of arms, also guarantees the right only to those individuals who are members of the militia. Had the Court viewed the Second Amendment as guaranteeing the right to keep and bear arms only to "all males physically capable of acting in concert for the common defense," it would certainly have discussed whether Miller met the qualifications for inclusion in the militia, much as it did with regard to the military value of a short-barrelled shotgun. That it did not discuss this point indicates the Court's acceptance of the fact that the right to keep and bear arms is guaranteed to each individual without regard to his relationship with the militia....

The author is arguing that the Supreme Court implicitly supports his interpretation of the Second Amendment: that it is the people in general, and not just a formal militia, that have been granted the right to bear arms.

Popularity

The right to keep and bear arms may not be undercut simply because that right may at the moment be unpopular to some. The Supreme Court has held time and again that "constitutional rights may not be denied simply because of hostility to their assertion or exercise."

Nor can constitutional rights be made dependent upon a popular consensus that there is a continued need for them. [As determined in *Martin v. Hunter's Lessee*,] "The Constitution of the United States was not intended to provide merely for the exigencies of a few years but was to endure through a long lapse of ages...."

Martin v. Hunter's Lessee was an 1816 case concerning ownership of a piece of land. The case's lasting legacy, though, is that it affirmed the power of the Supreme Court to override the state courts.

Indeed, it is precisely because the courts do not allow any contraction of the Bill of Rights that the evils contemplated by the Framers now seem so removed. As Justice Hugo Black stated:

Its [the Bill of Rights'] provisions may be thought outdated abstractions by some. And it is true that they were designed to meet ancient evils. But they are the same kind of human evils that have emerged from century to century wherever excessive power is sought by the few at the expense of the many.

From the above discussion, it should be readily apparent that the right to keep and bear arms, as guaranteed by the Second Amendment, is indeed a fundamental individual right which no amount of historical revisionism can deny. Thus, along with all other rights found in the Bill of Rights, it should be accorded a significant place in American jurisprudence.

Hugo L. Black (1886–1971) practiced law and served as a U.S. senator before being nominated as an associate justice of the U.S. Supreme Court in 1937 by President Franklin D. Roosevelt.

THE SECOND AMENDMENT: WHAT IT REALLY MEANS
Sarah Brady

James S. Brady was shot in the left temple and seriously wounded during the assassination attempt on President Ronald Reagan on March 30, 1981, by John W. Hinckley Jr. Brady recovered and returned to his job as White House Press Secretary.

Like many Americans, I never thought too much about the Second Amendment to the Constitution, until I experienced an incidence of handgun violence that changed my life and the lives of my family. As you know, in 1981, my husband, Jim Brady, White House Press Secretary, was shot during the attempted assassination of President Ronald Reagan. That shooting helped propel me into the battle for stronger federal gun laws.

My involvement in the handgun control campaign has encouraged me to examine more closely the Second Amendment, which in its entirety reads: "A well regulated Militia, being necessary to the security of a free state, the right of the people to keep and bear Arms, shall not be infringed."

The Founders were the delegates to the Constitutional Convention, the 1787 meeting at which the U.S. Constitution was drawn up.

When the Founding Fathers met at the Constitutional Convention in 1787 to create a government that would unite their separate states into a nation, a major issue debated was the extent of the federal government's control of military power. Federalists insisted on the need for a strong standing Army. Anti-federalists argued that individual citizens would continue to serve in state militias, and thus protect and defend the country.

Debate over amendment's meaning

"Ratification" means formal approval.

After the Constitution was signed, it was sent to state conventions for ratification, which occurred in 1788. From the debates in these conventions, there emerged a consensus that the Constitution should be amended to include a Bill of Rights. When the Bill of Rights was added in 1791, the Second Amendment addressed the issue of who should bear arms and for what purpose.

Over the years, there has been much debate over whether this "right" meant that individuals were guaranteed access to firearms under the Constitution. The National Rifle Association, which has emblazoned only the last fourteen words of the Second Amendment across its national headquarters, continues to argue that the Second Amendment guarantees the right of any American to own anything from handguns to machine guns.

However much debate there is among the general public, there is little debate in America's courts. In fact, the U.S. Supreme Court has interpreted the Second Amendment on five separate occasions. In addition, nearly forty lower court decisions have addressed the Amendment. All have ruled that the Second Amendment guarantees a state's right to maintain a militia—not an individual's right to own a handgun…

Three key cases heard by the Supreme Court were as follows: *U.S. v. Cruikshank*, 92 U.S. 542 (1876). In this case, Ku Klux Klansmen were charged with infringing the constitutional rights of black citizens to assemble and bear arms. Although this was primarily a civil rights case, the Justices did rule on the right of individuals to carry firearms by stating that the Second Amendment protects states' rights from the federal government, not individual rights.

Presser v. Illinois, 116 U.S. 252 (1886). Here, the defendant was prosecuted for leading a band of armed men in a parade without a license. The Court reaffirmed Cruikshank's holding that the Second Amendment was not a protection of individuals' rights, but instead states' rights.

And in the case of *U.S. v. Miller*, 307 U.S. 174 (1939), Jack Miller and a friend were arrested for violating the National Firearms Act by going from Oklahoma to Arkansas while carrying a double-barreled, sawed-off shotgun. The Supreme Court ruled that the weapon had no "reasonable relationship to the preservation or efficiency of a well-regulated militia" and thus, the laws relating to sawed-off shotguns did not violate the Second Amendment to the Constitution.

No support of handguns

Former Supreme Court Justice Lewis Powell echoed this view during a speech before the American Bar Association. Arguing that he found no Constitutional support for the private ownership of handguns, Powell said, "With respect to handguns … it is not easy to understand why the Second Amendment, or the notion of liberty, should be viewed as creating a right to own and carry a weapon that contributes so directly to the shocking number of murders in the United States." His audience no doubt agreed. The American Bar Association itself has stated: "Neither the United States Constitution nor any of its amendments grant any one the right to keep and bear arms."

Although the NRA continues to fight all forms of gun control measures with the claim that "the Second Amendment

The author argues that the U.S. courts are clear on the meaning of the Second Amendment: It guarantees a U.S. state's right to maintain a militia—not an individual's right to own a handgun.

Compare this author's view of U.S. v. Miller with that of Richard E. Gardiner on pages 153–155.

Lewis F. Powell Jr. (1907–1998) practiced law and was president of the American Bar Association (the organization of American lawyers, founded in 1878) before his nomination in 1971 by President Richard Nixon as an associate justice of the U.S. Supreme Court, on which body he replaced Justice Hugo L. Black.

is not limited by its language to the type of arms which the people have a right to own," Congress has already legislated some restrictions. In 1986, Congress outlawed the sale and manufacture of new machine guns. Two years later, over the objections of the NRA, President Reagan signed into law a bill preventing the sale of plastic, undetectable handguns.

Handgun Control Inc. (HCI) was formerly the National Council to Control Handguns. In June 2001 HCI was in turn renamed the Brady Campaign to Prevent Gun Violence.

Regardless of one's interpretation of the Second Amendment, the legislation I support would not prevent a law-abiding citizen's access to handguns. But I do not agree with the NRA that the Second Amendment guarantees the right of a John Hinckley to purchase a handgun. We at Handgun Control, Inc. do not advocate a handgun ban or handgun confiscation. Rather, we support common-sense measures to ensure that criminals cannot simply walk into gun stores and walk out with the tools of the trade. Our legislative agenda includes a national, seven-day waiting period before the purchase of a handgun, to allow for a criminal records check of the purchasers. We also support law-enforcement backed legislation to take paramilitary assault weapons of war off America's streets. In addition, we favor prohibiting the sale and manufacture of Saturday Night Specials—favored by criminals because of their concealability.

In general terms a handgun is a pistol or a revolver; a Saturday night special is a cheap, low-caliber, and easily concealed handgun; and an assault weapon is a military-style firearm—for example, an UZI, AK-47, or TEC-DC9.

Sensible handgun and assault weapon laws are on the books in cities and states across the country. Currently, 23 states have enacted some form of waiting period legislation. As mentioned above, federal law prohibits the manufacture and sale of new machine guns for civilians. If the gun lobby truly believed that such laws are unconstitutional under the Second Amendment, they would have challenged each and every law in the courts.

NRA failures

In fact, when the NRA has challenged these laws, they have lost. For example, in 1981, the town of Morton Grove, Illinois, passed an ordinance banning handguns. Exclusions were included for police officers, jail and prison authorities, members of the armed forces and licensed gun collectors and gun clubs. The Illinois Supreme Court ruled that the ordinance was a valid exercise of Morton Grove's police power under the Illinois state right to bear arms provision. The U.S. Seventh Circuit Court of Appeals also upheld the ordinance, stating that there is no individual right to keep and bear handguns under the Second Amendment. In October 1983, the U.S. Supreme Court declined to hear an appeal of this ruling, allowing the lower court ruling to stand.

The United States has 12 regionally based "circuit" courts of appeal that rank beneath the Supreme Court. The Seventh Circuit Court of Appeal is for Indiana, Illinois, and Wisconsin.

Clearly, there is little debate about the Second Amendment in the courts.

Even those who continue to maintain that the right to own a gun is guaranteed by the Second Amendment have to ask themselves how far this "right" goes. Surely no one would argue that felons, fugitives from justice, drug abusers or the adjudicated mentally incompetent should be given easy access to handguns. Yet that is just the situation we continue to allow in a country that sees 22,000 Americans lose their lives to these weapons each year.

The NRA and others who argue that the Second Amendment is limitless in its guarantees are clearly outside accepted constitutional thought and practice. Even they must accept the fact that with every right comes a responsibility. In the case of the Second Amendment, reasonable laws to protect the public safety, laws to deny easy access to firearms by those who would misuse them, laws to stop the sale of weapons of war—are obviously constitutional.

Do you agree with the author that "with every right comes a responsibility"?

Intent of the Founders

When the Constitution was drafted, our Founding Fathers foresaw a great nation of peace and tranquility. Part of the legacy of that vision is a nation free from violence—where the rights of individuals complement the quest for public safety. The Courts agree that nothing in the Constitution prohibits legislators from enacting common-sense restrictions on firearms. Clearly, our citizens agree. It is up to us to convince more legislators to translate that fact into action and pass a sensible federal gun policy which will make the nation safer for us all.

What do you think would constitute a sensible federal gun policy?

Summary

The Constitution of the United States primarily serves to defend and support the rights of the individual. The amendments have been open to interpretation, which has caused much debate. The Second Amendment "right to bear arms" has been used to defend the private ownership of handguns. Richard E. Gardiner argues that the distorted and wrongful interpretation of this amendment minimizes the "precious freedoms" guaranteed by the Bill of Rights and that the right to bear arms is a general right, not one limited to the militia. He argues that "the right to keep and bear arms, as guaranteed by the Second Amendment, is indeed a fundamental individual right which no amount of historical revisionism can deny." Sarah Brady, however, recounts how like most Americans, she was unmoved by the Second Amendment until her husband, Jim Brady, a former White House Press Secretary, was shot during the attempted assassination of President Reagan in 1981. That event led Brady to campaign for stricter gun laws. She argues that the Founders foresaw a land of peace and tranquility, and part of achieving this is to make the rights of individuals complement the quest for public safety.

FURTHER INFORMATION:

Books:

Cook, Philip J., and Jens Ludwig, *Gun Violence: The Real Costs*. New York: Oxford University Press, 2000.

Useful websites:

www.law.about.com/library/briefs/uc-ashcroft-guns.htm
Dave Workman, "Ashcroft Defends Individual Right-to-Bear-Arms."
www.vpc.org/press/0107hole.htm
Violence Policy Center response to John Ashcroft's letter to the NRA.
www.prospect.org/webfeatures/2000/07/mooney-c-07-20.html
Chris Mooney, "The Real Gun Crisis."
www.aclu.org/library/aaguns.html
American Civil Liberties Union on gun control.
www.prospect.org/print/V12/8/stone-p.html
Peter Jones, "Lethal Weapons."
www.mynra.com
National Rifle Association official site.
www.ichv.org/Articles.htm
Statistics on handgun use on Illinois Council against Handgun Violence site.

The following debates in the Pro/Con series may also be of interest:

In this volume:

IS GUN CONTROL UNCONSTITUTIONAL?

YES: The Second Amendment of the Constitution protects an individual's right to bear arms

YES: Violent crime is on the increase, and people have a right to protect their families and property

SECOND AMENDMENT
Does the Second Amendment protect the individual's right to bear arms?

CRIME
Is the private ownership of firearms necessary given rising crime?

NO: The United States has an extensive policing and law system; and if it is working properly, private firearm ownership should not be necessary

NO: Although the Second Amendment protects the right to bear arms, it was conceived for collective use, for state militias, and thus individual ownership is not protected by the Constitution

NO: Individuals do not have the right to take life or injure others even if they are protecting their property. The United States is a democracy and does not deal in "eye for an eye" rationales.

IS GUN CONTROL UNCONSTITUTIONAL? KEY POINTS

YES: The right training and education about use of firearms will prevent abuses

YES: Firearms are for protection and not for killing. If adequate gun laws are introduced that should be enough to prevent such abuses.

ABUSE
Is it possible to prevent abuses of firearms?

NO: The high incidence of gun-related suicide shows that it is impossible to preempt misuse

NO: We live in a society in which violence is glamorized by the media—tragedies such as the shootings at Columbine High School show that abuses will occur while people carry firearms

Topic 13

IS THE DEATH PENALTY EVER JUSTIFIABLE?

YES

"IN FAVOR OF CAPITAL PUNISHMENT"
SPEECH MADE TO HOUSES OF PARLIAMENT, APRIL 21, 1868
JOHN STUART MILL

NO

"THE DEATH PENALTY"
ACLU BRIEFING PAPER NO. 8
AMERICAN CIVIL LIBERTIES UNION

INTRODUCTION

The question of whether capital punishment should be used in society has always been a difficult one. Death penalty opponents, including individuals, religious and civil rights groups, and a growing number of law enforcement officials, argue that among other things, the death penalty is cruel and is in violation of the Eighth Amendment. Killing, whether carried out by the state or an individual, is wrong and cannot be condoned. Moreover, miscarriages of justice in which people have been executed for crimes they did not commit show that capital punishment is wrong. In 1999 the state of Illinois declared a moratorium on capital punishment after 89 people sentenced to death had their sentences quashed. Several other U.S. states are considering following suit.

Supporters of the death penalty argue that perpetrators of serious crimes must be punished. Capital punishment does act as a deterrent and is more humane than letting a prisoner sit in prison for the rest of his or her life. There is also the question of the victim's family, who are entitled to some redress.

Historically the first established death penalty laws date back to King Hammurabi of Babylon in the 18th century B.C., who codified the death penalty for 25 different crimes. It was used as part of the 14th-century B.C. Hittite legal code and the 7th-century B.C. Draconian code of Athens, which made death the punishment for any crime. In the 11th century A.D. hanging was the usual method of execution in Britain until William the Conqueror, after 1066, made it illegal except in times of war. By the 1700s 222 separate crimes were punishable by death in Britain, including felling a tree and robbing a rabbit warren.

The first recorded execution in the Americas was in 1608, when Captain George Kendall was killed for being a Spanish spy in Jamestown, Virginia.

Death penalty laws varied from colony to colony in early America. The Massachusetts Bay Colony held its first execution in 1630, and the New York Colony instituted laws in 1665 under which offenses such as striking one's mother could result in death.

Opponents of the death penalty in early America were influenced by the writings of Cesare Beccaria, among others. Beccaria wrote an essay, "On Crimes and Punishment," in which he argued that there was no justification for the state taking lives. His theory was taken up by intellectuals and abolitionists in Europe and America.

> *"There will be no lasting peace either in the heart of individuals or in social customs until death is outlawed."*
>
> —ALBERT CAMUS,
> *REFLECTIONS ON THE GUILLOTINE*

In the 19th century many states revised their policies on capital punishment and built state penitentiaries. Several states considered abolishing the death penalty. Others, however, adopted the electric chair after it was introduced in 1888. The 20th century began with six states abolishing the death penalty. However, following the Russian Revolution and outbreak of World War I, five reinstated it. Cyanide gas was introduced in 1924 as a more humane way of execution. The numbers of executions rose between 1920 and 1940. This was due partly to theorists' support for the death penalty, and also to the Depression, which drove some people to crime, and to gangster-related violence during the Prohibition. In the 1950s support for the death penalty waned, and many countries abolished it completely.

In the United States in the 1940s 1,289 people were executed; the total fell from 715 in the 1950s to 191 between 1960 and 1976. The execution in May 1960 of Caryl Chessman, convicted of robbery and rape despite his protestations of innocence, caused outrage, and public support for the death penalty waned. In 1972 the Supreme Court declared capital punishment to be unconstitutional. But later that decade high murder rates and political conservatism stimulated another growth in support. Capital punishment resumed in 1977.

In 1994 public support for the death penalty was at an all time high of 80 percent before questions about the fairness of the judicial system and the rate of wrongful conviction sapped support again. In April 2001 a poll showed that only 66 percent of U.S. citizens supported the death penalty, against 68 percent in Britain, which does not have capital punishment. But another poll at the same time showed that 22 percent of the people opposed to the death penalty still wanted Oklahoma bomber Timothy McVeigh to die, even though several of his victims' relatives opposed his execution.

In the following two extracts the British philosopher John Stuart Mill argues that the death penalty was necessary and that, if anything, laws should become more harsh. The ACLU argues that the death penalty is in fact inhumane and that its practice is both arbitrary and discriminatory.

IN FAVOR OF CAPITAL PUNISHMENT
John Stuart Mill

John Stuart Mill (1806–1873) was an English philosopher and economist.

☑ It is always a matter of regret to me to find myself, on a public question, opposed to those who are called … the philanthropists. Of all persons who take part in public affairs, they are those for whom, on the whole, I feel the greatest amount of respect.

Newgate was a London prison located at the foot of Ludgate Hill.

It is through their efforts that our criminal laws, which within my memory hanged people for stealing in a dwelling house to the value of 40 shillings—laws by virtue of which rows of human beings might be seen suspended in front of Newgate by those who ascended or descended Ludgate Hill—have so greatly relaxed their most revolting and most impolitic ferocity, that aggravated murder is now practically the only crime which is punished with death by any of our lawful tribunals; and we are even now deliberating whether the extreme penalty should be retained in that solitary case. This vast gain, not only to humanity, but to the ends of penal justice, we owe to the philanthropists; and if they are mistaken, as I cannot but think they are, in the present instance, it is only in not perceiving the right time and place for stopping in a career hitherto so eminently beneficial. There is a point at which, I conceive, that career ought to stop.

The need for indisputable evidence

When there has been brought home to any one, by conclusive evidence, the greatest crime known to the law; and when the attendant circumstances suggest no palliation of the guilt, no hope that the culprit may even yet not be unworthy to live among mankind, nothing to make it probable that the crime was an exception to his general character rather than a consequence of it, then I confess it appears to me that to deprive the criminal of the life of which he has proved himself to be unworthy … is the most appropriate, as it is certainly the most impressive, mode in which society can attach to so great a crime the penal consequences which for the security of life it is indispensable to annex to it. I defend this penalty, when confined to atrocious cases, on the very ground on which it is commonly attacked—on that of humanity to the criminal; as beyond comparison the least cruel mode in which it is possible adequately to deter from the crime. If, in our horror of inflicting death, we endeavour to devise some punishment for the living criminal which shall act on the human mind with a deterrent force at all comparable to that of death, we are driven to inflictions less severe indeed in appearance, and therefore less efficacious, but far more cruel in reality.

The alternatives to the death penalty

Few, I think, would venture to propose, as a punishment for aggravated murder, less than imprisonment with hard labor for life; that is the fate to which a murderer would be consigned by the mercy which shrinks from putting him to death. But has it been sufficiently considered what sort of a mercy this is, and what kind of life it leaves to him?

What comparison can there really be, in point of severity, between consigning a man to the short pang of a rapid death, and immuring him in a living tomb, there to linger out what may be a long life in the hardest and most monotonous toil, without any of its alleviations or rewards—debarred from all pleasant sights and sounds, and cut off from all earthly hope, except a slight mitigation of bodily restraint, or a small improvement of diet? Yet even such a lot as this, because there is no one moment at which the suffering is of terrifying intensity, and, above all, because it does not contain the element, so imposing to the imagination, of the unknown, is universally reputed a milder punishment than death—stands in all codes as a mitigation of the capital penalty, and is thankfully accepted as such.

Perceptions of the death penalty

There is not ... any human infliction which makes an impression on the imagination so entirely out of proportion to its real severity as the punishment of death. The punishment must be mild indeed which does not add more to the sum of human misery than is necessarily or directly added by the execution of a criminal. As my hon. Friend the Member for Northampton (Mr. Gilpin) has himself remarked, the most that human laws can do to anyone in the matter of death is to hasten it; the man would have died at any rate; not so very much later, and on the average, I fear, with a ... greater amount of bodily suffering. Society is asked, then, to denude itself of an instrument of punishment which, in the grave cases to which alone it is suitable, effects its purposes at a less cost of human suffering than any other; which, while it inspires more terror, is less cruel in actual fact than any punishment that we should think of substituting for it.

> Is that true? Is it a worse punishment to be incarcerated for life than to be executed? Make a list of the reasons for and against either alternative.

Then, as now, the death penalty was upheld as a way of deterring crime. Gilpin argued that the threat of execution has little power over hardened criminals—an argument still heard today.

My hon. Friend says that it does not inspire terror, and that experience proves it to be a failure. But the influence of a punishment is not to be estimated by its effect on hardened criminals. Those whose habitual way of life keeps them, so to speak, at all times within sight of the gallows, do grow to care less about it.... I can afford to admit all that is often said about the indifference of professional criminals to the gallows. Though of that indifference one-third is probably bravado and another third confidence that they shall have the luck to escape, it is quite probable that the remaining third is real. But the efficacy of a punishment which acts principally through the imagination, is chiefly to be measured by the impression it makes on those who are still innocent; by the horror with which it surrounds the first promptings of guilt; the restraining influence it exercises over the beginning of the thought which, if indulged, would become a temptation; the check which it exerts over the graded declension towards the state—never suddenly attained—in which crime no longer revolts, and punishment no longer terrifies.

Failure of the system

As for what is called the failure of death punishment, who is able to judge of that? We partly know who those are whom it has not deterred; but who is there who knows whom it has deterred, or how many human beings it has saved who would have lived to be murderers if that awful association had not been thrown round the idea of murder from their earliest infancy? Let us not forget that the most imposing fact loses its power over the imagination if it is made too cheap.

Is it, indeed, so dreadful a thing to die? Much has been said of the sanctity of human life, and the absurdity of supposing that we can teach respect for life by ourselves destroying it. But I am surprised at the employment of this argument, for it is one which might be brought against any punishment whatever. It is not human life only, not human life as such, that ought to be sacred to us, but human feelings.

The human capacity of suffering is what we should cause to be respected, not the mere capacity of existing. And we may imagine somebody asking how we can teach people not to inflict suffering by ourselves inflicting it? But to this I should answer—all of us would answer—that to deter by suffering from inflicting suffering is not only possible, but the very purpose of penal justice. Does fining a criminal show want of respect for property, or imprisoning him, for personal freedom? Just as unreasonable is it to think that to take the life of a man who has taken that of another is to show want of regard for human life. We show, on the contrary, most emphatically our regard for it, by the adoption of a rule that he who violates that right in another forfeits it for himself, and that while no other crime that he can commit deprives him of his right to live, this shall.

What about the innocent?

There is one argument against capital punishment, even in extreme cases, which I cannot deny to have weight—on which my hon. Friend justly laid great stress, and which never can be entirely got rid of. It is this—that if by an error of justice an innocent person is put to death, the mistake can never be corrected; all compensation, all reparation for the wrong is impossible.

Look at www.CNN.com, and find an example of a recent miscarriage of justice.

"I support the death penalty because I believe, if administered swiftly and justly, capital punishment is a deterrent against future violence and will save other innocent lives."

—GEORGE W. BUSH, 43RD U.S. PRESIDENT

No human judgment is infallible ... but in so grave a case as that of murder, the accused, in our system, has always the benefit of the merest shadow of a doubt. And this suggests another consideration very germane to the question. The very fact that death punishment is more shocking than any other to the imagination, necessarily renders the Courts of Justice more scrupulous in requiring the fullest evidence of guilt. Even that which is the greatest objection to capital punishment, the impossibility of correcting an error once committed, must make, and does make, juries and Judges more careful in forming their opinion, and more jealous in their scrutiny of the evidence.

Increasing punishment

I think ... there is more need of strengthening our punishments than of weakening them; and that severer sentences, with an apportionment of them to the different kinds of offenses which shall approve itself better than at present to the moral sentiments of the community, are the kind of reform ... which our penal system now [needs].

THE DEATH PENALTY
American Civil Liberties Union

Regardless of one's viewpoint about the morality or constitutionality of the death penalty, most people would agree that if we are going to continue executing people in the United States, we should be doing it fairly and rationally. However, three factors, unrelated to the crime itself, greatly influence who gets executed and who does not: poverty, race, and geography.

The quality of legal representation

The American Bar Association and many scholars have found that what most often determines whether or not a death sentence is handed down is not the facts of the crime, but the quality of the legal representation.

The overwhelming majority of death row inmates receive substandard legal representation at trial. Almost all capital-crime defendants are indigent when arrested, and are generally represented by court-appointed lawyers, who are inexperienced and underpaid.

Defending a capital case is time-consuming, taking about 700–1,000 hours. In some jurisdictions the hourly rates for appointed attorneys in capital cases are less than the minimum wage, and usually much less than the lawyer's hourly expenses. Moreover, courts often authorize inadequate funds for investigation and experts—or refuse to do so altogether. This is in the face of the almost limitless such funding for the prosecution.

Wealthy people who can hire their own counsel are generally spared the death penalty, no matter how heinous their crimes. Poor people [on the other hand] do not have the same opportunity to buy their lives.

Browse the Internet for information on the O.J. Simpson case. Why was he found innocent?

Racial bias

Death row in the United States has always held a disproportionately large population of people of color relative to the general population. Whereas African Americans constitute 12 percent of the U.S. population, they are 35 percent of those on death row; 9 percent are Native American, Latino, or Asian. The most important factor in levying the death penalty, however, is the race of the victim.

(Those who kill a white person are more likely to receive the death penalty than those who kill a black person.) A 1998 report by the Death Penalty Information Center summarizes the findings of several scholars which illustrates this point. The report also reveals a consistent trend indicating race-of-victim discrimination. For example, in Florida, in comparable cases, "A defendant's odds of receiving a death sentence are 4.8 times higher if the victim was white than if the victim was black. In Illinois the multiplier is 4, in Oklahoma it is 4.3, in North Carolina, 4.4, and in Mississippi, it is 5.5."

The author asserts that race is a key factor in whether defendants are sentenced to death.

Several studies show the effects of outright racial discrimination. [A] 1998 University of Iowa study of sentencing in Philadelphia showed that the odds of receiving a death sentence are nearly 3.9 times greater if the defendant is African American. These patterns of racial disparities are partly explained by the fact that the nation's prosecutors, who make the threshold decision about whether or not to seek the death penalty, are almost exclusively white men. [According to the study] of the district attorneys in U.S. counties using capital punishment, 98 percent are white, and only 1 percent are African American. New York State has only one African American district attorney.

Where you live matters

Whether someone convicted of a capital crime receives a death sentence depends greatly on the state or county in which the trial and conviction takes place. In some states, a death sentence is rare. Connecticut had five people on death row in 1999; Kansas, only two. Southern states, particularly Texas (443 death row inmates in 1999), hand down significantly more death sentences than those in the rest of the country. California, the state with the largest penal system, had 513 inmates on death row in the spring of 1999.

Which states use the death penalty? Which has the highest rate of execution?

Such state-to-state disparities exist because death penalty statutes are a patchwork of disparate standards, rules, and practices, and the consequence is the difference between life and death. Furthermore, some prosecutors are more zealous in seeking the death penalty than others—particularly if they are running for reelection.

In some states, inmates can be executed for crimes they committed at the age of 16; in others, only those who committed murder at age 18 or older are eligible for the death penalty. Some states, but not all, ban the execution of people with mental retardation. Some states include felony murder (unpremeditated murder committed in the course of

List reasons why those with "mental retardation" should not be executed.

another crime such as robbery or burglary) as a capital crime; others do not. In the 29 states that have a sentence of life without parole, 23 have statutes that bar judges from letting jurors know they have that sentencing option. Since studies consistently show that when given a choice between a death sentence and a sentence of life without parole, most people will choose the latter, failure to inform a jury of this alternative is tantamount to sending more people to the execution chamber.

How does this assertion relate to the views expressed in the previous article?

Social science research has discredited the claim that execution deters murder. The majority of murders are committed in the heat of passion, and/or under the influence of alcohol or drugs, when there is little thought given to the possible consequences of the act. "Hit men" and other murderers who plan their crimes beforehand, intend and expect to avoid punishment altogether by not getting caught.

"The benefits of capital punishment are illusory, but the bloodshed and the resulting destruction of community decency are real."
—HUGO ADAM BEDAU (ACLU PAPER)
THE CASE AGAINST THE DEATH PENALTY

Law enforcement officials know that the death penalty is not a deterrent. Imposing the death penalty more often was thought to be cost-effective by only 29 percent of 386 randomly selected U.S. police chiefs polled by Peter D. Hart Research Associates in 1995. States that have death penalty laws do not have lower crime rates or murder rates than states without such laws. And states that have abolished capital punishment, or reinstituted it, show no significant changes in either crime or murder rates.

Search www.cnn.com and www.washington post.com. for coverage of Timothy McVeigh's execution in 2001. Should families of victims be allowed to watch executions?

However satisfying vengeance may seem, a civilized society cannot accept an eye-for-an-eye, tooth-for-a-tooth delivery of justice. Although some families and loved ones of murder victims approve the death penalty, many others are against it. The irreversibility of the death penalty is especially significant in light of the percentage of [allegedly] innocent people on death row.

A study published in 1982 in the *Stanford Law Review* documents 350 capital convictions in which it was later proven that the convict had not committed the crime. Of those, 23 convicts were executed; others spent decades of their lives in prison. In a 1996 update of this study it was revealed that in the past few years alone, four individuals were executed although there was strong evidence that they were not guilty of the crime for which they were condemned. Since 1976, 77 persons have been released from death row because they were not guilty of the crime for which they had been condemned to death (33 of these releases have occurred since 1990).

A barbaric practice?

The United States is the only Western industrialized nation that practices the death penalty, and is by far the nation with the largest death row roster in the world. In comparison, all of Western Europe has abolished the death penalty, either by decree of law, or by practice. Fifty-seven nations and territories outlaw the death penalty for any crime, fifteen more allow it only for exceptional crimes such as military law or wartime crimes.

There are more than 3,700 death row inmates in the United States.

Another twenty-six countries and territories are abolitionist de facto, meaning they have not executed anyone during the past ten years or more, or that they have made an international commitment not to carry out executions. In numbers of people executed annually, the United States far exceeds the other 94 documented countries and territories that continue to deliver the death penalty.

Find out which countries execute criminals in significant numbers. How does their rate of execution compare with that of the United States?

Public attitudes to the death penalty

Various polls of public attitudes about crime and punishment found that a majority of people in the United States support alternatives to capital punishment.

According to the Death Penalty Information Center, when presented with possible sentencing alternatives, 50 percent of those surveyed chose life imprisonment without parole plus restitution to the victim's family as an alternative to the death penalty.

In 45 states, laws allow life sentences for murder that severely limit or eliminate the possibility of parole. Thirteen states impose sentences without the possibility of parole for 25–40 years, and all but three of the states that use capital punishment also have the option of life imprisonment with no possibility of parole. Although it is often assumed that capital punishment is less costly than life imprisonment, the opposite is true: in terms of dollars, in terms of crime control, and in terms of morality.

Summary

The death penalty has always been a contentious issue. In his speech to the British House of Parliament in defense of the death penalty the philosopher John Stuart Mill argues that society has a false horror of death and that the death penalty is a necessary punishment for those who have committed a crime. He also asserts that it is a deterrent to the criminally inclined. He even suggests that death itself is not so terrible a prospect for the condemned.

The American Civil Liberties Union, in its Briefing Paper No. 8 on the death penalty, argues that the death penalty is immoral and against civil liberties. The ACLU asserts that factors such as race, sex, the quality of legal representation, and where people live can have an effect on whether the death penalty is given or not. It further asserts that the United States is the only westernized country to still have a death penalty in place and that the majority of Americans would prefer an alternative to it.

FURTHER INFORMATION:

Books:

Bedau, H. (editor), *The Death Penalty in America*. New York: Oxford University Press, 1997.

Bohm, R., *Deathquest*. New York: Anderson Publishing, 1999.

Bosco, Antoinette, *Choosing Mercy: A Mother of Murder Victims Pleads to End the Death Penalty*. Maryknoll, NY: Orbis Books, 2001.

Cole, David, *No Equal Justice: Race and Class in the American Criminal Justice System*. New York: The New Press, 1999.

Lezin, Katya, *Finding Life on Death Row: Profiles of Six Inmates*. Boston, MA: Northeastern University Press, 1999.

Mears, Michael, *The Death Penalty in Georgia: A Modern History 1970–2000*. Atlanta, GA: Georgia Indigent Defense Division of Professional Education, 1999.

Sarat, Austin, *When the State Kills: Capital Punishment and the American Condition*. Princeton, NJ: Princeton University Press, 2001.

Schabas, W., *The Abolition of the Death Penalty in International Law* (2nd edition). Boston, MA: Cambridge University Press, 1997.

Useful websites:

www.aclu.org

American Civil Liberties Union site. Has section on death penalty. Useful for history and resources, etc.

www.web.amnesty.org

Amnesty International's website. Has a section on death penalty and executions.

www.coe.west.asu.edu/students/ahudson/WebQuest.html

A student assignment on this ethical debate.

www.deathpenalty.net

Site run by several anti-death penalty organizations.

www.politicalresources.net/c-death.htm

Death penalty information network.

www.thenation.com/doc.mhtml?i=20010806&c=1&s=shapiro

A European perspective on the U.S. death penalty.

www.w1.155.telia.com/~u15509119/ny_sida_1.htm

A site defending the death penalty.

The following debates in the Pro/Con series may also be of interest:

In this volume:

Topic 2 Is it possible to live in a nonracist society?

In *Science*:

Topic 10 Should doctors be able to assist in euthanasia?

IS THE DEATH PENALTY EVER JUSTIFIABLE?

YES: The perpetrator has given up any rights by committing the crime

YES: It is far more cruel to let a criminal linger indefinitely in prison

YES: It costs millions of dollars to keep criminals in jail

MORAL ISSUE
Is the death penalty justifiable within the terms of human rights?

ECONOMICS
Is it more economical to execute criminals than keep them in jail?

NO: The death penalty is a violation of human rights and dignity

NO: It is a barbaric practice and is prone to abuse

NO: Human life is at stake— money shouldn't be an issue

IS THE DEATH PENALTY EVER JUSTIFIABLE?

KEY POINTS

YES: There is a high incidence of criminals reoffending in societies lacking the death penalty

YES: Execution acts as a powerful deterrent to others

YES: The poor, along with ethnic minorities (which are often socially disadvantaged), have de facto higher crime levels

PUBLIC SAFETY
Should criminals be executed to protect the rest of society?

MINORITIES
Is application of the death penalty fair to all sectors of society?

NO: The "eye for an eye" adage is outdated and not fitting in a modern democracy

NO: What happens in the cases in which criminals are wrongfully convicted?

NO: That minorities figure abnormally highly in execution statistics is thanks largely to the all-whiteness of juries

THE DEATH PENALTY IN THE UNITED STATES

The first European settlers, influenced by existing British laws, brought capital punishment with them to the United States in the 1600s. The first recorded execution in the new colonies was that of Captain George Kendall, executed for being a spy for Spain, in the Jamestown colony in Virginia in 1608. Since independence different states have passed laws on the penalty. A strong anti-death-penalty lobby is calling for its total abolition.

"Under the laws of our land, the matter is concluded."
—GEORGE W. BUSH, 43RD U.S. PRESIDENT, ON THE EXECUTION OF OKLAHOMA BOMBER TIMOTHY MCVEIGH

1608 Captain George Kendall becomes the first recorded execution in the new colonies.

1612 Virginia governor Sir Thomas Dale enacts the Divine, Moral, and Martial Laws, which provide the death penalty even for minor offenses such as stealing grapes, killing chickens, and trading with Native Americans.

1632 Jane Champion becomes the first woman executed in the new colonies.

1767 Cesare Beccaria's essay "On Crimes and Punishment" theorizes that there is no justification for the state to take a life. In the late 1700s the abolitionist movement begins, heavily influenced by Beccaria's work.

Early 1800s Several states reduce their number of capital crimes and build state penitentiaries instead.

1834 Pennsylvania becomes the first state to move executions away from the public eye into correctional facilities.

1838 Discretionary death-penalty statutes are introduced in Tennessee and Alabama. This is seen as a victory for abolitionists because previously all states executed people convicted of a capital crime, regardless of circumstances.

1846 Michigan becomes the first state to abolish the death penalty for all crimes except treason. Later Rhode Island and Wisconsin abolish the death penalty for all crimes.

1888 New York builds the first electric chair.

1890 William Kemmler is the first person to die in the electric chair in New York.

Early 1900s The "Progressive Period" of reform in the United States begins.

1907–1917 Six states outlaw the death penalty. Three other states limit it to the crimes of treason and the first-degree murder of a law-enforcement officer.

1920 Five of the six abolitionist states reinstate the death penalty following panic after the Russian Revolution (1917) and World War I in Europe (1914–1918).

1924 Cyanide gas is introduced. Gee Jon is the first person to be executed by lethal gas.

1930s Executions average 137 per year—the highest levels in U.S. history.

1948 The Universal Declaration of Human Rights is adopted by the United Nations. It proclaims that everyone has a "right to life."

1966 A Gallup poll shows support for the death penalty at only 42 percent—an all-time low in the United States.

1968 In *Witherspoon v. Illinois* the dismissal of potential jurors who oppose the death penalty is determined unconstitutional.

June 1972 In *Furman v. Georgia* the Supreme Court voids 40 death-penalty statutes and suspends the death penalty.

January 17, 1977 A 10-year moratorium on executions ends with Gary Gilmore's death by firing squad in Utah.

1977 Oklahoma becomes the first state to adopt lethal injection as a means of execution. *Coker v. Georgia* holds that the death penalty is an unconstitutional punishment for rape of an adult woman when the victim is not killed.

December 2, 1982 Charles Brooks is the first person to be executed by lethal injection.

1984 Velma Barfield is the first woman to be executed since the death penalty resumes.

1986 The execution of the insane is banned in *Ford v. Wainwright*.

1988 *Thompson v. Oklahoma* upholds that executions of offenders aged 15 or under at the time of their crimes is unconstitutional.

1989 *Stanford v. Kentucky* and *Wilkins v. Missouri* decide that the Eighth Amendment does not prohibit the death penalty for offenders who commit crimes aged 16 or 17.

1989 *Penry v. Lynaugh* decides that the execution of mentally challenged people is not a violation of the Eighth Amendment.

1994 President Clinton enacts the Violent Crime Control and Law Enforcement Act, which expands the federal death penalty.

1998 Karla Faye Tucker and Judi Buenoano are executed. In November Northwestern University holds the first National Conference on Wrongful Convictions and the Death Penalty. Thirty former death-row inmates, who were freed because innocent, attend.

January 1999 Pope John Paul II visits St. Louis, Missouri, and calls for an end to the death penalty.

2000 A commission is appointed by the attorney general to investigate the death penalty in Arizona.

March/April 2001 Martha Barnatt, president of the American Bar Association, sends an open letter on behalf of 400,000 members asking for a moratorium on the federal death penalty.

July 11, 2001 Timothy McVeigh, the Oklahoma City bomber, is executed six years, one month, and 23 days after the bombing. The families of some of his victims watch online.

July 2001 There are 3,717 people on death row. A Harris Interactive survey shows 94 percent of Americans believe innocent people are sometimes convicted of murder.

Topic 14

SHOULD SOCIETY MAKE REPARATIONS TO THE DESCENDANTS OF SLAVES?

YES

"SLAVERY: LEGACY"

SPEECH TO HOUSE OF LORDS, BRITAIN, MARCH 14, 1996

LORD ANTHONY GIFFORD, QC

NO

"TEN REASONS WHY REPARATIONS FOR BLACKS IS A BAD IDEA

FOR BLACKS—AND RACIST TOO"

FRONTPAGEMAG.COM/HOROWITZSNOTEPAD/2001/HN01-03.HTM, JANUARY 3, 2001

DAVID HOROWITZ

INTRODUCTION

During the 20th century a growing number of people began to campaign for reparations—"the act of making amends for a wrong"—for descendants of Atlantic slaves. The debate has caused much discussion and division within both the African American community and society at large. International advocacy groups have yet to reach a consensus over the exact terms of reparations, but common among demands are that descendants receive formal apologies from the governments involved in slavery, that there be financial compensation for people whose ancestors were slaves, that "stolen" African antiquities be returned to their original countries, and that holocaust monuments be erected in memory of people who suffered and died as a result of slavery.

Advocates further argue that such compensation only goes a small way toward making up for the "genocide" and "crimes against humanity" suffered from the 16th century until 1865, when the United States abolished slavery. They state that other groups have received compensation for ill treatment and that their case is no different.

Opponents, however, who include well-known African Americans, argue that slavery happened a long time ago and that Africa also dealt in slaves. They assert that since the United States is a nation with a huge immigrant population, a large percentage of whom have no links to slavery, it would be unfair to make them foot the bill for any reparations made. Furthermore, reparations would solve very few of the problems existing today and would, if anything, lead to greater problems. Critics also argue that reparations would have a negative affect on how the African American community is perceived by other minority groups and the population at large.

The right to reparations is well established in international law. Its function, as defined by the Permanent Court of International Justice—the predecessor of the International Court of Justice—is to "as far as possible, wipe out all the consequences of the illegal act and reestablish the situation which would, in all probability, have existed if that act had not been committed." Mostly, however, reparation payments have fallen into two categories.

"An apology for slavery is a meaningless gesture."
—REVEREND JESSE JACKSON,
CIVIL RIGHTS ACTIVIST

The first relates to retribution pursued by states on behalf of their injured citizens against other states that have committed crimes against humanity. There have been substantial reparations payments in this area, most notably after World War II, when the Federal Republic of Germany paid some $2 billion to victims of Nazi persecution, which included $35.70 per month per inmate of concentration camps and $820 million for the resettlement of 50,000 Jews in Israel from lands formerly controlled by Hitler. Other undisclosed payments have since been made. Similarly, Japan has made reparations to countries that it occupied during World War II. More recently, the United Nations Security Council passed a resolution that requires Iraq to pay reparations for the invasion of Kuwait in 1990.

The second and probably more important category for the African American case is that of reparations made when a state has accepted its duty to make amends, not only to other states or countries, but to groups of people living within its own borders. In 1988 Congress passed the Civil Liberties Act, designed to make restitution for discriminatory acts carried out by the U.S. government to Japanese Americans interned during World War II. The terms of the act, which called for an apology "on behalf of the people of the United States" and provided for "restitution to those individuals of Japanese ancestry who were interned," are points that could equally be applied to African Americans.

Attorney Alexander Pires, a member of the Reparations Assessment Group, has stated that the government "has failed to enforce the Constitution equally for black people and that makes them liable." Pires argues that although slavery was legally abolished in the United States in 1865, and around four million African slaves were released from servitude, in reality little changed for them. Former slaves won no compensation, and many continued to live and work under discriminatory conditions. Even the Thirteenth, Fourteenth, and Fifteenth Amendments, which were passed to give African Americans rights of citizenship, have not ensured equality. Reparations would help right some of these wrongs.

The following extracts examine this issue. Lord Gifford presents a Jamaican-British perspective on why reparations should be made. The opposing piece caused a storm in 2001 when its author, David Horowitz, tried to have it run as an ad in campus newspapers across the United States.

SLAVERY: LEGACY
Lord Gifford QC

The author of this article, Lord Anthony Gifford, is one of Britain's most senior lawyers and a Jamaican attorney-at-law.

☑ The slavery experience has left a bitter legacy which endures to this day in terms of family breakdown, landlessness, underdevelopment, and a longing among many to return to the motherland from which their ancestors were taken. Once again, in the Caribbean the need to finance development programs has bound Caribbean governments and peoples in fresh shackles, the shackles of debt. In Jamaica, where I live, between 40 and 50 percent of the national budget has had to be paid out in debt servicing over the past 10 years. In many African countries, the proportion is much higher. The effects are crippling in that every public service, such as schools, health facilities, transport and roads, prisons and justice systems, is so squeezed that it is failing to deliver at even a minimum standard.

Britain and other European countries collaborated in the slave trade from the 16th century.

As well as the consequences in Africa and the Caribbean, there is a further element in the legacy of the slave trade which is the damage done within Britain, within the United States, and other Western societies. The inhuman philosophy of white supremacy and black inferiority was inculcated into European peoples to justify the atrocities which were being committed by a Christian people upon fellow human beings. That philosophy continues to poison our society today.

On one short visit back to Britain this month, I come across reports of racism in the armed forces and the police. Equal rights legislation has not been enough. It is necessary to look more deeply, to understand why the crimes of the past are poisoning the present for all people, white and black, and then to do something effective to repair the wrong. That will assist both African and European, black and white, to lance the poison and to heal the wounds.

The precedents of reparations

Germany has paid billions of dollars to Jewish people since World War II.

The concept that reparations are payable where a crime against humanity has been committed by one people against another is well established in international law and practice. Germany paid reparations to Israel for the crimes of the Nazi Holocaust. Indeed, the very creation of the State of Israel can be seen as a massive act of reparation for centuries of dispossession and persecution directed against Jews.

Japan apologized only last year, 50 years on, for its wartime atrocities and is still being urged, rightly, to pay compensation to the victims. The USA made apology and restitution for the internment of Japanese Americans during the Second World War. Going further back into history, Her Majesty the Queen, only last November in New Zealand, personally signed the Royal Assent to the Waikato Raupatu Claims Settlement Bill through which the New Zealand Government paid substantial compensation in land and in money for the seizure of Maori lands by British settlers in 1863. She apologized for the crime and recognized a long-standing grievance of the Maori people. Other indigenous peoples have similar, just claims for the dispossession which their ancestors suffered.

These examples suggest that there is no time limit on a nation's collective guilt for wrongs done to another nation or race. Do you agree?

African people, too, have a massive … grievance. It is no use saying that it all happened a long time ago, and we should just forget about it. The period of colonialism which succeeded the period of slavery continued the exploitation of Africa and the Caribbean in new ways. Further acts of brutality were committed, and the peoples of those regions, until recently, were denied the status of sovereignty and independence with which alone they could themselves demand the redress of the wrongs which were done.

But the wrongs have not been forgotten. The peoples of Africa and the Caribbean live with their consequences still. A group of eminent Africans under the auspices of the Organization of African Unity is beginning to articulate the claim for reparation.

Defining reparations

What is meant by the claim for reparations? The details of reparations settlement would have to be negotiated with an appropriate body of representatives of African people around the world. I would anticipate that some of the elements of an appropriate package would be, first, as with other precedents, an apology at the highest level for the criminal acts committed against millions of Africans over the centuries of the slave trade. His Holiness the Pope set the example when he visited the slave dungeons of Goree in Senegal in February 1992 when he said, "From this African sanctuary of black pain, we implore forgiveness from Heaven."

Secondly, there would be the cancellation of the intolerable burden of debt, which has overloaded the economies of Africa and the Caribbean. There are powerful economic and social arguments for debt cancellation which were most recently deployed by former President Kaunda of Zambia

COMMENTARY: Reconstruction's failure

One of the motives that drive activists to seek reparations for slavery is the failure of the 1865 Reconstruction to secure the full freedom of African slaves and grant them equal rights with whites under the Constitution. The importing of slaves had been outlawed by government in 1808, but a number of Southern states flouted the prohibition; perhaps a quarter of a million slaves were illegally imported from 1808 to 1865.

President Abraham Lincoln's Emancipation Proclamation of 1863 became a banner under which the Civil War, between Union and Confederacy, would be fought: it was a call for the freedom of the slaves who still toiled in the tobacco and cotton fields. As such, it enabled the Union to enlist blacks, some 170,000 of whom served in the Civil War. The death knell for slavery was sounded with the Union victory in 1865 and the ratification that year of the Thirteenth Amendment: "Neither slavery nor involuntary servitude ... shall exist within the United States."

However, Andrew Johnson, who succeeded to the presidency following Lincoln's assassination, was not the man to champion equality and enfranchisement for the four million or so black slaves who were now in legal terms, if not in any real sense, free. A Southerner, he showed consideration to the Confederates, returning their confiscated land. But in spite of Johnson, Congress pushed through further legislation to protect blacks. It passed the Civil Rights Act in 1866, granting citizenship to black Americans. Later that summer came the Fourteenth Amendment, guaranteeing equal protection under the law to all citizens; the Fifteenth (1869) conferred voting rights on black Americans.

The practicalities of helping the newly freed citizens from slavery to full citizenship were undertaken by the Bureau of Refugees, Freedmen, and Abandoned Lands, established by Congress in 1865. Usually known as the Freedmen's Bureau, it was in effect a welfare agency, providing health care and education for African Americans and securing labor contracts for those out of work. But the Bureau was poorly run by its governor, Oliver Howard, and it was especially ineffective on the issue of land ownership. Under a loose promise by General William Sherman of "40 acres and a mule" to each freedman's family, African Americans looked forward to a piece of America for themselves, and the Bureau had some 850,000 acres of land to apportion to them. But Johnson's restoration of land to Southerners made this effectively impossible, and the Bureau was summarily closed in 1872. Meanwhile, the Southern states enacted the so-called black codes, which set harsh penalties on African Americans for even minor misdemeanors, restricted their legal rights, and generally kept them inferior. The institutionalized racism persisted into the 20th century, to be swept away only in the 1960s. Today many reparationists refer to that old promise of "40 acres and a mule" in their demand that justice be done.

during a visit to Scotland in 1996. He said of the present state of Africa: "It is a human tragedy. People are dying by their thousands every day, children are dying. These things bring social disorder to countries."

Thirdly, there would be the return of treasures and works of art which come from the African continent, many of which are to be found in Britain's museums as a result of acts of theft. I refer, for instance, to the Benin Bronzes in the Museum of Mankind.

> Do you think that all such treasures, most of which were taken as the spoils of empire, should be returned to their native lands?

> *"Candidates run from the subject [of reparations]. But this is a subject that [we] cannot historically let slip through the cracks as we struggle with where we are now in our efforts to make America a true democracy."*
>
> —JOHN CONYERS, HOUSE JUDICIARY COMMITTEE

Fourthly, there would be measures to facilitate the repatriation and resettlement of those who wish to return to Africa. The word "repatriation" has an ugly ring in the mouth of racists who want to drive black people out of Britain. However, it expresses, too, a yearning among many descendants of Africans which is as powerful as was the yearning of the Jewish people for the Promised Land.

Fifthly, there would be a reparations settlement which would involve programs of development, without strings attached, in Africa, the Caribbean, Brazil, and elsewhere.

Bridging the divide

As we move to the next millennium, none of us can deny that there is a growing divide between north and south, between black and white, across frontiers and within frontiers. It is in the interests of all of us to recognize that the reasons for that divide lie in a shameful past.

If we realize that, we will be on the way to doing something to repair the wrong which was done, even though it may cost heavily in terms of pride and revenue. The steps to be taken will bring a happier world for all our children.

TEN REASONS WHY REPARATIONS FOR BLACKS IS A BAD IDEA *FOR BLACKS—* AND RACIST TOO
David Horowitz

NO

1. There is no single group clearly responsible for the crime of slavery

Does the first point imply that because almost everyone was implicated, no one is guilty?

Black Africans and Arabs were responsible for enslaving the ancestors of African Americans. There were 3,000 black slave owners in the antebellum United States. Are reparations to be paid by their descendants too?

2. There is no one group that benefited exclusively from slavery

The claim for reparations is premised on the false assumption that only whites have benefited from slavery. If slave labor created wealth for Americans, then obviously it has created wealth for black Americans as well. The GNP of black America is so large that it makes the African American community the 10th most prosperous "nation" in the world. American blacks on average enjoy per capita incomes in the range of 20 to 50 times that of blacks living in any of the African nations from which they were kidnapped.

3. Only a tiny minority of white Americans ever owned slaves, and others gave their lives to free them

Is it possible to establish whether Union soldiers died to liberate slaves or to save the Union?

Only a tiny minority of Americans ever owned slaves. This is true even for those who lived in the antebellum South, where only one white in five was a slaveholder. Why should their descendants owe a debt? What about the descendants of the 350,000 Union soldiers who died to free the slaves? They gave their lives. What possible moral principle would ask them to pay (through their descendants) again?

4. America today is a multiethnic nation and most Americans have no connection (direct or indirect) to slavery

The two great waves of American immigration occurred after 1880 and then after 1960. What rationale would require

Vietnamese boat people, Russian refuseniks, Iranian refugees, and Armenian victims of the Turkish persecution, Jews, Mexicans, Greeks, or Polish, Hungarian, Cambodian, and Korean victims of Communism, to pay reparations to American blacks?

5. The historical precedents used to justify the reparations claim do not apply, and the claim itself is based on race not injury

The historical precedents generally invoked to justify the reparations claim are payments to Jewish survivors of the Holocaust, Japanese Americans and African American victims of racial experiments in Tuskegee, or racial outrages in Rosewood and Oklahoma City. But in each case, the recipients of reparations were the direct victims of the injustice or their immediate families. This would be the only case of reparations to people who were not immediately affected and whose sole qualification to receive reparations would be racial. During the slavery era, many blacks were freemen or slave owners themselves, yet the reparations claimants make no distinction between the roles blacks actually played in the injustice itself. Randall Robinson's book on reparations, *The Debt*, which is the manifesto of the reparations movement, is pointedly subtitled "What America Owes to Blacks." If this is not racism, what is?

How might the subtitle of The Debt *be construed as racist?*

6. The reparations argument is based on the unfounded claim that all African American descendants of slaves suffer from the economic consequences of slavery and discrimination

No evidence-based attempt has been made to prove that living individuals have been adversely affected by a slave system that was ended over 150 years ago. But there is plenty of evidence the hardships that occurred were hardships that individuals could and did overcome. The black middle class in America is a prosperous community that is now larger in absolute terms than the black underclass. Does its existence not suggest that economic adversity is the result of failures of individual character rather than the lingering after-effects of racial discrimination and a slave system that ceased to exist well over a century ago? West Indian blacks in America are also descended from slaves but their average incomes are equivalent to the average incomes of whites (and nearly 25 percent higher than the average incomes of American-born blacks). How is it that slavery adversely affected one large group of

Given the wealth disparity between African Americans and whites today, how do you view this claim for "failures of individual character"?

descendants but not the other? How can government be expected to decide an issue that is so subjective—and yet so critical—to the case?

7. The reparations claim is one more attempt to turn African Americans into victims. It sends a damaging message to the African American community.

Do you think reparations would create a "renewed sense of grievance" or placate existing grievances?

The renewed sense of grievance—which is what the claim for reparations will inevitably create—is neither a constructive nor a helpful message for black leaders to be sending to their communities and to others. To focus the social passions of African Americans on what some Americans may have done to their ancestors fifty or a hundred and fifty years ago is to burden them with a crippling sense of victim-hood. How are the millions of refugees from tyranny and genocide who are now living in America going to receive these claims, moreover, except as demands for special treatment, an extravagant new handout that is only necessary because some blacks can't seem to locate the ladder of opportunity within reach of others—many less privileged than themselves?

8. Reparations to African Americans have already been paid

The author refers in part to affirmative action programs, which, say some, should be abolished if slavery reparation payments are made. Would that be fair?

Since the passage of the Civil Rights Acts and the advent of the Great Society in 1965, trillions of dollars in transfer payments have been made to African Americans in the form of welfare benefits and racial preferences (in contracts, job placements, and educational admissions)—all under the rationale of redressing historic racial grievances. It is said that reparations are necessary to achieve a healing between African Americans and other Americans. If trillion-dollar restitutions and a wholesale rewriting of American law (in order to accommodate racial preferences) for African Americans is not enough to achieve a "healing," what will?

9. What about the debt blacks owe to America?

Slavery existed for thousands of years before the Atlantic slave trade was born, and in all societies. But in the thousand years of its existence, there never was an antislavery movement until white Christians—Englishmen and Americans—created one. If not for the antislavery attitudes and military power of white Englishmen and Americans, the slave trade would not have been brought to an end. If not for the sacrifices of white soldiers and a white American president who gave his life to sign the Emancipation Proclamation, blacks in America would still be slaves. If not for the dedication of Americans of all ethnicities and colors to a society based on the principle that all men are created equal,

> *"I never owned a slave. I never oppressed anybody. I don't know that I should have to pay for someone who did before I was born."*
>
> —HENRY HYDE, HOUSE JUDICIARY COMMITTEE

blacks in America would not enjoy the highest standard of living of blacks anywhere in the world, and indeed one of the highest standards of living of any people in the world. They would not enjoy the greatest freedoms and the most thoroughly protected individual rights anywhere.

Look for some logic behind Horowitz's argument. (What, according to him, have African Americans to be grateful for?)

10. The reparations claim is a separatist idea that sets African Americans against the nation that gave them freedom

Blacks were here before the Mayflower. Who is more American than the descendants of African slaves? For the African American community to isolate itself even further from America is to embark on a course whose implications are troubling. Yet the African American community has had a long-running flirtation with separatists, nationalists, and the political left, who want African Americans to be no part of America's social contract. African Americans should reject this temptation.

For all America's faults, African Americans have an enormous stake in their country and its heritage. It is this heritage that is really under attack by the reparations movement. The reparations claim is one more assault on America, conducted by racial separatists and the political left. America's African American citizens are the richest and most privileged black people alive—a bounty that is a direct result of the heritage that is under assault. The American idea needs the support of its African American citizens. But African Americans also need the support of the American idea. For it is this idea that led to the principles and institutions that have set African Americans—and all of us—free.

Horowitz claims that the campaign for African American identity has been hijacked by separatists.

Summary

After slavery was abolished in the 19th century in Britain and in the United States, no formal recompense or apology was given to the communities who had suffered humiliation, abuse, and loss of rights. It is this issue that Lord Gifford, who lives in Jamaica, addresses in his speech on "Slavery: Legacy" to the House of Lords. Gifford argues that slavery has left a bitter legacy, and the effects of it have not been forgotten by the African community. He gives several examples of recent reparations and suggests that the reparations needed to allow descendants of Atlantic slaves to move on include a formal apology, financial compensation, and repatriation if they want it.

David Horowitz, however, argues that slave reparations are not only wrong but also racist. He argues that Africans also took part in the slave trade and are therefore complicit in it. In addition, today it is impossible to finger one single group who benefited from slavery. Only a small number of white Southerners, he says, were ever slave owners, so it is unreasonable to expect white America to pay for reparations. Horowitz further asserts that reparations will harm African Americans by turning them into victims, and that sends a detrimental message to the black community. The call for reparations, he suggests, is being orchestrated by a minority of separatist extremists and will harm everyone—African Americans included.

FURTHER INFORMATION:

Books:

Barry, Brian, *Culture and Equality: An Egalitarian Critique of Multiculturalism.* Cambridge, MA: Harvard University Press, 2001.

Robinson, Randall, *The Debt: What America Owes to Blacks.* New York: Plume, 1999.

Useful websites:

www.arm.arc.co.uk/legalbasis.html
An essay by Lord Anthony Gifford on the legal basis for reparations.

www.ncobra.com
Site of N'COBRA, the National Coalition of Blacks for Reparations in America.

www.news.mpr.org/features/200011/13
williamsbreparations/
Brandt Williams, "The Case for Slave Reparations" at www.salon.com/news/feature/2000/06/05/
reparations/index.html

Earl Ofari Hutchison "Debt Wrong: David Horowitz is incorrect. It's time for the U.S. to pay up for slavery."

The following debates in the Pro/Con series may also be of interest:

In this volume:

Part 1 Issues in equality and inequality, pages 8–9

Topic 1 Is inequality a problem?

Topic 2 Is it possible to live in a nonracist society?

Topic 6 Should affirmative action continue?

In *Government*:

Topic 2 Are all human beings created equal?

SHOULD SOCIETY MAKE REPARATIONS TO THE DESCENDANTS OF SLAVES?

YES: Millions of Africans were forcibly abducted from their homes and were sold into slavery. They had no rights and were treated as less than human. That is a crime.

YES: This would emphasize how wrong slavery is and provide a precedent for other countries in which slavery is still an issue

YES: Other communities and groups have received reparations payments, such as Japanese Americans interned during World War II; this is no different

NO: Africans and Arabs also participated in the slave trade; should they pay too?

BLAME
Should white people today be held responsible for the crimes of their ancestors?

DEFINITIONS
Does slavery count as a crime against humanity?

NO: Only a small minority of people took part in the slave trade, so that is unfair on the majority

NO: Slavery was wrong, but it would be inadmissible to compare it to the Holocaust or occurrences of ethnic cleansing

NO: The United States is a country of immigrants, so would they all have to pay for events that happened centuries before they emigrated?

SHOULD SOCIETY MAKE REPARATIONS TO THE DESCENDANTS OF SLAVES?

KEY POINTS

YES: It would inevitably lead to resentment and to calls from other groups, such as Native Americans, for reparations for similar offenses

YES: The money could be put into funds for use in education and business rather than allotted on a person-by-person basis

INTEGRATION
Would reparations harm black/white relations?

GRIEVANCES
If reparations were made, would it help black communities?

NO: It would help African Americans put the past behind them and move on

NO: Advocates of reparations do a disservice to successful African Americans by assuming that all African Americans need help

Topic 15

IS ABORTION A RIGHT?

YES

"THE RIGHT TO CHOOSE AT 25: LOOKING BACK AND AHEAD"
ACLU REPRODUCTIVE RIGHTS UPDATE, JANUARY 1998
AMERICAN CIVIL LIBERTIES UNION

NO

"ABORTION—IT'S WRONG"
UNIVERSITY OF AUCKLAND
DR. RACHEL SIMON KUMAR

INTRODUCTION

Abortion refers to the premature expulsion of a human fetus either in a naturally spontaneous way, such as through a miscarriage, or by artificially induced methods. When people discuss abortion today, they usually refer to the latter definition. Almost 93 percent of all abortions are induced and are performed for nonmedical reasons.

According to the Center for Disease Control and Prevention, 36 million abortions are carried out worldwide each year, about 17 percent of an annual figure of some 210 million pregnancies. In most U.S. states abortion may be legally performed in cases in which there has been rape or incest, the fetus is severely deformed, the pregnant woman's health is at risk, or her age or social situation render her an unsuitable mother. The precise legality of abortion varies from one state to the next. In some states it is available on demand simply because a woman requests it.

The abortion debate is emotionally charged, with prolife groups, women's rights groups, civil liberties groups, and religious groups offering entrenched opinions from both sides. Prolifers argue that a fetus has full human rights. Some prolife groups are even prepared to go as far as violence and murder in defense of the unborn child. Between 1993 and 1998 seven people were killed in antiabortion murders. Doctors have been threatened and clinics bombed, although legislation has been passed to protect clinic attendees.

Prochoicers argue that a woman should have the right to choose whether or not to carry a baby to full term—that at the end of the day, if she judges herself incapable of dealing with a baby, she should not be forced to do so by the law. The church has further moral opinions on the subject of abortion. Catholics especially oppose abortion, citing the explicit views of the Pope that it is a sin against God.

Abortion has had a checkered past in the United States. Legal until the mid-19th century, it was later outlawed by physicians, religious groups, and racial purists, who cited a varying range of reasons for their opposition.

The 20th century also saw change. In 1965, 17 percent of all pregnancy-related deaths in the United States were the result of illegal abortions. In 2000, according to the organization Planned Parenthood, abortion was 10 times safer than childbirth. The Alan Guttmacher Institute has estimated that around 1,500 pregnancy-related deaths were prevented by abortion in 1987, and that from 1965 to 1985 the rate of infant deaths dropped from nearly 25 per 1,000 live births to 7.6 per 1,000.

"America needs no words from me to see how your decision in Roe v. Wade *has deformed a great nation. The so-called right to abortion has pitted mothers against their children and women against men. It has portrayed the greatest of gifts—a child—as a competitor, an intrusion, and an inconvenience."*

—MOTHER THERESA

The most important legal case in abortion history in the United States was *Roe v. Wade*. On January 22, 1973, the Supreme Court announced its decision on a case filed by one Jane Roe, who wanted to safely and legally terminate her pregnancy in Texas, a state that had a statute making abortion illegal unless the woman's health was at risk. The court sided with Roe and overrode the Texas statute. At the time nearly two-thirds of states had outlawed abortion—although Alaska, Hawaii, New York, and Washington had repealed abortion bans—but the *Roe* decision made existing laws unconstitutional.

At the start of the 21st century public opposition to abortion appears to be increasing, and prolifers are asking for stronger legislation to sweep away the freedom granted under *Roe*. Antiabortion groups, such as the National Right to Life, assert that there are around 3,000 Crisis Pregnancy Centers in the United States, willing to give advice to pregnant women and show them their options, including adoption, and how to continue studying after the baby is born. They argue that abortion clinics have a financial incentive to perform abortions and do not offer alternative advice to women.

As governor of Texas George W. Bush made clear his antiabortion stance. Vice President Dick Cheney stated that the president had stated that he would reduce the incidence of abortion if possible. Once president Bush stopped funding to family-planning groups operating abroad that advocated abortion. In July 2001 the *Washington Post* reported that the federal government had rejected all pending requests by states to increase family-planning services to poor women. Physicians are reporting a decrease in routine training services for abortion.

The following articles—the ACLU report and Dr. Rachel Simon Kumar's "Abortion—It's Wrong"—examine both sides of this highly emotional debate in which there appears to be little common ground.

THE RIGHT TO CHOOSE AT 25
American Civil Liberties Union

On January 22, 1973, the United States Supreme Court announced its landmark rulings that legalized abortion, *Roe v. Wade* and *Doe v. Bolton*. Two days later, a *New York Times* editorial predicted that the decisions offered "a sound foundation for final and reasonable resolution" of the abortion debate.

Yet, in fact, the struggle that had resulted in the Supreme Court victories was far from over. Few in 1973 could have anticipated how explosive the issue of abortion would become and how difficult the right would be to retain. Nor could anyone then have known how much the availability of safe legal abortion would contribute to women's social, economic, and political advancement in the next quarter of a century.

1. Establishing the right to choose in U.S. law

Abortion was not, in fact, illegal in most states until the second half of the nineteenth century. Before then, medical experts and other commentators believed that abortion was commonly sought and widely available. By their estimates, there was one abortion for every four live births.

But from the mid-nineteenth century, opposition to abortion began to emerge from several directions. Physicians charged their competitors—midwives and folk healers—with performing too frequent and unsafe abortions.... Professional organizations of physicians sought criminal bans. A vocal group of native-born, white Americans condemned abortion as "race suicide" because it lowered their birth rate at a time when they feared being outnumbered by immigrants. Still others, reacting to the new movement for women's suffrage and other rights, worried that continuing access to abortion would permit women to stray from their traditional roles as wives and mothers. As a result of these converging sentiments, by the end of the century every state had enacted a law criminalizing abortion. Most made an exception only for abortions undertaken to preserve a woman's life.

These laws did not end abortion but merely sent it underground. The unsafe and unsanitary practice of illegal abortion maimed and killed thousands of women. Finally, in

Find out how the objections to abortion often given today compare with those of the past. Has public opinion changed?

the 1960s, an outcry arose to make abortion legal again. The outcry came from doctors, legal reformers, clergy, and women themselves. The ACLU was in the forefront of this movement.

Led into the struggle by board members like Dorothy Kenyon, a feminist lawyer and judge, the ACLU was the first organization to call for a woman's right to choose abortion. Kenyon began pressing the issue as early as 1958, and she persisted until 1967, when the board affirmed "the right of a woman to have an abortion." She also brought the issue to the public, appearing on television talk shows and in print, where she called for an end to "cruel and unconstitutional abortion laws." Kenyon ... died at the age of 84 in 1972, a little too soon to see the fruition of her work. In 1973 the Supreme Court decided the two cases that upheld a woman's right to abortion, *Roe v. Wade* and *Doe v. Bolton*.... The ACLU was involved in both cases.

Roe v. Wade

Roe v. Wade challenged a Texas law prohibiting all but lifesaving abortions. The Supreme Court invalidated the law on the ground that the constitutional right to privacy encompassed a woman's decision whether or not to terminate her pregnancy. Characterizing this right as "fundamental" to a woman's "life and future," the Court held that the state could not interfere with the abortion decision unless it had a compelling reason for regulation.

See box on page 10 for a fuller account of Roe v. Wade and its importance in abortion law.

In *Doe v. Bolton* the Supreme Court overturned a Georgia law regulating abortion. The law prohibited abortions except when necessary to preserve a woman's life or health or in cases of fetal abnormality or rape. Among other conditions, the law also required that all abortions be performed in accredited hospitals and that a hospital committee and two doctors in addition to the woman's own doctor give their approval. The Court held the Georgia law unconstitutional because it imposed too many restrictions and interfered with a woman's right to decide, in consultation with her physician, to terminate her pregnancy.

The Supreme Court's decisions in *Roe v. Wade* and *Doe v. Bolton* had nationwide impact. After the Court ruled the Texas and Georgia abortion laws unconstitutional, no other states could enforce similarly restrictive laws. When the Court made its landmark rulings, it was in step with public opinion. Public attitudes had shifted as a result of the decade-long campaign to legalize abortion. In 1968, only 15 percent of Americans favored liberalizing abortion laws; by 1972, 64 percent did.

Can you discover in what ways the court rulings were in step with advances in the feminist movement?

2. What legalization has meant for women

The legalization of abortion has dramatically improved women's health. Abortion services moved from the back alleys into hygienic facilities staffed by health professionals. High-quality training, the ability of professionals openly to share their expertise with one another, and the development of specialized clinics all enhanced the safety of abortion services. In the early part of this century an estimated 800,000 illegal abortions took place annually, resulting in 8,000–17,000 women's deaths each year. Thousands of other women suffered severe consequences short of death, including perforations of the uterus, cervical wounds, serious bleeding, infections, poisoning, shock, and gangrene. After legalization, deaths as a result of abortion greatly declined. In 1991, for example, 11 women died as the result of complications arising in legal abortions. Today, one death occurs in every 167,000 legal abortions, compared with one in every 30,000 in 1973.

Quoting statistics is an effective way of supporting your argument.

Once *Roe* made it possible to obtain safe legal abortions, women have been having abortions earlier in their pregnancies when the health risks are the lowest. In 1973, only 38 percent of abortions were performed at or before eight weeks of pregnancy; in 1997, this percentage has risen to 52, and 89 percent of all abortions occur in the first 12 weeks. Only one percent takes place after 21 weeks. Today [in 1998] abortion is one of the most commonly performed surgical procedures and is ten times safer than carrying a pregnancy to term.

The availability of safe legal abortion is a cornerstone that supports the remarkable advances women have made in American society in the past quarter of a century. As the Supreme Court observed in reaffirming *Roe* in 1992, "The ability of women to participate equally in the economic and social life of the Nation has been facilitated by their ability to control their reproductive lives."

How does the author reinforce the argument by quoting the Supreme Court?

3. Defending reproductive freedom

[Since] 1973, the ACLU Reproductive Freedom Project and our sister organizations have worked continuously to defend and expand reproductive rights. Our greatest challenge has been to try to assure that the right to choose extends to those whose lack of political power makes them easy targets for lawmakers: low-income women and young women.

[A]s our efforts to protect the rights of the most vulnerable women continue, the backlash against reproductive choice has escalated on other fronts. Beginning in the mid-1980s, vandalism, bombings, arsons, and assassinations threatened to shut down many abortion providers. Clinics, doctors, and other advocates of choice demanded federal protection and helped to persuade Congress to enact the Freedom of Access to Clinic Entrances Act of 1994 (FACE). This statute prohibits force, threats of force, physical obstruction, and property damage intended to interfere with people obtaining or providing reproductive health services. It does not apply to peaceful praying, picketing, or other free expression by antichoice demonstrators—so long as these activities do not obstruct physical access to clinics. FACE has reduced but by no means eliminated clinic violence. Thus the struggle … goes on, both to counter persistent attacks and to advance an affirmative agenda of enabling people to make informed and meaningful decisions about reproduction.

The right to speak out on any subject is upheld by the First Amendment.

"Under our Constitution, the right of a woman to choose [abortion] is protected. But President Bush thinks it's wrong for people overseas even to discuss this right. That's crazy. And women will die because of it."

—MADELEINE K. ALBRIGHT,

FORMER U.S. SECRETARY OF STATE

---

4. Preserving the right to choose

We must defend abortion as a moral choice. Opponents want to return to the time when abortion was illicit. They portray women who have abortions as immoral, inhumane, and irresponsible. We must respond with a clear moral defense of abortion. We must remember that it is an act of violence to force an unwilling woman to bear an unwanted child. We must cultivate respect for women as moral actors who make their childbearing decisions based on profound concerns about their own lives and the lives of their families. Women make these decisions within the framework of their own religious beliefs and conscience. Abortion is a responsible choice for a woman who is unwilling to continue a pregnancy and unprepared to care for a child.

Why is it difficult to defend freedoms on moral grounds?

ABORTION—IT'S WRONG
Dr. Rachel Simon Kumar

NO

The "right" to abortion became a reality in legislation when the U.S. Supreme Court, in 1973, ruled in the case of *Roe v. Wade* that women had the "right to privacy" in matters relating to marriage, family, and sex. The battle to legalize abortion came in the wake of the feminist campaign in the 1960s and 70s to establish that women had "reproductive rights"; rights to choose what was best for their bodies. Antiabortion or prolife arguments raise critical and valid points against legalizing abortion. The act of abortion cannot be merely seen as an issue where the state provides for a medical procedure. Abortion involves the killing of life and as such holds deep emotional, spiritual, and moral consequences.

Kumar makes her position in the argument clear from the start

There is abundant evidence drawn from women's narrations of their abortion experiences that it has left them emotionally scarred. Prolife groups have also demonstrated that the act of abortion is not a painless one for the fetus. The forced expulsion of the fetus from the womb, even under legal conditions, is often unsuccessful and messy. Yet, the legal grounds for abortion are firmly entrenched in the "right of privacy." Are the rights of privacy and choice so basic to women's survival that it is sufficient to justify the termination of another life?

William Rehnquist was a conservative during an era noted for liberalism on the Supreme Court. He was appointed chief justice in 1986 by Ronald Reagan.

Justice Rehnquist, who dissented at the verdict of *Roe v. Wade*, noted that "the asserted right to an abortion is not 'so rooted in the traditions and conscience of our people as to be ranked as fundamental.'" The most vocal challenge to abortion rights have come, unsurprisingly, from the Catholic Church. However, prolife feminists have also contributed to the debate. Together, they provide powerful arguments for reevaluating the moral grounds for appraising rights; both of the mother and of the fetus.

Value of life: The Church's view

The substance of the Church's stand on abortion is based on Bible's clear statements that life that is given is from God and can only be taken away by him. All life is an expression of God ("so God created humankind in his image" Gen. 1: 27) and it is sin to kill ("Thou shalt not kill" Exod. 20:13). The

Church recognizes that human life begins at the moment of conception ("Before I formed you in the womb I knew you and before you were born I consecrated you" Jer. 1:5) and [that] the fetus is entitled to the rights that are applicable to all members of society. The fetus is a potential person, and although not a fully contributing member of society, deserves the rights accorded to other weaker segments of society like the aged, handicapped, or mentally challenged.

Kumar compares the fetus to such people because like them, it cannot speak for itself. Ronald Reagan once said, "Abortion is advocated only by persons who have themselves been born."

Thirty-seven million lives have been lost since Roe v. Wade became the law of the land."
—SENATOR JOHN ASHCROFT, U.S ATTORNEY GENERAL

In 1974 the Vatican issued a Declaration on Procured Abortion, wherein it stated that "the first right of the human person is the right to life … this one is fundamental—the condition of all others. Hence it must be protected above all others. It does not belong to society, nor does it belong to public authority in any form to recognize this right for some and not for others." The Vatican also states categorically that abortion, both for the person who conducts it and on whom it is conducted, is a grievous sin against God. Recently, in 1995, Pope John Paul II in his Evangelium Vitae (The Gospel of Life) made a specific address to post-abortive women emphasizing that abortion was an act of sin. "Certainly what happened was and remains terribly wrong…." The Church, therefore, disallows any moral ground that takes away the right of the fetus to life.

Value of justice: A prolife feminist argument

Sidney Callahan's (1996) essay offering a case for "Pro-Life Feminism" argues against abortion not so much from the viewpoint of the fetus, but more strongly from the perspective of women's rights. Her charge against prochoice feminists is that their demands are "inconsistent with feminism's basic demands for justice." Feminism, she argues, seeks to ensure full social equality or personal development. By endorsing a right to abortion, she argues, feminist will make "a woman's body … more like a man's." It strengthens negative cultural norms around pregnancy and childbirth— that it is burdensome, and undesirable…. Callahan also argues that the right to abortion can easily be exploited by men who can now engage in sexuality without responsibility. *Roe v.*

Sidney Callahan is the author of several essays on topics involving bioethics and Christian issues.

COMMENTARY: *Roe v. Wade*

The 1973 Supreme Court ruling on *Roe v. Wade*, in combination with its contemporaneous ruling on *Doe v. Bolton*, heralded an era of legal abortion on demand for American women.

Jane Roe was the pseudonym adopted for the case by the plaintiff, one Norma McCorvey, a single woman living in Dallas County, Texas. Aged 21 at the time, McCorvey was on her third pregnancy and too poor to pay for the abortion she sought (then illegal in her home state except in a life-or-death situation). She filed a suit against Texas law. The court threw it out, but the Supreme Court heard her appeal. On the same day it heard the similar case of Sandra Benson, who was acting under the pseudonym Mary Doe.

Verdict and consequence

On January 22, 1973, the Supreme Court decided 7–2 in favor of McCorvey; Benson also won. In writing the decision on *Roe*, Justice Harry Blackmun found that existing abortion law infringed a woman's right to privacy—and thus her right to abortion—under the Fourteenth Amendment.

For Blackmun the critical decision lay in determining the fetus's viability—when it was capable of surviving outside the womb, and therefore when it might be assumed to have the same human rights as an individual living in society. He placed viability at 28 weeks, though he conceded that the timing might be flexible. Blackmun divided the nine-month pregnancy term into three equal trimesters. He decreed that a woman might freely have an abortion on demand, with the proviso that she obtain consent from her physician in the first trimester, from an accredited clinic in the second, and from the state in the third. The state, according to the verdict, had the right (though not the obligation) to proscribe abortion in the third trimester. In reality, then as now, third-trimester abortions were rare.

McCorvey's victory, which effectively legalized abortion nationwide, was celebrated by prochoice activists. It chimed with a general shift in U.S. opinion toward freer sexual mores and a stronger public voice for women. However, more recent Supreme Courts have swung back toward a more conservative outlook, and there are regular attempts to rerestrict abortion.

For McCorvey herself life took a series of unexpected twists. Like Benson, she never had an abortion; her daughter was given up for adoption. After a series of low-key jobs she ended up living next door to some prolife activist led by the Rev. Phillip Benham. He befriended his neighbor and in 1995 helped her become a Christian. She then became a staunch prolife activist and confessed to having lied at the trial. Dismissing the significance of such events, prochoicers point to the wider implications of *Roe v. Wade*—better women's health. Roughly the same number of women have abortions today as did before 1973; the difference, say activists, is that most of the operations are now legal and safe, not illegal and life-threatening.

Wade, she contends, "removed the last defense women possessed against male sexual demands."

Instead, a model of a feminist society that truly liberates women would seek to change social organization so that women are supported through pregnancy, not isolated. The Official Statement of Feminists for Life of America, a prolife group, notes that a just world for women would be "a world in which pregnancy and motherhood are accepted and supported". Pregnancy should not be seen as solely the responsibility of women, but rather of society as a whole. The Feminists for Life of America state that "No woman should be forced to choose between relinquishing life and career plans or suffering though a humiliating, invasive procedure and sacrificing her child. Abortion is a last resort, not a free choice." The debate that women should rightly engage in, therefore, is the state's responsibility to provide day care and child support, not to endorse abortion rights. In the end, Callahan argues, it works to women's advantage to link their rights with fetal rights.

> *Kumar is implying that abortion freedom and childcare support are mutually exclusive. Is this necessarily true?*

Morality and the definition of rights

The prolife position on abortion, therefore, does not position rights as absolute but as contingent on the various relationships and responsibilities that tie people in society together. In relation to abortion, specifically, there are, as Lisa Cahill points out, "duties or obligations that can bind humans to their fellows in ways to which they have not explicitly consented … the mother-fetus relation is characterized by obligations of this sort, as are all parent-child relations." Rights cannot be assumed by the individual without thought to the impact of the exercise of rights on the larger community. Rights of the individual should be interpreted from within a framework of responsibility, obligations and duty. The foundations of rights should shift from a view of self-centeredness to an expanded moral and social responsibility. Those in favour of abortion may argue that religious sentiments and social mores may not be a sound foundation for a legal ruling that enables people to act freely in society. However, it is precisely to ensure that society is guided by the ethics of fairness and justice that it is important to bring legislation in tune with values about sanctity of life that transcend time and space. The world we live in is increasingly aware of the need to protect life regardless of color, race, religion, or sex. The right to abortion must be seen as contrary to the just world that we envision.

> *Kumar defines rights that are relative to those of others (including the fetus). How does this fit your understanding of constitutional rights?*

Summary

In the ACLU report on the 25th anniversary of *Roe v. Wade* the organization outlines the main reasons for supporting abortion as a right. The ACLU argues that legalized abortion has led to improved women's health and lower rates of death from botched abortions, and has allowed women to participate equally in economic and social affairs by giving them the ability to control their reproductive lives. Dr. Simon Kumar, however, argues that abortion involves killing and as such holds deep emotional, spiritual, and moral consequences for the women involved. She argues that only God can take life away and that it is a sin to kill, and that today's society is increasingly aware of the need to protect life. Therefore, she concludes, abortion on demand is contrary to "the just world that we envision."

FURTHER INFORMATION:

Books:

Grant, George, *Grand Illusions: The Legacy of Planned Parenthood*. Franklin, TN: Adroit Press, 1992.

Gorney, Cynthia, *Articles of Faith: A Frontline History of the Abortion Wars*. New York: Simon & Schuster, 1998.

Olasky, Marvin, *Abortion Rites: A Social History of Abortion in America*. Wheaton, IL: Crossway Books, 1992.

Articles:

Cahill, L. S., "Abortion, Autonomy, and Community," in L. Steffen (editor), *Abortion: A Reader*. Cleveland, OH: Pilgrim Press, 1996.

Callahan, Sidney. "Value Choices in Abortion," in *Abortion: Understanding Differences,* edited by Sidney Callahan and Daniel Callahan. New York: Plenum Press, 1984.

Callahan, S., "Feminists and the Sexual Agenda: A Case for Pro-Life Feminism," in *Abortion: A Reader*, edited by Sidney Callahan and Daniel Callahan. Cleveland, OH: Pilgrim Press, 1996.

Useful websites:

www.abortionfacts.com/index2.asp
Information supplied by a prolife organization.
www.aclu.org
The civil liberties site features reports on abortion, reproductive rights, and women.
www.roevbush.com
Site on abortion policies of President George W. Bush.

www.naral.org/
Site of the National Abortion and Reproductive Rights Action League (NARAL), a prochoice organization.
www.prochoice.about.com/library/blabqandawhylegal.htm
A page of prochoice views and resources supplied by about.com.
www.villagevoice.com/features/9845/gonnerman5.shtml
A *Village Voice* series on abortion and terrorism.

The following debates in the Pro/Con series may also be of interest:

In this volume:

IS ABORTION A RIGHT?

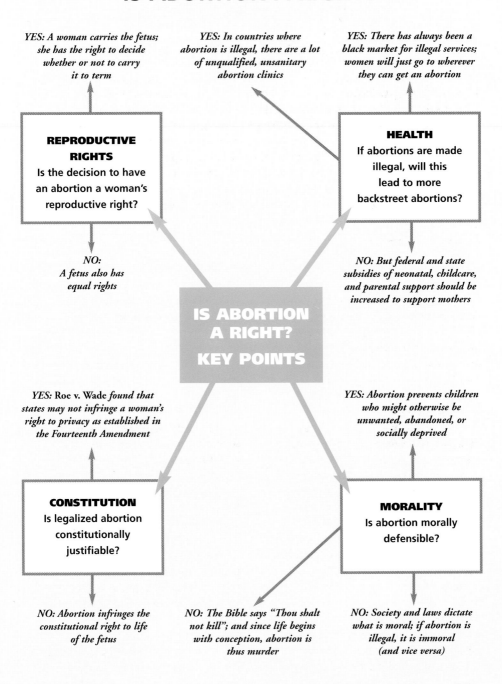

YES: A woman carries the fetus; she has the right to decide whether or not to carry it to term

YES: In countries where abortion is illegal, there are a lot of unqualified, unsanitary abortion clinics

YES: There has always been a black market for illegal services; women will just go to wherever they can get an abortion

REPRODUCTIVE RIGHTS
Is the decision to have an abortion a woman's reproductive right?

HEALTH
If abortions are made illegal, will this lead to more backstreet abortions?

NO: A fetus also has equal rights

NO: But federal and state subsidies of neonatal, childcare, and parental support should be increased to support mothers

IS ABORTION A RIGHT? KEY POINTS

YES: Roe v. Wade found that states may not infringe a woman's right to privacy as established in the Fourteenth Amendment

YES: Abortion prevents children who might otherwise be unwanted, abandoned, or socially deprived

CONSTITUTION
Is legalized abortion constitutionally justifiable?

MORALITY
Is abortion morally defensible?

NO: Abortion infringes the constitutional right to life of the fetus

NO: The Bible says "Thou shalt not kill"; and since life begins with conception, abortion is thus murder

NO: Society and laws dictate what is moral; if abortion is illegal, it is immoral (and vice versa)

ABORTION IN THE UNITED STATES

A woman's right to have an abortion is a hotly debated issue in the United States, and the history of our abortion laws reflect the opposing views. Some people argue that only a woman has the right to decide what happens to her body. Others say that life begins from conception and that no one has the right to "play God."

1820s The first abortion laws appear, forbidding abortion after the fourth month of pregnancy.

1859 The American Medical Association condemns abortion apart from cases in which the birth threatens the mother's or child's life.

1875 Every state in the U.S. adopts laws banning abortion.

1900 Most abortions in the U.S. are outlawed by pressure from physicians, the Medical Council Association, and legislators.

1916 Margaret Sanger, Ethel Byrned, and Fania Mindell establish the first birth-control clinic in Brooklyn, New York. It is closed by the police after 10 days.

1921 Margaret Sanger establishes the Birth Control League, now known as Planned Parenthood, to promote abortion and contraception.

1959 The American Law Institute suggests a model penal code that recommends, among other things, that abortions be carried out in licensed hospitals and be allowed for cases including rape and incest.

1965 All 50 states ban abortion, with the exceptions of threats to the mother's life, cases of rape or incest, or if the fetus is deformed. *Griswold v. Connecticut* invalidates a Connecticut statute that prohibits the use of contraceptives. The Court rules by 7–2 that the statue violates the constitutional right to marital privacy.

1968 Pope Paul VI issues *Humanae Vitae*, which restates the Catholic Church's condemnation of artificial birth control.

April 11, 1970 New York allows abortion on demand up to the 24th week of pregnancy. Similar laws are passed in Alaska, Hawaii, and Washington State. Hawaii becomes the first state to repeal a criminal abortion law.

1972 *Eisenstadt v. Baird* makes invalid a Massachusetts law that prohibits the distribution of contraceptives to unmarried people and establishes that constitutional rights to privacy extend to the reproductive decisions of both married as well as unmarried people. The government reports 39 deaths resulting from illegal abortions.

1973 In *Roe v. Wade* the Supreme Court's decision legalizes abortion under the constitutional "right to privacy" and gives women in the U.S. an absolute right to abortion in the first three months of pregnancy when it affects the mother's health. In *Doe v. Bolton* the court declares that "health" covers all factors of a woman's health, physical and mental.

1977 The Hyde Amendment prevents federal Medicaid from being used on abortions except when the mother's life is in danger.

1979 In *Bellotti v. Baird* the Supreme Court overturns a Massachusetts law that requires parental consent for abortions sought by women under age 18. Pregnant minors are able to petition a court to have an abortion without parental notification.

1980 In *Harris v. McRae* the Supreme Court upholds the Hyde Amendment of 1977.

1984 Operation Rescue is founded and led by Randall Terry. On Christmas Day three abortion clinics are bombed, and those convicted call the bombings "a birthday gift for Jesus."

1989 In *Webster v. Reproductive Health Services* a Missouri law barring the use of public money, facilities, or employees for abortions is upheld by the Supreme Court. States are given significant rights to regulate abortion. The court also orders doctors to test any fetus older than 20 weeks for viability.

1990 In *Ohio v. Akron Center for Reproductive Health* the Supreme Court upholds a state statute that requires a physician to give notice to a parent that a minor intends to have an abortion. The means by which a minor can bypass the judiciary notice by demonstrating evidence of hardship is also declared constitutional. Planned Parenthood reports that the number of federally funded abortions plummeted from 294,600 in 1977 to 165 in 1990.

1992 In *Planned Parenthood v. Casey* the framework of the *Roe v. Wade* decision is replaced by the Supreme Court with the "undue burden" test. States may enact abortion laws providing no substantial obstacles are placed before a woman seeking an abortion.

1993 President Clinton lifts a ruling that forbids doctors in federally funded clinics from presenting abortion as an option. On March 10 Michael Griffin kills Dr. David Gunn in Pensacola, Florida—the first murder of a doctor by an antiabortionist.

1994 The Hyde Amendment is altered by Congress to allow states to be able to pay for Medicaid abortions in cases of rape or incest, as well as to save the life of the mother. President Clinton signs the Freedom of Access to Clinic Entrances Act (FACE) into law that makes obstruction of "reproductive health care" providers a federal crime.

1995 The 104th Congress passes HR 1833, which outlaws "partial-birth abortion." President Clinton later vetoes the legislation, saying the procedure needs to be allowed to protect a woman's health as well as her life. Congress fails to override the veto.

1997 Clinton vetoes legislation that would have banned a type of late-term abortion. On July 11 a National Council of Churches official responsible for Christian education endorses a Planned Parenthood video aimed at young people that promotes abortion as being safe.

1998 Alfred E. Smith, a prochoice activist, is found guilty of murdering his ex-girlfriend, Deena Moody. He killed her because she refused to have an abortion. A study finds that 80 percent of women obtaining abortions are under 30 years old, and women aged 18–19 have a higher rate of abortion of any other age group.

June 2001 A Centers for Disease and Control report concludes that U.S. teenagers were less likely to become pregnant in 1997 than in 1976, when the first national figures became available.

Topic 16
IS SURROGATE MOTHERHOOD WRONG?

YES
"SURROGACY IS NOT A RIGHT"
DR. RACHEL SIMON KUMAR

NO
"WHY LEGISLATORS SHOULD PASS POSITIVE LEGISLATION REGARDING SURROGACY"
WWW.OPTS.COM, SEPTEMBER 2, 1997
LAWRENCE A. KALIKOW

INTRODUCTION

Surrogacy is an issue of ethical debate that goes to the heart of motherhood and the relationship between parents and their children. A surrogate mother is a woman who carries a pregnancy for another woman. Most commonly, this other woman is in a relationship in which her male partner is fertile, but she has problems conceiving. The surrogate mother may be artificially inseminated with the sperm of the man in question, or she may be impregnated with an embryo produced by the woman or another woman's ovum. Opponents argue that surrogacy has been subject to abuse in the past and that it is equivalent to buying and selling a human being as a commodity. Supporters of surrogacy argue that infertility is emotionally destroying, and adoption is often difficult. Surrogacy gives couples who want children but cannot have them—an estimated 10 to 15 percent of all married couples—the hope and possibility of having a family.

In most cases a surrogate mother has no genetic ties to the offspring. Eggs and sperm both come from donors and are *in vitro* fertilized (fertilized in a test tube or similar laboratory vessel) and implanted into the uterus of the surrogate. This type of surrogacy usually assumes that the couple wanting the surrogate child cannot have children naturally. The woman usually has a medical disorder that affects the ovaries, such as endometriosis, early menopause, or has a genetic disorder.

In a typical surrogacy arrangement the couple who want to have a child and the surrogate mother enter into a contract. On one hand, the contract guarantees that the surrogate will behave as if the pregnancy were her own. It stipulates, for instance, that she must eat certain things but not others, that she will refrain from taking drugs, take a certain amount of exercise, quit smoking or drinking alcohol, and so on. In return, the contract stipulates the fee the surrogate will receive. There are also clauses stipulating what will happen in the case of, say, a miscarriage. Usually the surrogate mother receives nothing if there is a problem with the pregnancy.

Surrogacy remains relatively rare. The U.S. Congress Office of Technology Assessment estimated in 1988 that only around 600 babies had been born through surrogacy. Although the figure may be low, the practice of surrogacy raises serious issues.

The issues surrounding surrogacy include its physical and emotional implications. How will the surrogate mother cope with giving up the child she has been carrying at the end of the pregnancy? What will happen if she reneges on the contract and tries to keep the baby? What would be the potential problems if a couple refused to accept a surrogate child who was sick or handicapped? On the other hand, the rejection of sick and handicapped babies is a potential problem that is by no means confined to surrogate parents.

"Hiring a surrogate mother can be viewed as part of a constitutional right of married couples to reproduce."
—JOHN ROBERTSON,
LAW PROFESSOR

There is also an issue of basic morality. Some opponents to surrogacy see the hiring of a woman as the equivalent of buying and selling a human being. That was outlawed in the United States by the Thirteenth Amendment, passed in 1865. Surrogate mothers can be paid as little as $10,000. Some opponents argue that

a fee of $10,000 for nine months works out only at around $1.33 per hour, which is well below the minimum wage. Surrogate mothers are the victims of exploitation, they say. Supporters of surrogacy admit that it has been open to abuse in the past. They point out, however, that statistical evidence does not support the caricature of better-off couples hiring surrogates who are desperate for money. Most surrogate mothers have 13 or more years of education and are financially secure. They are motivated, supporters say, not by financial gain but by the humanitarian desire to help another woman have a child.

The surrogacy debate also raises issues about the child's rights. Some people argue that surrogacy may result in confusion or emotional problems for a child as he or she grows up. What is the emotional impact on existing children in a family? There is no guarantee that the new child would not be resented or made to feel inferior. Supporters, however, argue that a child who is a product of surrogacy is loved by its parents in exactly the same way as any other child, and that a couple seeking surrogacy have normally explored other options and thought the procedure through. They also argue that a proper system could be introduced to protect the rights of the child in question.

The following two articles examine the main issues in the debate. Dr. Kumar asserts that surrogacy is morally wrong because it commercializes childbirth. She draws on arguments used by the Catholic Church, among others. Lawrence Kalikow, on the other hand, argues that surrogacy is vital because everyone should have the right and opportunity to have children.

SURROGACY IS NOT A RIGHT
Dr. Rachel Simon Kumar

YES

The ethics of surrogate motherhood—the practice of impregnating a woman to have a baby explicitly for the purpose of being adopted by a childless couple—burst into American public debate in 1986 with the much-publicized case of "Baby M."(see page 206).The legal battles that followed the biological mother's refusal to hand over the baby after birth, although she had signed a contract to that effect, has raised questions about the morality of this practice. Surrogacy—often labeled "baby selling" and "wombs for hire" by its critics—has raised fundamental questions about an individual's abuse of the freedom to make choices about one's body and the nature of contracts one can enter into.These agreements are seen as harmful to children, exploitative of women, and degrading to society as a whole.

How far do one's rights to freedom of choice extend? Does the act of surrogacy infringe the rights of the unborn child?

Commercializing children

Surrogacy is widely criticized because it is seen as commercializing the act of childbirth. A typical arrangement involves payments to the mother and an agency that negotiates the deal, apart from medical costs, all of which are borne by the childless couple.The Roman Catholic Church in a statement responded to the Baby M. case, focusing on the commercial aspects of surrogacy, that it "promotes the exploitation of women and infertile couples and the dehumanization of babies ... what is being paid for is a living child." Medical ethicists have also raised concern that humans and body parts ought not to be treated like "mere meat" that can be produced and sold to the highest bidder. A Kentucky court, upholding a surrogacy contract, argued that the view of "baby selling" was an overreaction because a father cannot be accused of buying his own child.Yet, in most surrogacy contracts, there are finer clauses which note that lesser amounts of money only need be paid if the child is stillborn or born impaired.

Medical ethicists are concerned with the ethical issues or moral principles arising from new techniques or discoveries in the world of medicine.

Women as vessels

Like children, women too are open to exploitation in the commercial contracts of surrogacy. Surrogacy undeniably constitutes a form of "slavery," making clear distinctions between rich women who can pay for children and those from lower economic classes for whom the huge amounts transacted are an inducement to enter into such contracts. In the mid-eighties, a typical arrangement averaged around U.S. $25,000. Surrogate mothers are usually poor, uneducated, either at home raising their own children or on welfare payments. One author questions if women, who agree to be surrogates, can in such unequal financial circumstances, give "informed consent."

At another level, the commercial nature of surrogate arrangements encourages the stereotyping of women as reproductive machines. Margaret Atwood's influential novel *A Handmaid's Tale*, set in the near future where women are maintained in society solely for their ability to reproduce, emphasizes the fear that women could be reduced to being "breeding machines" not persons. In the Baby M. trial, a physician report referred to the biological mother as a "surrogate uterus and not a surrogate mother." Clearly, although women seem to be making choices about their bodies, in the larger perspective, surrogacy clearly denies them the legitimacy of their motherhood.

What are the conflicts between commerce and morality? Can surrogacy be viewed as simply an occupation?

Moral questions

There is a whole slew of moral questions that surrogacy evokes which are not contained within the ambit of a legal contract. For instance, Cahill (1990) points to the moral deficiencies in the decision "(1) to conceive a child one does not intend to raise, or to induce another to do so; and (2) to enter into a reproductive relationship with an individual with whom one has no significant and enduring interpersonal relationship, especially when one is already married to someone else." Surrogacy is not quite the same as adoption, where the decision to give up the child comes after the conception has taken place. In surrogacy, the mother conceives, usually from a man with whom she has no relationship, knowing full well that she is not going to raise the child. In effect, the child is instrumental to the biological parent, that is, it is the means to obtain an end (whether money or even a sense of satisfaction that one has acted for the benefit of other people). The Catholic bishops in New Jersey emphasized this point in their submission—"in surrogacy, a child is conceived precisely in order to be abandoned to others and his or her best interests are the last to be considered … [t]here is great potential for psychological injury to the child when he realizes that he was born, not of a loving relationship, but

For an overview of surrogacy, with arguments for and against, articles, and an annotated bibliography, visit www.udayton.edu/ ~gender/biblio/ 97miller.htm.

COMMENTARY: The Baby M. Case

The Baby M. case gave rise to a landmark court ruling on the issue of surrogacy. On February 6, 1985, Mary Beth Whitehead entered into a contract with Elizabeth and William Stern to conceive Mr. Stern's child and at birth to hand the child over to the couple, relinquishing all her parental rights. For this service Mrs. Whitehead was to be paid a sum of $10,000 by the Sterns. When the child was born, Mrs. Whitehead decided that since the baby looked just like her, she would keep it. She and her husband were recorded as the parents on the birth certificate, and she fled with her family from New Jersey to Florida. The Sterns appealed for help, and the police went to Florida to take the child by force. The matter was then taken to court, where Mrs. Whitehead's parental rights were legally terminated.

However, Mrs. Whitehead appealed the decision in the New Jersey Supreme Court. In 1988 the court ruled that surrogacy contracts are illegal and unenforceable because they violate the public policy of the state. The court saw the contract as, in effect, an agreement by Mrs. Whitehead to sell her baby, an act prohibited by New Jersey law. The court further ruled that Mrs. Whitehead had been coerced into promising to surrender her baby to the Sterns. Accordingly, her parental rights as birth mother were reinstated. Mr. Stern, as Baby M.'s father, was awarded custody, but Mrs. Whitehead was granted full visitation rights. There have been no significant developments in the law affecting surrogacy since this case.

from a cold, usually financial relationship." The morality of such contracts is questionable.

In the same way, the relationships—legal and otherwise—that the child has with the various actors involved are very unclear. In the case of Baby M., the surrogate was also the biological mother but not the parent raising the child. The initial court did not recognize her rights to her baby over and above the surrogate contract. Even though the New Jersey Supreme Court ruled that she was the natural mother, it was felt that the adoptive parents were more suited to the baby's "best interests." Baby M. was relatively straightforward; in other cases, as for instance in *Johnston v. Calvert* (1993), the surrogate was not biologically related to the baby at all; she carried to term an embryo that was fertilized with the wife's egg and father's sperm. In this case, the surrogate demanded to be recognized as the child's natural mother because she carried the baby and would give birth to it. The court denied her request, referring to her as the "gestational surrogate," or in other words, the hired womb. In an even more bizarre

Anna Johnston was a black woman who, in 1990, gave birth to a baby for the Calverts, who were of European and Philippine ancestry. The fee involved was $10,000.

incident in 1987, a forty-eight year old woman became the surrogate for her daughter's infants. She was impregnated with the embryo from her son-in-law's sperm and daughter's egg. Such controversial arrangements contest the relationships of family that keep society together and deny the child born out of such arrangements the potential of stable and balanced relationships.

Legal difficulties

Finally, the surrogacy contracts are filled with legal loopholes. Although the Constitution permits all individuals the right to enter into contracts, and upholds them, surrogacy has failed to fit neatly into the framework of a contract. Legally, there have been many unresolved issues in surrogacy. In case of the "breakdown" of a contract, as happened in the case of Baby M., several issues remain unclear. Who has the legal guardianship of the child in question? In case the biological mother decides against giving up her child, should courts enforce a contract? If it is suspected that the fetus has genetic defects, can the biological father, under the contract, enforce the mother to undergo abortion? If the surrogate decides against continuing with the pregnancy, can she be prohibited from having an abortion? These are among the huge "grey" areas in these contracts that have not been addressed within legal debates.

Is it possible to draw up general legislation on the issue of surrogacy, or should each case be judged on its own merits?

Best interests?

In conclusion, it must be emphasized that the terms of surrogacy are morally complex. For individuals living in a free society, there is an obligation to respect certain boundaries. All transactions that humans enact in a lifetime cannot and must not be subject to the influence of market commerce. Individual freedoms alone cannot be the dictating factor in permitting all forms of contracts and exchanges in society. Freedoms can and must be exercised within the framework of responsibility to others. In the end, arrangements such as those in surrogacy threaten the best interests of society itself.

Does surrogacy undermine the traditional family unit, or is it a positive step for society?

WHY LEGISLATORS SHOULD PASS POSITIVE LEGISLATION REGARDING SURROGACY
Lawrence A. Kalikow

NO

Surrogacy, as a family-building option, implicates both the right of privacy and procreative freedom. Recognition … was well expressed by a number of distinguished state senators from Pennsylvania, who in 1991, co-sponsored a surrogate parenting bill (Pennsylvania Senate Bill No. 269 of 1991) that expressly set forth the following finding:

"…an individual's decision regarding whether or not to bear or beget a child falls within the constitutionally protected right of privacy, and, therefore, the Commonwealth may not prohibit the practice of surrogate parenting or enact regulations that would have the effect of prohibiting that practice."

The term "Commonwealth" is the official designation (rather than "state") of four states: Pennsylvannia, Kentucky, Massachusetts, and Virginia.

In order to properly understand surrogacy, one must first have an understanding of infertility. Few things can touch an adult human being more intimately or affect him or her more pervasively than the inability to have a child. The psychological and emotional consequences can be devastating. Infertility often consumes those afflicted by it, leaving in its wake emptiness, grief and despair. Those who have been blessed with children can only imagine the deep void that would exist in their lives without them.

Does everyone have a right to have a child; no matter what the social costs may be?

While conventional adoption may be a viable alternative for some infertile couples, there are significant limitations with adoption as a family-building option. For many couples, age restrictions, costs, the limited number of adoptable children (particularly healthy newborns) and the prospect of a protracted emotional "roller coaster" may effectively foreclose adoption. Moreover, conventional adoption will not result in a genetically related child. Often, surrogacy alone provides that possibility. The desire to have a genetically related child is deeply rooted in the human psyche and should be neither condemned nor denigrated. Undeniably, few couples of the fertile world would choose to forego having their own genetic offspring in favor of adoption.

Surrogacy is clearly consistent with and, indeed, furthers deeply held societal values. Because it is the very means through which an infertile couple brings a child into the world, surrogacy is inherently pro-family and is, in the truest sense, emphatically pro-life. Properly done, surrogacy is a carefully structured collaborative creative effort that holds the potential for great joy and happiness, and for the development of a unique and truly wonderful set of human relationships. Few of our social institutions—indeed, few human endeavors—can boast a success rate approximating that of surrogacy. Of thousands of surrogate parenting arrangements that have been entered into, only a small handful (far fewer than one percent) have resulted in litigation over custody. The vast majority are glowing success stories. Unfortunately, however, such happy outcomes are not likely to make their way to prime time television.

Should a child be told of his or her biological origins?

That surrogacy is so successful as a family-building option is not surprising. Most couples who choose to pursue surrogacy do so only after lengthy infertility treatment, followed by careful study and reflection. Many receive some form of counseling or other professional guidance even before embarking on the process. Overwhelmingly, those intending to parent through surrogacy are in stable, long-term marriages and are responsible, law abiding, and productive members of society. Above all else, they share an intense desire to have a child and become a family. Surrogacy is rarely undertaken without extensive preparation, screening and planning. Indeed, the typical surrogate parenting arrangement involves far more medical and psychological screening prior to achieving a pregnancy than does conventional conception or conventional adoption, and includes a comprehensive written agreement, memorializing the intentions, as well as the respective obligations, of the intended parents and the surrogate mother. Hence, in a very real sense surrogacy is the ultimate in planned parenthood.

Would those people planning to employ a surrogate make better parents than people who have benefited from natural conception?

The perceived problem with surrogacy is one largely created by distorted, sensationalized media coverage of a few aberrational cases and by some bioethicists, cloistered in ivory towers and insulated from real life experience. It is clearly anomalous to judge surrogate parenting based upon its very few failures. Surely, no one can seriously maintain that conventional adoption ought to be condemned because so many adoptions ultimately fall through or that marriage ought to be condemned because of a growing incidence of spouse abuse or a spiraling divorce rate. Measured against any objective standard—and, especially, when compared with other practices and institutions—surrogate parenting has not posed a significant problem in any state.

In the absence of an amply demonstrated compelling need to rectify an actual rather than a perceived problem, lawmakers should shun legislation that intrudes upon the right of privacy and curtails procreative freedom. While legislatively imposed restrictions on any human activity always exact a price in terms of diminished freedom and narrowed choices, the price exacted by banning or unduly restricting surrogate parenting will for many of those affected be tragically high: the dream of having a child

Is a person's freedom to employ a surrogate mother a moral or a legal question? What role does morality play in the framing of new laws?

A mother and her young daughter play together in the grass. Surrogate motherhood is a complex issue, from both a legal and an ethical perspective.

and becoming a family. Wisdom and compassion, as well as sensitivity to the constitutional rights implicated, dictate a different approach.

Presently, the majority of states have not enacted laws that ban or severely restrict surrogate parenting.... Any legislation that would prohibit the payment of compensation would have a devastating impact upon surrogacy: it would effectively foreclose surrogacy as a lawful family-building option for most couples. Moreover, criminalizing the payment of compensation would inevitably make criminals of otherwise honest, law-abiding, productive citizens, whose only "crime" would be attempting to create a biologically-related family. It would also cruelly stigmatize many children who have already been born of successful surrogacy arrangements that involved the payment of compensation.

Contrary to what some bioethicists have suggested, neither the payment nor acceptance of compensation for a surrogate mother's participation in a surrogate parenting arrangement can reasonably be viewed as the "buying" or "selling" of a baby. Particularly in light of the tremendous amount of time, energy and effort that the surrogate mother necessarily expends in any surrogate parenting arrangement, reasonable compensation is both fair and appropriate.

Although surrogacy is intensely important to those infertile couples who already have created a family through that option or who hope to do so in the future, it is clearly not viewed as an important issue by the vast majority of the electorate. Unlike so many problems, such as crime, teen pregnancy, and child abuse, that do regularly adversely affect the general public, surrogacy has had virtually no discernible negative impact. Rather, it has provided the means through which some very good citizens have been able to fulfill the dream of creating a family.

As the public learns more about infertility in general and surrogate parenting in particular, support for anti-surrogacy legislation is likely to continue to wane.

Far from benefiting anyone, the enactment of anti-surrogacy legislation is certain to cause grief and despair. Can anything be more devastating to flesh and blood human beings than the death of the dream of creating a family? Any lawmaker considering anti-surrogacy legislation should give ample thought to that question before casting his or her vote. On the other hand, sponsoring and/or supporting salutary legislation that preserves surrogate parenting as a viable family building option can help others realize that dream and the great happiness that flows from it.

The Law Research Library is a useful starting point for learning more about surrogacy legislation. Visit their website at www.law research.com.

Will anyone benefit from antisurrogacy legislation? Should adoption procedures be made simpler in order to reduce the need for surrogacy?

Summary

Surrogacy is an emotional issue. It brings into question all kinds of ethical, moral, and legal matters, such as reproductive rights, the rights of the child, the natural right of anyone to have children, and the economic and social cost. It is, however, a system that has existed since ancient times—there is even reference to it in the Bible.

In the first of the articles Dr. Rachel Simon Kumar argues that surrogacy is wrong—that children are not commodities to be bought and sold, and that surrogacy commercializes the act of childbirth. She describes the inequality of rich couples paying poorer women to bear their children, and sees this as exploitation of women who become little more than "breeding machines." Overall, Dr. Simon Kumar contends that the emotional and psychological implications of the system far outweigh its benefits. There is also an overview of the Baby M. case—a landmark legal ruling in the New Jersey Supreme Court that found surrogacy contracts to be illegal, and that asserted the parental rights of surrogate mothers.

In the second article the lawyer Lawrence Kalikow argues that to understand surrogacy properly we have to understand how traumatic and dreadful infertility is. He asserts that instead of proposed negative anti-surrogacy legislation, the United States should have positive laws to support this system that gives thousands of couples the "dream of creating a family." The key map opposite sums up some of the major issues in this debate.

FURTHER INFORMATION:

Books:

Field, Martha A., *Surrogate Motherhood*. Cambridge, MA: Harvard University Press, 1988.

Gostin, L. (editor), *Surrogate Motherhood*. Bloomington, Indiana: Indiana University Press, 1990.

Hauser, B. R. (editor), *Women's Legal Guide: A Comprehensive Guide to Legal Issues Affecting Every Woman*. Colorado: Fulcrum Publishing, 1996.

O'Neill, Terry (editor), *Biomedical Ethics: Opposing Viewpoints*. San Diego, CA: Greenhaven Press, 1994.

Pence, Gregory, E., *Classic Cases in Medical Ethics*. New York: McGraw-Hill, 1995.

Useful websites:

www.kluge.net/~mrv/class/py2713-1.html
Michelle Vadeboncoeur, "Paper 1: Surrogate Motherhood." November 16, 1995.

www.surrogacy.com
Articles on the legal aspects of surrogacy.

www.udayton.edu/~gender
Book reviews and articles on the ethical and legal issues raised by surrogacy.

www.csun.edu/~pdy453/surrog_y.htm
Article on the argument for "Should Surrogate Motherhood Be Legal."

The following debates in the Pro/Con series may also be of interest:

In this volume:

Topic 8 Should people have to obey unjust laws?

Topic 15 Is abortion a right

IS SURROGATE MOTHERHOOD WRONG?

YES: Everyone should have the right to have children, and surrogacy provides a useful and compassionate service to people who are unable to do so

YES: Adoption can be difficult, and surrogacy gives childless people another option

YES: Surrogacy provides a vital service, and the natural mother should be rewarded for it

BUSINESS
Should a woman receive payment for carrying a surrogate baby?

INFERTILITY
Should surrogacy be legal as it helps people who cannot have children?

YES: Whatever the reasons for agreeing to do the arrangement the natural mother is essentially giving up almost a year of her life

NO: Human beings should not be bought and sold

NO: Parenthood is not a natural right—not everyone is suitable

IS SURROGATE MOTHERHOOD WRONG?
KEY POINTS

YES: Keeping a natural mother and her child together is the best for all concerned

YES: No one can predict how the real mother will feel until she gives birth

NATURAL RIGHTS
Should the natural mother have the right to change her mind after the birth?

NO: The woman has entered into the agreement having weighed up all the pros and cons of giving away/selling her child. She should not have the right to change her mind.

NO: The people taking the child have rights too—that would be too cruel

GLOSSARY

abortion the premature delivery of a human fetus, either naturally through miscarriage or by artificial methods. Usually the term refers to the latter definition. *See also Roe v. Wade.*

ACLU the American Civil Liberties Union, a nonprofit, nonpartisan organization with a mission to fight civil liberties violations and protect America's original civic values.

affirmative action a set of public policies and initiatives designed to end discrimination based on race, color, gender, or religion. Also known as "positive discrimination."

Amish a Christian sect that shuns the conveniences of the modern world and follows a simple, agricultural lifestyle.

anti-Semitism hatred or hostility toward Jewish people, expressed either in speech or behavior by individuals or as official government policy.

apartheid the official policy of separating the races in South Africa from the mid-20th century until 1990. It discriminated against nonwhites both economically and politically. *See also* racism, segregation.

assimilation a condition under which the traditions and culture of a minority ethnic group are absorbed by a dominant culture.

bilingualism the ability to speak two languages. The term is also used in the U.S. to describe a system of education in which non-English speakers are taught in their native language.

Bill of Rights a bill ratified in 1791 that contains the first 10 amendments to the U.S. Constitution; four other amendments were added later. The amendments protect certain rights of the people, such as freedom of speech, assembly, and religion. *See also* civil rights, freedom of speech, First Amendment, Second Amendment, Fourth Amendment.

Black Panther Party an organization formed in 1966 by young militants who advocated armed struggle and violence in support of gaining civil rights. *See also* civil rights.

Black Power the name given to the political and social movement, led by Malcolm X, that struggled for economic and political power for blacks during the civil rights movement. *See also* civil rights.

capital punishment the legal ending of a person's life as punishment for a serious, or "capital," offense.

civil rights rights guaranteed to the individual by certain laws, such as the right to vote and equal treatment of all. *See also* Bill of Rights.

civil society a community of citizens that shares religious or moral values, or a sense of duty or responsibility, other than the laws of the state.

discrimination the act of treating others unfairly on the basis of their race, color, gender, sexuality, nationality, religion, education, or economic status.

ethics the system or code of morals of a particular person, group, or organization, or the practice of examining those standards of conduct or moral codes.

ethnic cleansing action intended to remove or extinguish members of a minority ethnic group from a country or region.

feminism the organized activity to attain equal rights and opportunities for women.

First Amendment an addition to the U.S. Constitution that protects an individual's right to freedom of speech, the freedom of the press, freedom of assembly, and the freedom to practice one's own religion.

Fourth Amendment an addition to the U.S. Constitution that protects, among other things, the privacy of persons, homes, and papers from unreasonable searches.

freedom of speech the right to freedom of expression of one's views and opinions, and freedom of the press, protected by the First Amendment. *See also* hate speech.

gender the economic, social, cultural, and political attributes that are associated with being either male or female.

genocide action intended to destroy or kill an entire national or ethnic group. *See also* ethnic cleansing.

hate speech any expression that ridicules, degrades, or reviles a person, institution, or group on the basis of their race, creed, sexual orientation, religion, handicap, national origin, or economic condition. *See also* freedom of speech.

inequality disparity in distribution of a specific resource or item, such as income, education, employment, or healthcare.

integration a condition under which different races live side by side in the same society, allowing free and equal association; the opposite of segregation.

morality standards of conduct or moral codes that establish the principles of right and wrong behavior.

multiculturalism the policy or practice of fostering the cultural contributions and representing the cultural needs of all groups in society.

noncooperation a philosophy of peaceful, nonviolent resistance to oppression and encouragement of social change, developed by the Indian leader Mahatma Gandhi and later taken up by the black civil rights leader Martin Luther King, Jr.

positive discrimination *see* affirmative action.

prejudice an opinion formed about someone, something, or a group that is not based on knowledge of the facts but on irrational hatred, intolerance, or suspicion.

prochoice the belief that a woman should have the right to choose whether or not to carry a baby to term.

prolife an antiabortion movement in which the members believe that human life begins at conception and that a fetus has full human rights.

racism a belief that some races are inherently and naturally superior to others, which often gives rise to discrimination against or harassment of certain races. *See also* apartheid, segregation.

reparations the act of making amends for a wrong, usually by paying a financial sum, as Germany was forced to do after World War II.

Roe v. Wade a case in which the Supreme Court ruled in 1973 that the constitutional right to privacy included a woman's decision whether or not to end a pregnancy—that is, a woman had a constitutional right to abortion. Before that time abortion was illegal in most U.S. states except in cases of rape, incest, or in which the woman's life was at risk.

Second Amendment an addition to the U.S. Constitution that protects the right to keep and bear arms, and which states that a well-regulated militia is necessary for the security of the state.

segregation the official or unofficial practice of limiting physical contact or personal interaction between the races. Official segregation occurred in the southern states until the mid-1950s, and segregation continued unofficially until the 1960s. *See also* apartheid, racism.

social responsibility a set of behaviors and beliefs that includes a commitment to fostering the well-being of everyone in society, to resolve conflict peaceably, to foster cooperation and community, to value diversity and difference, and to counter bias and prejudice.

society part of a community bound together by common interests and standards or a group of interdependent persons that form a single community.

surrogacy the practice of being a substitute or stand-in. A surrogate mother conceives and bears a child on behalf of another woman, usually for a fee.

xenophobia fear, hatred, or hostility toward strangers or foreigners. *See also* ethnic cleansing, prejudice, racism.

Acknowledgments

Topic 1 Is Inequality a Problem?

Yes: From "Dollars Count More than Doctors" by Bonnie Lefkowitz, May 2000 (www.inequality.org/healthdc. html). Copyright © 2000 by Bonnie Lefkowitz. Used by permission.

No: From "Solving the New Inequality" by Richard B. Freeman, *Boston Review*, December 1996/January 1997. Copyright © 1996 by Richard B. Freeman. Used by permission.

Topic 2 Is it Possible to Live in a Nonracist Society?

Yes: From *Killing Rage, Ending Racism* by bell hooks. Copyright © 1995 by Gloria Watkins.

No: From *The Granta Book of Reportage*. Copyright © 1992 by Richard Rayner.

Topic 3 Are Women Still the Second Sex?

Yes: From *The Second Sex* by Simone de Beauvoir, translated by H.M. Parshley. copyright 1952 and renewed 1980 by Alfred A. Knopf, a division of Random House, Inc. Used by permission of Alfred A. Knopf, a division of Random House, Inc.

No: From "War against Boys, Part 1" by Christina Hoff Sommers, *Atlantic Monthly*, May 2000. Copyright © 2000 by Christina Hoff Sommers. Reprinted by permission of Christina Hoff Sommers, American Enterprise Institute, Washington, D.C. 20036.

Topic 4 Should the Constitutional "Right to Privacy" Protect Homosexual Conduct?

Yes: From *Bowers v. Hardwick*, 478 U.S. 186 (1986), Justice Harry Blackmun.

No: From *Bowers v. Hardwick*, 478 U.S. 186 (1986), Justice Byron White.

Topic 5 Should Gay Men and Women Be Allowed to Marry?

Yes: From "Gay Marriage: Should Lesbian and Gay Couples Be Allowed to Marry?", ACLU Answers, June 1998. Copyright © 1988 by American Civil Liberties Union. Used by permission.

No: From "A Critical Analysis of Constitutional Claims for Same Sex Marriage" by Lynn D. Wardle, *Brigham Young University Law Review*, Issue 1, 1996, page 1. Copyright © 1996 by Lynn D. Wardle. Used by permission.

Topic 6 Should Affirmative Action Continue?

Yes: From "Give Affirmative Action Time to Act" by William Darity, Jr., The Chronicle of Higher Education, December 1, 2000. Copyright © 2000 by William Darity, Jr. Used by permission.

No: "Don't Encourage Inequality" by Alex Braithwaite. Copyright © 2001 by Alex Braithwaite. Used by permission.

Topic 7 Should English Be the Official Language in the United States?

Yes: From "Bilingual Education: A Critique" by Peter Duignan, Hoover Institute (www.hoover.stanford.edu/publications/he/22/22g.html). Reprinted from *Bilingual Education* with the permission of the publisher, Hoover Institution Press. Copyright © 1998 by the Board of Trustees of the Leland Stanford Junior University.

No: From "English Only," ACLU Briefing Paper, 1996. Copyright © 1996 by American Civil Liberties Union. Used by permission.

Topic 8 Should People Have to Obey Unjust Laws?

Yes: Statement by Eight Alabama Clergymen, April 12, 1963, (www.du.edu/~airvine/teaching/mlk/public_statement.htm).

No: From "Letter from a Birmingham Jail" by Martin Luther King Jr. Reprinted by arrangement with The Heirs to the Estate of Martin Luther King Jr., c/o Writers House as agent for the proprietor, copyright © 1958 Martin Luther King Jr., renewed 1996 Coretta Scott King.

Topic 9 Should There Be a Right to Violate Laws for Religious Reasons?

Yes: *Wisconsin v. Yoder*, 406 U.S. 208 (1972), Chief Justice Warren Burger.

No: From *In Defense of Liberal Democracy* by Walter Berns, originally published by Regnery Gateway (Chicago) 1984. Copyright © 1984 by Walter Berns.

Topic 10 Is Violent Protest Ever Justified?

Yes: "The Case of the Civil Rights Movement and Apartheid" by Alex Braithwaite. Copyright © 2001 by Alex Braithwaite. Used by permission.

No: From "Violence and Terrorism" by Mahatma Gandhi, (www.mkgandhi.org/nonviolence). Copyright © 2001. Reprinted with the permission of Navjeevan Publishing House, Ahemadabad 14, India.

Topic 11 Is Hate Speech a Right?

Yes: From "Hate Speech on Campus," ACLU Briefing Paper, 1996. Copyright © American Civil Liberties Union. Used by permission.

No: From "Hate Speech: The Speech that Kills" by Ursula Owen, *Index on Censorship* 1/98, the magazine for free expression (www.indexoncensorship.org). Copyright © 1998 by Index on Censorship. Used by permission of Index on Censorship.

Topic 12 Is Gun Control Unconstitutional?

Yes: From "To Preserve Liberty—A Look at the Right to Keep and Bear Arms" by Richard E. Gardiner, *Northern Kentucky Law Review* 10/1. Copyright © 1992 by *Northern Kentucky Law Review*.

No: From "The Second Amendment: What It Really Means" by Sarah Brady, *San Francisco Barrister*, December 1989.

Topic 13 Is the Death Penalty Ever Justifiable?

Yes: From "In Favor of Capital Punishment" by John Stuart Mill, made to Houses of Parliament, April 21, 1868.

No: "The Death Penalty," ACLU Briefing Paper No. 8. Copyright © 1999 by American Civil Liberties Union. Used by permission.

Topic 14 Should Society Make Reparations to the Descendants of Slaves?

Yes: From "Slavery: Legacy" by Lord Anthony Gifford, QC, speech to the House of Lords, Britain, March 14, 1996. Courtesy of the House of Lords.

No: From "Ten Reasons Why Reparations for Blacks Is a Bad Idea *for Blacks*—And Racist Too" by David Horowitz, (frontpagemag.com), January 3, 2001. Copyright © 2001 by David Horowitz. Used by permission.

Topic 15 Is Abortion a Right?

Yes: From "The Right to Choose at 25: Looking Back and Ahead," ACLU Reproductive Rights Update, January 1998. Copyright © 1998 by American Civil Liberties Union. Used by permission.

No: "Abortion—It's Wrong" by Rachel Simon Kumar. Copyright © 2001 by Rachel Simon Kumar. Used by permission.

Topic 16 Is Surrogate Motherhood Wrong?

Yes: "Surrogacy is Not a Right" by Rachel Simon Kumar. Copyright © 2001 by Rachel Simon Kumar. Used by permission.

No: From "Why Legislators Should Pass Positive Legislation Regarding Surrogacy" by Lawrence A. Kalikow, September 2, 1997. Copyright © 1997 by Lawrence A. Kalikow. Used by permission.

Brown Partworks Limited has made every effort to contact and acknowledge the creators and copyright holders of all extracts reproduced in this volume. We apologize for any omissions. Any person who wishes to be credited in further volumes should contact Brown Partworks Limited in writing: Brown Partworks Limited, 8 Chapel Place, Rivington Street, London EC2A 3DQ, U.K.

Picture credits

Cover: Image Bank: Terje Rakke; **Corbis:** Bettmann Archive 76, 103, 200–201; Owen Franken 210; Robert Maass 44; Sayrr 26; **Hulton/Archive:** Archive Press 40; Central Press 6–7, 104; Picture Post 112–113; Richard Saunders 34–35; The Observer 84–85; Three Lions 122; **PA Photos:** 56; European Press Agency 174–175

SET INDEX